PAPUA NEW GUINEA'S
LAST PLACE

For mum and dad

PAPUA NEW GUINEA'S LAST PLACE

*Experiences of constraint in a
postcolonial prison*

by
Adam Reed

Berghahn Books
New York • Oxford

First published in 2003 by

Berghahn Books
www.berghahnbooks.com

First paperback edition published in 2004
Reprinted in 2006

Library of Congress Cataloging-in-Publication Data
Papua New Guinea's last place : experiences of constraint in a postcolo nial prison / Adam Reed.
    p.cm.
Includes bibliographical references and index.
ISBN 978-1-57181-581-1 (cl.: alk.paper) — ISBN 978-1-57181-694-8 (pbk.: alk.paper)
    1. Bomana Major Central Area Correction Institution (Port Moresby, Papua New Guinea) 2. Prisons--Papua New Guinea. 3. Prison psychology--Papua New Guinea. 4. Prison discipline--Papua New Guinea. 5. Prisoners--Papua New Guinea--Social conditions. I. Title

HV9916.5 .P677 2003
365'.99545 21
                                                                    2003052213

British Library Cataloguing in Publication Data
A catalogue record for this book is available from the British Library

Printed on acid-free paper

ISBN 978-1-57181-581-1 hardback
ISBN 978-1-57181-694-8 paperback

Contents

List of Figures

List of tables

Acknowledgements

This book is based on fourteen months' (from October 1994 to December 1995) fieldwork in Port Moresby, Papua New Guinea. It would not have been possible without the support and cooperation of prisoners and staff at Bomana Major Central Area Correctional Institution. I remain immensely grateful for the insight inmates gave me into gaol life and the ordeal of living in Papua New Guinea's last place. The men and women I met wanted their stories to be told and their names to be published (I have not used pseudonyms). In particular, I wish to thank Alex Aputi, Max Manale, Abui Oba, Laurence Martin, Mosley Bore, Fred Heni, Aumari Ai, Lucas Pena, Kapal Wai, Simon Kaluwin, Ted Lahui, Johnson Yawa, Winston Pondo, George Hetau, Bala Vele, Andrew Aisa, Billy Kawa, Caspar Goro, Larry Jack, Joe Pondo, Napoleon Allen, George Kalupi, Ebon Kasagoraga, Antony Ume, Timothy Kola, Ann Laiam, Clara Poia, Mary Pulah, Rose Maia and the late Kenneth Baupo. Thanks to Stuart Fancy for the tea and biscuits, and the conversations about home. For their assistance, patience and continued friendship, I am most indebted to Jerai Bawai and Jeffrey Malepo. Among the staff at Bomana, I especially wish to thank Michael Joseph and Ned Gong, but also Geoffrey Moduwa, Napoleon Koda, Henry Levi, Alfred George Noine, Agatha Peng, Ito Fareho, Jacqueline Makon, Ericton Sariri and Julie Aka. As well as a supportive contact, Cyprian Wunum was a good friend; I am grateful to him and his family for all their hospitality. For permission to work at Bomana, I must thank the then Commissioner Sam Nuakona and the then gaol commander Geoffrey Niggins. At Correctional Institution Service headquarters in Port Moresby, I am grateful to Philip Eka; without his guidance, support and enthusiasm I am not sure the project would ever have gained approval.

During my time in Port Moresby I lived with the Dominican community of St Martin's Priory at the Bomana Catholic Seminary (a ten-minute walk from the gates of the prison complex). Everyone at that house welcomed me with great warmth and made me feel at home. I wish to express particular thanks to Father

David Halstead for the invitation, his many kindnesses and the eagerly awaited Sunday meal! It is with much affection that I now recall our many conversations. My appreciation is extended to the late Father Ambrose Loughton, Brother Noah, Brother Francis and Brother James. I also wish to thank the members of the Passionist community, especially Father Kevin Henessey and Brother Caspar, and my seminarian friend Brother (now Father) Alphonse. In Port Moresby city I remember with fondness the friendship of Cecilia Ronderos and her family. Finally, I should like to thank Cyndi Banks for her assistance, kind hospitality and intellectual company during my time there and since.

I am grateful to the Papua New Guinea Post-Courier newspaper in Port Moresby for permission to reproduce images from the front page of one of their issues and to Jada Wilson for agreeing to draw the cartoon illustrations. Melissa Vieceli is owed special thanks for stepping in and redrawing the map illustrations at such short notice. The expense of fieldwork was made possible by grants from various bodies at the University of Cambridge: the Smuts Memorial Fund, Bartle Frere Fund, Antony Wilkin Fund, Eddington Fund and William Wyse Fund. In addition, I received monies from the Emslie Horniman Fund, administered by the Royal Anthropological Institute. For financial support throughout fieldwork and the period of writing-up, I am grateful to the officers of the Prince of Wales Scholarship Fund, at the Cambridge Commonwealth Trust and to Trinity College, Cambridge. Further support came from a postdoctoral research fellowship at Clare College, Cambridge.

For her guidance and support throughout this project, I will always be indebted to Marilyn Strathern. Despite sometimes acting as a bit of a 'loose body', I remain very aware of everything she has done for me. I am also deeply indebted to Tony Crook, Eric Hirsch and Annelise Riles. There are many other friends and colleagues to whom I owe a great deal: Sarah Green, Andy Holding, Rupert Houghton, Julia Lawton, Robert Marsh, Nick Mellor, Hiro Miyazaki, Barbara Placido and Karen Sykes. I am grateful to Michael O'Hanlon for providing a forum to meet other anthropologists working in Melanesia and to Sean Kingston for his editorial comment. I would also like to thank Debbora Battaglia, Don Brenneis, Sinclair Dinnen, Keith Hart, Stuart Kirsch, James Leach and Peter Fitzpatrick. For their constant support, I thank my parents (to whom this book is dedicated) and my sisters. Finally, I thank Shari Sabeti for her love and patience (and tireless editing).

Prologue

―――――――――――― ⁊ ――――――――――――

The last place

Talk drifted once more, our attention diverted by the sight of new inmates entering Bomana. Bewildered, these men ran, stumbled and hurried again, propelled forward by the weight of warders' shouts and insults. They ran bare-chested, sweating, with civilian shirts and shoes – earlier removed for inspection – clasped awkwardly in their arms. On their heads they seemed to carry too much hair. The men passed on, out of sight, to the reception office and we returned our attention to the interview. This time the convict before me wore a different, more puzzling expression; the face of his round and shaven head revealed both smile and frown. 'This, this is the last place', he muttered, 'the very last place in the country'. The convict paused and surveyed the compound yard around us, as if to confirm that he was indeed talking about the prison. 'Here', he continued, 'everything is left behind. There is no beer or tobacco, no women. You cannot see your forest, your rivers, mountains and rocks. You cannot see your children. In this kind of place you are abandoned'. These sad thoughts were followed by silence. Then he straightened, cleared his throat and returned the conversation to an earlier inquiry.

Police vans dump new male inmates at the gates of the main compound of the gaol (Bomana holds on average 700 men and thirty women, both convicts and those held on remand). These men are shuffled into lines and counted. Warders then escort them to an inspection hut next to the gate and instruct them to remove their clothes. Fingers struggle with awkward button-holes; knees bend and sway as men step out of trousers. With garments littered on the concrete floor, they stand cross-armed or with hands shyly covering sexual organs. Some men try to retain their underpants, but warders shout and kick them until these too are pulled down (experienced prisoners call this stuffy, breezeblock hut the 'naked beach', an ironic reference to the strips of coastal sand outside where boys leave their clothes before running, screaming and laughing, into the sea). Once undressed, these inmates are ordered to turn around and spread their hands against the wall. The row of naked men, with their buttocks raised, are ready for inspection. Warders walk down the line, checking hair and mouth for smuggled items such as tobacco, marijuana or rolls of money; sticks, used to fish around for contraband, are inserted up the anus. Nervously, inmates wait. They listen for the sound of footsteps or the slap of rubber hosing against guards' thighs. If something is discovered, the smuggler is dragged from the line, cursed and hit. Angry warders sometimes whip everyone, drawing screams from inmates as the strips of hose lash the back of their legs. The inspection is over quickly. Sore and bruised, men put on their trousers and gather up remaining clothes. Once outside, warders count them again and then send them off to be processed at reception (Figure 1).

Figure 1 *Arrival*

New inmates, still panting from the run, must stand to attention and answer the questions put to them by the registration clerk. He demands to know details about their marital status, the name of their village and province, and the address of designated next of kin. This information is recorded in an intake document and then filed away. The duty warder instructs the men to forget their lives outside and instead concentrate on following the rules of prison. He orders them to remove their trousers and underpants, empty their pockets of property, and then hand the bundle over for storage. In return, men are issued with uniform waistcloths, red for convicts and blue for those on remand. The former are also given a bar of soap and razor, told to shave and cut their hair short (legal provision protects remand inmates from these restrictions). Convicts' dreadlocks, beards and moustaches must disappear, only to return, with their civilian clothes, when their term of sentence is completed.

For prisoners at Bomana, this ceremony of arrival is crucial. They distinguish their experience of incarceration on the basis of that moment of dramatic separation, in terms of those things that are taken away. Inmates complain that the gaol is a place without kin, spouse, partner or children. It is a place without money, alcohol, popular music and custom (*kastom*), without favourite foods or familiar landmarks. Although the gaol is only a fifteen-minute bus ride from Port Moresby, the national capital and largest urban centre in Papua New Guinea, prisoners claim to feel isolated, as if lost in a deep forest. The convict who told me that Bomana was the country's 'last place' (*las ples*), a popular expression among inmates, was drawing attention to that dilemma. To him, it appeared that life was taking place elsewhere. Prisoners share this sense of omission, of being cut off or exiled from those they know outside the gaol. They believe their prison lives are shaped by what is missing.

As the designation 'last place' highlights, prisoners' thoughts on imprisonment are often presented through a meditation on place (*ples*). Bomana is said to be unlike any other place they know; in fact it is the very opposite of what place means to them outside the jail. Anthropologists working in the region point out that people are usually concerned to demonstrate how they are made visible in the land (Schieffelin 1976; Feld 1996). Places take form and significance through the history of life activity that marks them – the gardens people make, the houses they build, the paths they use, the everyday acts of feeding and sharing (Weiner 1991; Kahn 1996; Leach 2003). Particular landmarks – a river, a group of stones or a mountain – reflect peoples' memories of those events and remind them of obligations.[1] Sets of relations animate those places, just as places animate those relations. It is through their connection to the land that people articulate who they are; as Kahn (1996: 180) states, to be without a place is to be humiliated, to exist at the limits of conventional social life.

Although Bomana is acknowledged to be a 'place of law' (*ples blong lo*), established and governed by agents of the State, prisoners prefer to emphasise the negative dimensions of place in gaol. They fail to see themselves reflected in the prison landscape.

Bomana is a place where prisoners claim they have no memories to draw upon, no evidence of the past inscriptive activity of kin or other familiar persons. The gaol is known as Papua New Guinea's last place because it is hardly a place at all (the last place any of them want to be). Nevertheless, the peculiar attribute of placeness at Bomana is what defines prison life. Inmates state that all aspects of their imprisonment can be understood by asking what it means to live in the last place. During my time at Bomana, I was invited to explore the different dimensions of this relationship (one of the themes that structure the chapters of my book), the multiple ways in which people experience (sense) place in prison.

Under constraint

This prison ethnography is about the constraint of place (and the sets of relations place reflects); in particular, it is about the constraint of living in the last place. The book examines the series of negations that prisoners characterise as the principle of their penal lives. These restrictions are coerced and painful to bear; they appear as obvious artifice. Indeed, at Bomana prisoners regard their location as something they have to negotiate; they feel that they are being punished with place (both the place they are given and the place that is taken away). The situation they describe offers a challenge to anthropologists working in the region – as Papua New Guinea's last place, Bomana is a site of radical perspectives – as well as a challenge to those working in the multidisciplinary domain of prison studies.

Although not articulated through the notion of place, those working in the field of prison studies have long been concerned to explore the consequences of the act of detention. The sociological tradition of description and analysis of prison experience really starts, or restarts (cf. Clemmer 1940), with Sykes's now classic work, *The Society of Captives* (1958). Heralded by the author himself as a new kind of penal account, this book cast a shadow over all future renderings of the genre. It encouraged an immediate outpouring of sociological monographs on individual prisons, both in the United States (Giallombardo 1966; Heffernan 1972; Carroll 1974) and Europe (Morris and Morris 1963; Mathiesen 1965; Cohen & Taylor 1981; Moczydlowski 1992), which organised their descriptions around, and in reaction to, the principles that Sykes laid down. It also influenced a growing interest in the study of the 'total' power exercised by these institutions (see Goffman 1961). Sykes outlined the problem, as he saw it, for those who would wish to study the experience of incarceration – how to explain the emergence of inmate society and culture? This question was premised on another insight that Sykes presented as original, namely, that prisons produced their own coherent form of society, one quite distinct from that found outside the prison (1958: xii). That unique type, he argued, was deserving of separate scholarship; prisons provided what Giallombardo would describe as 'an ideal social laboratory in which to test sociological theories' (1966: 2; and cf. Heffernan 1972: 2–3). Imprisonment was held to be special then because it appeared to allow sociologists to watch society making in progress.

What I want to highlight is the emphasis drawn on the links between the pains of imprisonment and the nature of inmate culture. If society existed in prison, it did so, according to Sykes, as a response to the constraints of that life. Faced with a series of attacks on their self-image, prisoners turned to society making as a coping mechanism (1958: 82); the idiosyncrasies of inmate culture emerged out of that adjustment or substitution. Sykes proceeded to outline what those painful constraints might be. He listed a number of 'deprivations' that he claims prisoners at the New Jersey Maximum Security Prison, where he conducted research, identified. These included a 'deprivation of liberty' (loss of freedom of movement and exile from family), a 'deprivation of goods and services' (loss of possessions and material benefits), a 'deprivation of heterosexual relationships' (loss of sexual access and the company of the opposite sex), a 'deprivation of autonomy' (loss of control over personal actions and choices) and a 'deprivation of security' (loss of protection from violent or aggressive behaviour) (1958: 65–77). It was these pains, according to Sykes, that needed to be offset and mitigated by the construction of society (as solidarity increased among inmates, so the distress caused by imprisonment diminished), an adaptation that he believed also gave back to prisoners a sense of self-worth.

Sykes's theory about the constitution of prison society was soon heavily contested (an argument raged about whether prison society was unique or in fact continuous with society outside the gaol). The influence of his work did mean, however, that those conducting research in prisons felt compelled to record the complaints of inmates and describe, if only briefly, the restrictions they felt. Sociological studies started to include chapters with headings such as 'The experience of imprisonment' (Morris and Morris 1963), where testimonies of constraint could be found. Uppermost among these were complaints about the lack of access to family and friends,[2] and in particular the frustrations felt by inmates at their inability to influence the course of events outside the gaol. Prison studies and memoirs repeatedly highlighted the distress caused by worrying about this state of affairs: whether a spouse would be faithful, the family evicted and property pawned, a child sicken or a relative die. In this description, imprisonment began to be articulated as a form of punishment grounded in confinement, in the experience of what has been taken away.

However, despite the recorded testimonies of prisoners, such constraints never seemed to become the proper subject of inquiry. Gradually, the focus of prison studies shifted from the prisoners' experience of detention (and its deprivations) to their experience of the institution's system of disciplinary management. Punishment became increasingly perceived as an issue of 'mortification' (Goffman 1961) or normative subject control (Foucault 1977; Sim 1990), often seen less as a result of confinement and more as the outcome of internal routine and surveillance. In place of society making, sociologists discovered that gaol was a site of identity making, viewed as a contested process over which inmates and prison authorities continually struggled for control (Díaz-Cotto 1996; Bosworth 1999). In these accounts, prison culture is built around things made present (the people and regime of gaol), rather than those things that are absent (the people and way of life outside the gaol). Where discussed, the experience of being separated from people outside the gaol was usually understood as a straightforward negative, a loss whose significance begins and ends at the moment of withdrawal.

In this book, I aim to recuperate the ongoing centrality of enclosure and dispossession, to make these experiences current and the focus of my prison analysis. The experience of living in Papua New Guinea's last place leads prisoners to privilege those things that are absent; life at Bomana appears premised on the constraint of forced separation. As Sykes pointed out, the deprivations of confinement remain at the heart of prison life (even if they are not mechanisms for society making). Inmates' stories about gaol are always also stories about those simple sets of restrictions: no kin, no women (or men), no money and no familiar landmarks. The places and persons from whom they are separated provide them with the background to every action. At the same time those absent things are thrown into relief, allowing prisoners to assess their usual orienting presence (their benefits and costs). Conventional sets of relations, and the obligations that accompany them, become the subject of debate and reflection. Imprisonment makes prisoners aware not just of what they are missing, but of constraints that exist everywhere (and of their artifice); in their discussions, the deprivations of detention become different in degree, rather than kind, from those faced by people outside the gaol. One of the lessons of prison life is that the imposition of constraint (whether voluntary or coerced) has its own potential.[3]

Forgetting

Imprisonment was, of course, a totally new idea to the native. At first it was a complete failure. The prisoners fretted, lost courage, pined, sickened, and died. *(British New Guinea Annual Report 1897–1898: 47)*

Examining early government reports for the colonial period, I was struck by the frequency of statements like the one above. In these reports officers complained of mysteriously high death rates in their prisons, of inmates who would arrive healthy and strong but within a few weeks would sicken and expire. The puzzle, for these gaolers, was that penal discipline offered a regime specifically crafted to produce quite the opposite effect – clean and well-managed bodies. What force, they therefore asked themselves, could resist such a well-intentioned programme? The answer they invariably provided was home-sickness or too much fretting about absent things.

When I later asked prisoners at Bomana to give their own comment on these deaths, they told me that 'worry must have killed them' (*wari mas kilim ol*). Explanations would continue thus: 'such people did not understand the ways of the white men. When they were taken from their home and imprisoned they felt alone and scared. They thought about their parents, their brothers and sisters, garden food and all the good things left at home. So they worried and died'. Prisoners state that they still suffer from 'worry' (*wari*); for them this emotion embodies the pains imprisonment causes. Indeed, upon arrival in gaol a new inmate is said to feel nothing else. He or she may refuse prison food and spend the first days lying in a cell corner, crying and sleeping fitfully. Although worry no longer kills prisoners, I was told it continues to upset their composure.

In the security office at Bomana, an old black and white photograph is pinned to the notice board. Prominently exhibited, it shows a man dead, hung by the neck. The shaven figure wears only a waistcloth and appears bent double as if in prayer. His neck, caught by a leather strap, seems extended and directs the downward angle of his blank gaze. From the evidence of the photograph, this death scene, a presumed suicide, took place in a cubicle of the outside toilet block. It is a pathetic, miserable image. Indeed, that is the very reason for its display. Warders want prisoners to realise the consequences of too much worry (some prisoners referred to this photograph when answering my questions about the high death rate in colonial prisons). They fear that this sentiment, if left unchecked, may lead to trouble; not just the harm inmates may inflict on themselves, but also the danger that worry may spark quarrels, fights and, most seriously (as far as staff are concerned), attempts to escape.

In an attempt to curb these anxieties, warders at the welfare office reserve several hours each morning for hearing prisoners' concerns. Those who visit the office are known as the 'worry people' (*wari lain*). They come either on their own initiative or through the representation of guards and other inmates. During these interviews staff are unusually receptive, permitting each prisoner full time to express their worries. These tend to revolve around a sense of frustration at his or her inability to meet obligations to people outside the gaol. 'Who', it is typically asked, ' will look after my parents? How will my wife survive in the city without me? How can I prevent my husband from running away with another woman? What will happen to my garden, my pigs and property? Who will pay my children's school fees?' Prisoners are also concerned about the worry their kin may suffer as a consequence of their detention; in particular, the commonly expressed fear that it may affect the health of elderly parents. If regret is expressed for the pain their actions have caused, it is directed towards these people rather than the victims of their offence. Prisoners fear the anger of kin outside the gaol; especially remand inmates, who often sit around and speculate about why their bail fee has not been paid (as a punishment, parents may wait weeks or months before paying the fee and getting them released). Sometimes inmates determine to keep their detention secret, in the hope that they will quickly be discharged. Those who do want to inform kin may be prevented by the swiftness of their arrest, so that they are never quite sure if anyone outside the gaol actually knows.

The contribution warders can make to the management of worries is limited; ultimately, it is up to prisoners to keep these feelings in check. This is achieved by learning to forget or 'lose thoughts' (*lus tingting*). Prisoners tell each other to stop thinking and talking about events outside the gaol. They try to lose memories, to disregard kin and other persons they miss. Indeed, inmates claim that they no longer die from worry precisely because they have learned how to forget. When a prisoner appears alone and depressed, others will approach and offer their company; the dejected man or woman, bombarded with jokes and stories, is comforted and encouraged to lose his or her thoughts. The worries that cause pain are thus disremembered. At Bomana forgetting is presented as a deliberate act, one that requires the constant vigilance and hard work of inmates. Almost any activity – card games, penal labour, reading, song writing, sports, church worship and so on – can be motivated by this ambition. Male prisoners say that the very best way to forget is smoking: either tobacco or marijuana, both of which are contraband and must be smuggled into gaol. When an inmate's worries grow out of control, he can inhale on a cigarette until his head starts to spin and his thoughts settle. Prisoners are impressed by the capacity of these drugs to 'kill their memory' (*kilim dispela memori sens belong yu*), and thus provide solace from prison despair.

While the constraint of living in the last place may be coerced, it is also in some respects voluntarily imposed. For inmates must try and forget those persons and places left outside the gaol, to put them out of mind. This denial of what is missing is an active, ongoing struggle. Inmates must learn to place a limit on their thoughts, to stop themselves dwelling on a range of conventional subjects. They must themselves enact a disappearance. Giallombardo (1966: 133), writing about the Federal Reformatory for Women in Alderson, West Virginia, speaks of the prison as an 'as if' world, one that is premised on continual efforts of disremembering. At Bomana these efforts are directed at denying the failure of obligation. Prisoners attempt to live together *as if* nothing is wrong, *as if* the separation from loved ones hasn't happened, even *as if* kin never existed. Through their acts of forgetting they try to constitute Bomana as the *only* place in Papua New Guinea. Inmates do not believe they 'make' prison society, but they do believe their work allows certain sets of relations to be acknowledged. The form that prison life takes is presented as the outcome both of detention and of the constraint that prisoners impose on themselves.

Anthropologists working in Papua New Guinea and the broader region of Melanesia have no history of direct investment in prison studies.[4] However, the idea that experiences of loss may be at the centre of gaol life would come as no surprise to them. Melanesian societies are judged to be unusually concerned with the relationship between what is made visible and what is kept hidden; people are said to be always aware of what needs to be forgotten in order for something else to appear. Events such as ritual exchange, mortuary and initiation ceremonies have been presented as deliberate attempts to reconstitute sets of relations by formal acts of separation (cf. Clay 1977; Wagner 1977; Feld 1982; Mosko 1985; Küchler 1987 and 1988; Strathern 1988; Battaglia 1990; Weiner 1991, 1993 and 1995; Mimica 1992; Gillison 1993). Indeed, Battaglia suggests that there exists what she calls a 'practical nostalgia' (1995: 77), concern for what absent things evince as well as disallow. She believes that in these societies loss carries 'active' or 'positive' potentialities (1990: 196): it directs people to the present (and future) states of social relations.

Her description draws self-consciously upon the scholarly tradition of deconstructive practice (1990: 7). That critique of positivism – the idea that every assertion or positive presence is always an act of deferment – seems to correspond in certain ways with the principles of indigenous performance. However, Strathern (1992a: 73–74) cautions against the use of that analogy. She points out that deconstructive practice, which targets totalising constructions, is based upon an assumption that social worlds are built or made. Strathern suggests that rather than uncovering the traces of lost positions, Melanesians might better be imagined as seeking to hide or disguise what is present and near. It is this attributed social behaviour that may help to inform an understanding of what incarceration means to prisoners at Bomana.

Indeed, the anthropological contribution to my genealogy of constraint comes from the work of Strathern (1988, 1992a, 1992b, 1995a). Her writing strategies seek to illustrate the power of indigenous practice by making it the basis of her methodology.[5] In *The Gender of the Gift* (1988), she is concerned to write a text whose significance and rigour derives from what it omits. Orienting dichotomies of social analysis such as Individual and Society, Nature and Culture, Domestic and Public, are missing; in fact they are deliberately hidden. *The Gender of the Gift* is a book about that disappearance, one that speaks of its own constraint.[6] It invites the reader through demonstration, as well as explication, to consider the contours of these absent dichotomies. On the basis of this omission Strathern puts forward an experimental sociality,[7] one that privileges another analytic limit: the Relation (see 1995a). Much of her subsequent work is a gymnastic display of the constraint she has imposed upon herself, not only what it allows but also what it prevents.

Strathern weaves her experiment by drawing upon and taking apart the anthropological canon from Melanesia. Her text operates as a parasite upon that material, using it first to describe the dichotomies and then reworking it, imposing her own constraint, in order to make the canon demonstrate what it actually obscures. Thus *her* Melanesians fail to recognise the conventional categories of anthropological representation. Instead of socialisation, they consider rituals such as male initiation as acts of decomposition (1988: 3). Instead of disorder, they consider fighting as another form of exchange. Instead of contract, they consider marriage as converting sameness into difference. Instead of society making, they consider action as working upon relations that are already given.[8] Her experimental subjects enact the consequences of the anthropologist's avoidance of certain analytic limits. They are themselves demonstrations of constraint, both because of what they recognise (the Relation) and what they hide (Individual and Society, Nature and Culture, Domestic and Public).

Strathern's writing strategy is sympathetic to any account of constraint as mode of living (including the constraint of living in the last place that prisoners at Bomana suffer). Yet at the same time her experimental sociality presents my prison ethnography with certain problems. While her subjects are engagingly subversive for anthropology, their analytic power is precisely what creates difficulties. As embodiments of a limit imposed by the anthropologist, they deserve more respect than simple emulation. In this book I will focus on the constraints that prisoners identify (coerced or voluntarily imposed) in order to demonstrate the ways in which their practice simultaneously reproduces and displaces the sociality she describes.

Sneeze

'Achoo! Achoo!, Who', Don asked, 'calls out my name?' The convict, from Tari in the Southern Highlands, reacted to his bout of sneezing by tensing his body and throwing back his arm until it reached his ear. He then proceeded to extend his arm with sudden violent thrusts back and forth; each downward extension begins a revolution, turning the body in a clockwise movement. When his elbow bone cracked (*bun paiap*) Don stopped, thus freezing the position of the extending limb, which now pointed in one direction (Figure 2). This arm, Don held, marked the bearing or location of those persons outside the gaol whose thoughts had caused his nasal expulsion. However hard inmates try to forget the fact of their confinement events like sneezing are said to return that separation to mind. In this way missing persons and places declare their presence (absence) and so risk unravelling the 'as if' world prisoners establish by their acts of forgetting.

When someone outside Bomana worries about a prisoner, that person is said to literally 'send thoughts' (*salim tingting*) to him

Figure 2 *Sneeze*

or her. This transmission may cause the inmate to sneeze, but also to develop skin itches, headaches, pulsating veins or ringing ears.[9] Gabriel, a remand inmate from the Goilala region of Central province, took his involuntary gulps or hiccups as evidence that kin were talking about him. At such moments he stopped and called out their names, waiting until the spasms ended and the identity of the concerned persons were thus revealed. Troubling events are also said to leave their mark on the bodies of prisoners. Numb limbs or reflex kicks of the leg during sleep are taken to indicate a death or injury outside the gaol. When cold air currents descend on Bomana, causing men and women to shudder and their arm hairs to stand on end, some inmates grow anxious. They believe that the change in weather denotes misfortune, and in response they throw worried questions into the wind: 'Is someone injured at home? Has fighting returned? My father, is he dead'? If the gusting currents cease to blow, then the prisoner knows that he has asked the right question.

I remain behind the fence here.	*Mi stap long banis hia*
I look at the blue hill here.	*Mi lukim blu maunten hia*
I think of the cold place,	*Mi tingting long kol ples*
And that is all.	*Na em tasol*
I worry here.	*Mi wari hia.*
	(Clare Poia.)

I live in Bomana.	*Mi stap long Bomana*
When I turn and see Bisoke hill,	*Taim mi tainim na mi lukim maunten Bisoke*
I am sorry and cry.	*Mi sori na karai.*
	(Timothy Kola.)

Inmates may also see reflections of absent places in the prison landscape. Around Bomana, the ground undulates gently between flat expanses; most of the year it is brown and torn. Only one hill scars the horizon. Prisoners, adopting the local language name, call this earth form Bisoke. From the small female wing it is seen to rise most dramatically, towering above the dusty plateau as if intent on eating the sky. Bisoke is a lowland hill, but to those from the Highlands region it seems familiar. For them, the mountainous proportions recall their own

home scenery, that 'cold place', and with it those persons they
have left behind. Double exposure: Bisoke is strange, yet so
familiar that it makes them cry. Clara – a convict from the
Western Highlands – waited to hear if she would be transferred
back home. She told me that she found the delay upsetting and
the sight of Bisoke amplified her distress. Timothy – a remand
inmate from the province of Simbu – expected to receive a long
sentence. The blue hill reminded him of what he would be
missing and his song evoked that sadness.

But the most common form of thought transmission is held
to be dreams. Prisoners believe that faraway events are often
revealed to them during sleeping hours. Peter – another inmate
from the Goilala region – claimed to learn of a death outside the
gaol in this way. He told me his dream.

He sits by the side of a city road, holding the corpse of a man. A car approaches
and Peter hails the driver. When the vehicle's tinted window slides down, he sees
that the driver is a white man. Peter asks him to take them to the hospital. He
complains that the buses refused to stop. The white man agrees to help and
leaves the two of them outside the morgue. When Peter sees the dead body lying
out on the metal slab, he cries.

The morning after this dreaming, Peter received news that a
gang mate had been shot and killed by police in Port Moresby.
Other dreams may inform prisoners about the injury of kin, a
quarrel or fighting between clans at home. The problem,
however, is that the cause of dreams is not always clear. Many
times, prisoners are left to speculate about the nature of the
event described. Thus, Kubu, a convict from Balimo on the coast
of Western province, remained puzzled by his dream experience.

He turns to find a stranger facing him. This man stands with a straight back
and to Kubu seems sad. The stranger hesitates and then speaks. 'Your sister', he
says, 'is dead. She lies in the snow. Go and fetch her'! Shaken, Kubu sets off.
Soon he finds his sister, her dead body cushioned by a blanket of snow. The
landscape is everywhere blindingly white. Kubu lifts the body and carries it
home. His kin start to wail over the corpse.

Although the dream seemed ominous, he had received no news
from home to support it. Before Bomana, Kubu was imprisoned at
Daru, the administrative centre of his province, and his sister used
to visit him regularly, but since his transfer he had heard nothing
from her. The dream itself appeared very strange – a missing sister
from a hot, coastal village, where winter scenes could only be
viewed in photographs, found dead in the snow! Kubu hoped that

his sister's thoughts of him had sparked the dream, but he knew it might signify something worse. He tried to push that prospect aside, but everyday he expected to receive bad news.

Dreams, then, have the capacity to exacerbate prisoners' worries. If one dreaming experience is verified, others immediately take on new significance. For instance, a convict who dreams of her younger sister having sex with an unknown man, and subsequently hears that her sibling is pregnant, will begin to treat other dreams more seriously. If she next dreams that her husband is being unfaithful, the convict will become unsettled and anxious. The worries caused by sending thoughts work in both directions. When prisoners dwell too long on people outside the gaol, they too can be affected; a male inmate who worries about his parents may cause them to dream about him. Prisoners are therefore concerned that their own worries do not upset kin and friends (female inmates instruct those among them that are mothers not to think too much about their children outside Bomana, for fear that their thoughts will damage the children's minds and make them ill). The imperative to forget extends beyond the welfare of inmates.

Prisoners also remain ambivalent about receiving letters and visits. While they look forward to both events, and get angry if they do not eventuate, at the same time they know such occasions upset their composure and risk aggravating worries. Very often visitors arrive completely unexpectedly; even when their appearance is planned, the meeting is charged with the prospect of departure (visits take place on the weekend and last for half an hour only). As they sit and eat food together, both parties are already considering the negotiation of goodbyes (Figure 3). Inmates are hungry for news about life outside the gaol, but as they listen to their guests' accounts they know that this information will disturb them. Sometimes they claim that it is better to refuse weekend visits and therefore avoid the tearful face and catalogue of woes that visitors too often relate. Prisoners say that it can take days for them to recover from a letter or visit, to put aside memories of all they have read, heard or seen.

These worries may finally lead inmates to try and escape. Topkein, a convict from Kiunga in Western province, one day took off from a work party after receiving a letter that informed him his mother was ill. He fled to Port Moresby and waited in hiding until his brother sent him money to buy an air ticket back

Figure 3 *Visit*

home. When the aeroplane landed at Kiunga Township, the fugitive rushed to the local hospital in order to visit his mother. There he remained, protected and concealed by kin in the surrounding forest, until the day she recovered. In order to avoid getting his supporters in trouble, Topkein then returned to Port Moresby, where he was soon apprehended and sent back to Bomana. Indeed, during the first ten months of my fieldwork a total of forty-five male inmates ran away! Upon recapture they are usually punished by a term of solitary detention. But at many provincial gaols (and until recently at Bomana as well), these prisoners are forced to wear the letter E sewn on their uniform, a character (E for escape) whose placement is designed to cause shame and make the wearer more easily identifiable. The recaptured inmate walks around as a living embodiment of disruption, a subject whose very presence threatens the limits imposed by detention.

Prisoners then are faced not just with constraint, but also with its interruption. Weekend visits, escapes, dreams, earaches, nasal expulsions etc. all act to challenge the form that life takes at Bomana. Those persons who are locked outside the gaol continue to make elusive and brief appearances, often evading the control of both prison authorities and inmates. As a result the work of forgetting is constantly disturbed; inmates are reminded that living in the last place means living in exile. Yet without these interruptions prisoners' lives would ultimately be diminished. They do not really wish to be completely forgotten; the actions caused by the worries of people outside the gaol can be comforting, taken as evidence that love and concern for them still persists. These transmissions are also proof that detention *remains* a punishment, the orienting dimension of incarceration. It seems that only with the possibility (or threat) of displacement does the imposition of constraint gather power.[10]

The example of interruptions or flaws in penal confinement, which at once undermine and exacerbate the need for the setting of limits, might be taken to provide a challenge both for anthropology and prison studies. I am asked to describe a place whose form is premised on what is taken away, yet continually ruptured by what returns. This dilemma leads me to question the portrayal of prisons as 'total' environments (Sykes 1958; Goffman 1961) and of inmates as subjects who primarily suffer from the strictures of discipline within an enclosed, self-contained regime (Foucault 1977). The fact that the thoughts of missing persons are held to affect the constitution of prisoners, and vice versa, should be taken as evidence that imprisonment may always be considered as a mediated experience. Perhaps what is at issue is the degree of separation from those left outside the gaol. Prison life gains and loses its coherence as a result of that constraint and its interruption. This is where inmates' attention begins and ends.

And what of anthropology? Does it need to learn how to pay attention to its own narrative sneeze? Not just to the descriptions that may emerge as a consequence of imposing constraint, but also to those that may keep returning long after their apparent disappearance? For inmates at Bomana the persons and places made absent by their confinement do not simply vanish. Rather their displacement figures a shifting significance. In the same way the *as if* world established by writing constraints should always provide anthropologists with a route back to what is erased and which, as a result, now carries a quite different analytic weight. If imprisonment highlights both the pain and inventiveness derived from taking something away, it also cautions against placing too much faith in what that omission allows.

Notes

1   Kahn (1996: 168) claims that for the Wamira people, who live on the south-eastern tip of Papua New Guinea, places are ultimately 'emotional territories'. They capture the past interactions of people and thus act as memorials and moral landscapes, conveying stories about collective history and social responsibilities.

2   Morris and Morris (1963: 164) quote from the testimony of an anonymous inmate in Pentonville prison, England, to demonstrate where prisoners locate the pains of imprisonment. The inmate states, 'as time goes on it seems very long, and even the bitterness fades. But all one's worries are magnified 100 times. The biggest punishment is being away from home; as for prison itself, there's nothing to it'.

3   To me, the emphasis of prisoners on the potential of constraint recalls the literary practice of the Oulipo (Ouvrior de de Littérature Potentielle) group (see Motte 1986a; Bellos 1995). Rather than assuming that 'inspiration', an old and tired mythology, is the basis for literary expression, members of the group advocated an aesthetic of formal constraint (Motte 1986b: 10). Only by continually imposing new limits on their writing, a voluntary and deliberately rigorous submission to experimental form, did they believe it possible to release imagination. Members highlighted constraining forms in all literature, but criticised the academy for converting them into natu-ralised rules (Bénabou 1986: 41). The point of their endeavour was to recover consciousness of choice in the selection of writing forms; an aware-ness of what constraint enabled and disallowed, of the potential that lay within newly imposed limits. Among the constraints favoured by the Oulipo was the 'lipogram' ('lipo' means lacking, 'gram' means letter), a text in which a given letter of the alphabet does not appear. The purpose of such an experiment, and indeed of all Oulipian forms, was to produce a literary work that spoke of its own constraint. In a sense, this is what incarceration achieves for prisoners at Bomana; they live in a place that continually reminds them of its limits, of the deprivations they must endure in order to experience it.

4   Imprisonment does figure in the history of the foundation of Melanesian anthropology. Early ethnographers in the region often viewed the colonial prison as a resource; it was one of the first places they visited upon arrival, assured of finding subjects upon whom they could practise interview tech-niques (I am grateful to Professor Michael Young for first bringing this connection to my attention). Thus, Seligman spent many days interview-ing prisoners and measuring their heads on Samarai Island (*Journal for New Guinea 1904:* 61 and 116), in what was then the colonial Territory of Papua, followed a decade later by Malinowski on his way to conduct fieldwork in the Trobriand Islands (Malinowski 1967: 45–47). Of course neither of them were interested in what prisoners had to say about their captivity. Instead

inmates stood for them as types of cultural groups, plied for information about customary practice at home. For anthropologists, as voyeurs of what they took to be society making outside the gaol, the world of inmates only held value as a microcosm of that wider social laboratory.

5 The methodology of Strathern contrasts with much reflexive writing in anthropology. While others set about critiquing anthropological representations that rely on idioms of totality, unit and presence by highlighting what they take to be the ambiguous, continually deferred and transient ground of cultural practice (Clifford and Marcus 1986; Clifford 1988 and 1997; Taussig 1992 and 1993), she takes constraint itself as her operating principle. Strathern is suspicious of claims that make literary techniques such as collage or narrative evocation the key to closer correspondence; to effect ambiguity does not in her view achieve much of a revolution (it is not clear how that effect resolves the dilemma of representation).

6 I believe that *The Gender of the Gift* might usefully be considered as a kind of lipogram (a text that is written with the constraint that a given letter of the alphabet may not appear). Members of the Oulipo group chose Georges Perec's novel, *La Disparition* (A Void, 1995) as the most distinguished example of this experiment, since it was written without using the letter E, the most important vowel in the French language. Its success lay not just in the concealed qualities of language that emerged as a result of this violent erasure or 'disappearance', but also in what that absence said about the letter's usual orienting presence. *La Disparition* is held to exist in two dimensions, as the story of what is portrayed and that of the constraint that allowed it to be recounted (Motte 1986b: 12). The same, I believe, might be said of Strathern's text.

7 Strathern (1988) uses the term 'sociality' as a descriptive device that allows her to talk about a Melanesian social imagination that does not incorporate anthropological assumptions about the relationship between Individual and Society.

8 Strathern (1988) argues that in Melanesia it might be more profitable to imagine the person as a composite of these relations, what Wagner (1991: 163) terms 'an entity with relationship integrally implied'. Sets of relations and the social order are given, and embodied in the person.

9 Sneezes and other physical reactions exemplify the ways in which for prisoners absent persons and places are felt as well as heard or seen. Feld (1996) highlights this multisensory conceptualisation of place among the Kaluli people of Bosavi. He calls for anthropologists to pay attention to all the senses that are used when people evoke place (not just the preference for visualism that dominates the European concept of landscape) (94).

10 Members of the Oulipo group held that no system of constraint should be taken as completely coherent or imposed without a nod to its own transgression. They advised that readers should be aware of interruptions or 'anti-constraints' as well (Motte 1986b: 19). Indeed, Motte asks whether creative freedom might be assured not by constraint itself, but rather by the flaw it necessarily contains (1986b: 20).

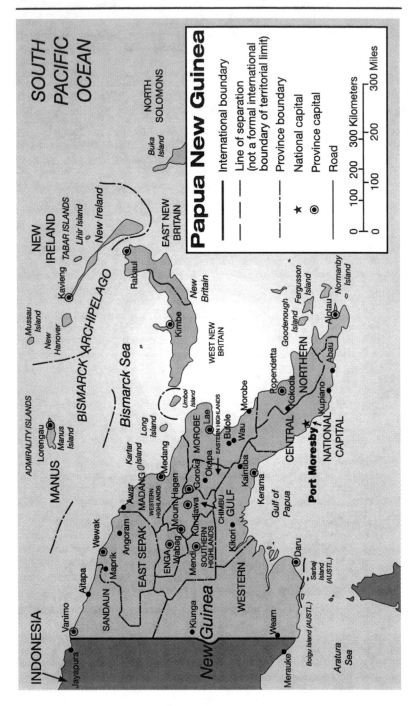

CHAPTER 1

Dark Place

Out of sight

Bomana Major Central Area Correctional Institution (Figure 4) is the largest prison in Papua New Guinea (it usually holds between 600 and 700 inmates, supervised by nearly 200 warders). Contained within its extensive grounds are not just prison compounds, but also housing for staff and a national training centre for new recruits. The prison complex is divided into general sections, including A Compound for male national prisoners (550 to 600 inmates), E Division for expatriate male prisoners (one to five inmates) and a juvenile compound for boys (twenty to thirty inmates).[1] These sections are each surrounded by their own cyclone wire fence (eight feet high), but together are enclosed behind a perimeter fence (nineteen feet high). A Compound contains by far the largest number of cells at Bomana. Constructed of breeze-blocks with corrugated iron roofs, concrete walls and floors, barred ventilation windows just below ceiling level, back rooms with drop toilets and taps for washing, and a single heavy metal door at one end, these barrack rooms or dormitory-style houses usually hold between thirty and eighty men. Some of them run back-to-back, joined and separated by small detention or punishment cells. A Compound itself is further divided into three adjacent sections, each with its own yard and cyclone wire fence (Figure 5). There is a section for remand inmates (200 to 250 inmates), which has three cells, and two sections for convicts (300 to 400 inmates serving sentences ranging from a few weeks to life terms); the larger one has ten cells and the other, designed for those classified as well behaved, has two. Within the Compound there is also a mess hall where convicts and remand inmates collect and eat their meals and a large communal toilet block with showers. Just outside the gate of A Compound are a guardhouse and watchtower, the prison library and chapel, and behind it a sloping grass parade ground, where every morning and afternoon roll call is taken.

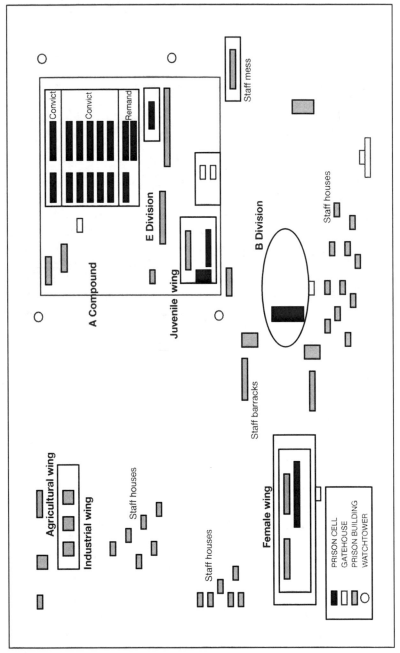

Figure 4 *Map showing Bomana Major Central Area Correction Institution*

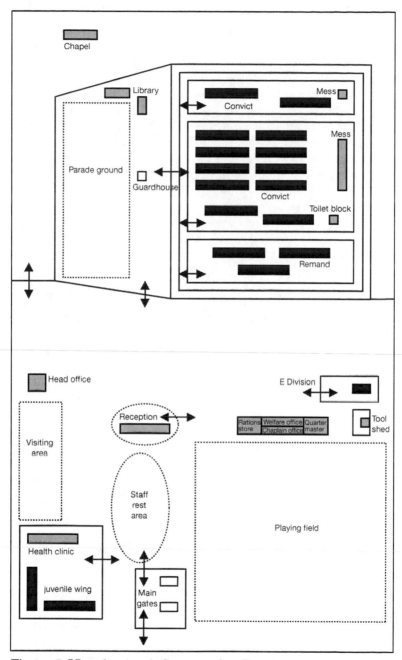

Figure 5 *Map showing A Compound at Bomana*

The rest of the area within the high perimeter fence is shielded from A Compound by a corrugated iron wall. Directly behind it, is E Division, a small house, divided into individual barred rooms, with its own shower, raised toilet and cooking facilities. The staff buildings are also breeze-block and include the reception office and property room, as well as a narrow single-storey structure that contains the rations store, the quartermaster store and cramped rooms for the chaplain and welfare office. Another building, a two-storey wooden villa, holds offices for the jail commander and his deputy, the security officer and civilian secretaries. On its ground floor is an interrogation room, where prisoners are searched after receiving weekend visitors and punishment beatings are some-times carried out. A single-lane macadam path, wide enough for vehicles to go up and down, leads from these offices to the main gates of the high perimeter fence. On one side of the path is a full-sized playing field, where prisoners play soccer and touch rugby, and large events such as group baptisms or customary dance competitions are held. The other side of the path is lawn, bordered with flowers and arranged with wind and sun shelters for the comfort of staff and waiting visitors. Behind it is another grassed area, where ecumenical Christian services and conversion crusades take place, and visitors sit down with prisoners. Tucked into the far corner of the high perimeter fence, and as far as possible from A Compound, is the juvenile wing. This contains two dormitory cells, one occupied by teenage male offenders and the other by those adult convicts and remand inmates who are considered to be at risk of personal attack. This compound yard also houses the prison health clinic, run by a single paramedic guard who is responsible for treating the wounds and ailments of the entire prison population. Watchtowers, falling back on one side to the Laloki River and on the other to a small artificial lagoon, ring the high perimeter fence.

The road beyond the high perimeter fence is lined with mango trees and eventually leads out, via a sentry post and lift gate, to the civilian parts of Bomana (a Catholic seminary, two high schools, an agricultural college, a Second World War cemetery for Australian service men, a police training academy and the edges of Port Moresby settlements). But before leaving the prison complex, this road passes what is known as B Division (ten to thirty inmates), the only maximum-security institution in the country. Some ten minutes' walk from the high perimeter fence that encloses the other male inmate compounds, B Division houses those men who are considered especially dangerous or deserving of extra punishment, such as recaptured fugitives, well-known prisoner rapists, the protagonists of fights and riots, and those caught with weapons and illegal contraband. A tall corrugated iron wall (fifteen feet high) that prevents outside observation encircles the unit itself. Inside men are locked in a single building that contains two rows of individual, windowless cells. During the day they may be brought out for exercise in the small yard or placed in individual open cages. Prisoners are expected to use the bucket provided in their cell as a toilet and to shower in public, whenever guards decide to open the shower taps in the yard. The female wing is a further ten-minute walk, back behind the maximum-security institution. This installation is surrounded by staff housing and cannot be viewed from any of the male compounds. A double cyclone wire fence (eight feet high) contains one dormitory cell, holding both remand (five to ten inmates) and convict women (fifteen to twenty inmates), a mess hall and a converted cell used as a leisure room and workshop. There is a small gatehouse, but no watchtowers. The rest of the prison complex is given over to industrial and agricultural training facilities. These include fields for growing crops and raising cattle, a piggery and chicken farm, as well as a garage and electrical, welding and joinery workshops. Staff housing is spread across the complex, divided between officers and guards, and then between single men or women, who live in barrack rooms or studio blocks, and those who live in married quarters.

Reasons	*rison*
I have been living in a dark place.	*mi bin stap long peles tudak*
I have no friends.	*mi no gat ol poroman*
They have forgotten me.	*ol lus tingting long mi*
Another day is hot,	*narapela san i hat*
Another night is cold.	*narapela nait i kol*
What can I do?	*bai mi olsem wanem*
The air is full of strange behaviour.	*win pulap long kain kain pasin*
Some will win, some will lose.	*sampela win, sampela lus*
Tell me your reasons,	*telim mi rison blong yu*
And I will tell you mine.	*na mi bai telim yu mine*
I don't care if it is wrong.	*mi no care em i rong*
I don't care if it is right.	*mi no care em i rait.*

(Antony Ume)

A remand inmate, who awaits the outcome of his court case and, like those around him, suffers from the uncertainty of his penal situation, wrote the song above. For him the experience of separation from those he knew outside the gaol is best evoked by appeal to metaphors of darkness. The inmate regrets the absence of friends, his inability to view them or in turn to be viewed, and as a result feels abandoned. Indeed, prisoners often describe Bomana as a 'dark place' (*dak ples*). It is dark because it leaves the inmate unsighted, his or her gaze blocked and the prisoner himself or herself veiled from public view. In particular inmates focus on the missing face (*pes*), that which might be looked upon and thus evoke response and that which might look back. The architecture at Bomana is distinguished on the basis of what it hides or conceals (see Reed 1999).

This sense of darkness pervades the analogies that prisoners sometimes draw. Koivi, for instance, a convict from Baimuru in Gulf province, compared the prison to the men's ceremonial house that once stood in his village. As a boy, he recalled hearing stories about customary initiation. Old men, he was told, would escort male youths to this ceremonial house, which sloped down like a sagging triangle from the top of a support post. Through a small door the party would crawl inside and find themselves in a dark, windowless interior. There, invisible to one another and those outside, the boys would live for the next month and listen to the disembodied voices of the old men. During that time they would receive little food and be forced to have their ears cut and bled. When they eventually left the men's house, the boys would be greeted with cheers and admiring comments. Koivi stated that although he never experienced the ceremony, old men in his village still talked about it and themselves made direct comparisons to incarceration. Locked inside the men's house, the convict explained, boys were unable to see the face of their father, mother, brothers or sisters (*no lukim pes blong papa, mama, brata, susa*), like prisoners they ate little and lived without viewing the sun rise or set.

Peter, a remand inmate from Pityilu Island in Manus province, drew a different comparison. He suggested that prison seemed like a customary mourning ceremony. Peter explained that when someone dies on his island the head of the grieving spouse is shaved and that person is then dressed in black and raised up onto a high platform house. There he or she remains for three to six months, abstaining from certain foods, covered over in rags and hidden from public scrutiny. At the end of that mourning period a feast is held and the grieving spouse is led down from the platform and taken to the sea in order to wash. Once clean, his or her black clothes are removed and mourning is said to end. Peter regarded the grieving spouse, restricted in movement and concealed from view, as akin to a prisoner at Bomana. Indeed, he reported that people at home regarded the ceremony as a form of captivity, the widow or widower described as 'locked up above' (*kalabusim em antap*).[2] In this analogy, and that drawn to initiation at the ceremonial men's house, prisoners display a concern for the shadows thrown by the act of confinement. The prisoner is characterised as someone unseen.

More generally, however, prisoners are reluctant to suggest analogies. They perceive the conditions at Bomana as unique and without precedent. The ultimate site of this removal from public gaze is held to be B Division, for men there are confined and separated not just from people outside the prison, but also from fellow inmates. Locked up for three-month periods and denied access to weekend visitors (and also to anthropologists!), these prisoners are said to reside in a place quite unlike the rest of Papua New Guinea, one where 'all relationships are broken'. Men who return to A Compound after a term in the maximum-security unit often complain at their inability there to see anything beyond the tall corrugated iron wall. They complain that they couldn't see Bisoke hill or the road along which work gangs and weekend visitors walk as they make their way back and forth to the high perimeter fence that surrounds the other male compounds. When they looked up from the unit's yard, these inmates recall, they saw nothing but blue sky and beating sun, and the faces of warders, who stared down from an observation platform that circles the top of the wall. Being in B Division, several male inmates claimed, was like living 'under the ground' (*aninit long graun*), lost in a deep, dark hole.[3]

But darkness is not just a condition imposed by the force of prison authority. Inmates themselves claim to favour unseeing lives. They tend to walk around the compound yards with slumped shoulders and downcast eyes. Prisoners warn newcomers to act 'humble', to avoid direct eye contact with others, not to stare or 'place their eyes' (*putim ai*), and thus prevent the risk of confrontation. Just as the weeping face of a parent on a weekend visit might cause the inmate to worry, so to gaze upon the unknown or hostile visages of strangers might provoke unwelcome response. Prisoners advise that 'face to face' (*pes pes*) living at Bomana is dangerous.

To reduce the impact of challenging gazes, male inmates hang blankets in their dormitory cells to act as screens. Indeed, from any cell doorway one usually only sees a narrow corridor of blankets leading to the bathroom at the other end. Behind these screens further hanging blankets slice the space into smaller divisions known as 'cubes' or 'dark rooms' (*dak rum*). There, hidden from the view of cellmates, four to nine men live together.[4] Before entering another cube they must ask permission. Without these dark rooms, male prisoners claim, fights would break out all the time. If forced to live face-to-face, cellmates would overhear private conversation and witness private actions. It is said that they would start to steal from each other, to argue over food rations and grow angry from disturbed sleep. By throwing shadows, the cube keeps potential enemies apart (Figure 6).

These veiled spaces have another purpose. They also hide men from more welcome faces and the obligations that accompany

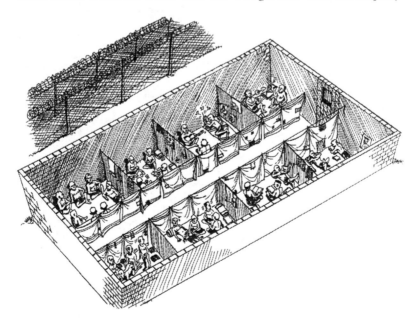

Figure 6 *A men's prison cell*

that sight. Male inmates complain that they never have enough supplies of tobacco, marijuana and home-brew alcohol to share around. When smoking a cigarette or eating a stolen tin of fish meat an inmate is aware of those he excludes from the feast. Should he share the items with one man, then others who might demand a claim will go without. In a cell with no cubes this situation would become impossible. Too many demands would be made obvious and as a result somebody would always be left unsatisfied. The dark room allows goods to be consumed in private and thus leaves competing obligations safely juggled.

Of course, cubes also block the gaze of warders. Behind these screens men break prison rules and conduct themselves without fear of observation. So protected, they smoke, etch tattoos, listen to smuggled radios, beat up suspected informers, cut their foreskins, discuss plans for future robberies or escapes, rape others, cook food and gamble. Warders tolerate the existence of these hidden spaces because they acknowledge that without them tensions would increase. Unless the offence takes place in full view, guards generally do not feel compelled to intervene. Only the 'big head' (*bik het*) or stubborn inmate, who defies rules in public, provokes their punishment. Indeed, the men of A Compound are left relatively unsupervised. The dormitory cell itself provides no outside peephole in which to observe events inside. Watchtowers are rarely occupied and surveillance tends to be casual rather than systematic. In the same way male prisoners often forgive warders their beatings as long as they take place out of view. It is the public sight of struck blows and bloodied faces that demand response and can spark riots.

The constraint of separation prompts inmates to adopt metaphors of darkness when describing prison experience. Bomana is a dark place because it blocks the exchange of gazes with people outside the gaol. Yet enclosure is also a technology that prisoners come to value. By hiding or making themselves unseen, they learn to strategically manage sets of relations within Bomana. The restrictions on sight that casting darkness provides allows inmates to measure, and thus gain relief from, the weight of obligation.

Supervision

The margin by which the prison exceeds detention is filled in fact by techniques of a disciplinary type. And this disciplinary addition to the juridical is what, in short, is called the 'penitentiary'. (Foucault 1977: 248)

The metaphor of darkness chosen by prisoners at Bomana seems out of sympathy with the emphases placed on penal routine and discipline by historians of incarceration in Europe and North America. Imprisonment, as an act of separation and enclosure, tends to be ignored in favour of accounts that describe the emergence of this technical administration. As the story goes, at some point, usually said to be the late eighteenth century, a break in the culture of punishment occurred. Rather than viewing prison as just a staging post in the spectacle of legal sanction, which is properly exercised upon the body of the criminal (whippings, executions, tortures, the stocks), people start to consider prison itself as the appropriate focus of punishment and at the same time eschew the public act of judicial violence (see Rothman1971 and 1980; Foucault 1977, Ignatieff 1978; Spierenburg 1984; Hirsch 1992; Friedman 1993). No longer a dungeon or holding house, the prison becomes the site for extraordinary interventions on what is regarded as the soul or self of the criminal.[5] While historians acknowledge a period of great confinement, their attention falls not on the dimensions of concealment but rather on the regime that removal is held to allow. In particular, Foucault is suspicious of any claim that relegates the penal experience to the moment of enclosure, to what he terms the legalistic definition of punishment as 'mere deprivation of liberty' (1977: 257). For him the penitentiary is crucially detention *plus* discipline. It is this extra judicial aspect of imprisonment that Foucault is concerned with and whose impact he believes supersedes the pains of confinement.

The history that Foucault presents is tied into a wider project that seeks to undermine the post-Enlightenment claims made for vision (cf. Jay 1993). He is especially concerned to challenge the ideal of transparency, a notion that it is possible or desirable to strive for total visibility, presence or clarity (Levin 1997: 412). This ideal, Foucault argues, informs the motivation for modern knowledge practice and has real political consequences. For the modern attitude is said to govern by illumination, to convert vision into supervision (Flynn 1993: 281) or make visibility a trap (Foucault 1977: 200). Foucault seized upon the designs put forward by Bentham for a Panopticon precisely because they seemed to validate the dangers he saw in an ocular centric bias. Prison reforms that introduced penal discipline operated on the basis of first making subjects visible. Far from being a place where offenders were hidden away, Foucault argued that the penitentiary brought them to light and made them objects of attention. In his own words, techniques 'were being elaborated for distributing individuals, fixing them in space, classifying them, extracting from them the maximum in time and forces, training their bodies, coding their continuous behaviour, maintaining them in perfect visibility, forming around them an apparatus of observation, registration and recording, constituting on them a body of knowledge that is accumulated and centralised' (1977: 231). To Foucault, these activities were what marked the experience of imprisonment as something more than detention. He notes the emergence of the idea that a subject's behaviour could be transformed by the discipline of visibility. While Foucault recognises that enclosure took place (he could hardly do otherwise), he never grants that constraint has the same productive power.

Perhaps this omission is the consequence of working with archive material and nonethnographic resources. A study of dominant discourses provides cultural representations of both 'prisoner' and 'prisons', but does not necessarily suggest the nature of the penal experience. Sloop (1996: 6), who provides a genealogy of popular media rhetoric on prisoners in the United States since the Second World War, argues that these representations carry social force and thus gain materiality. He claims that subject disciplining is the outcome of such rhetoric as well as institutional practice (9). For Sloop both the consciousness of prisoners and their forms of punishment are shaped by these discursive manoeuvres. But this idea is problematic, especially when transferred to the discursive environment of colonial and postcolonial government records. Representations of prisoners and prisons seem exclusive or interest-group specific. It is harder to make claims for their translation as a force or instrumentality upon the subject position of inmates. When reading the archive of annual reports on colonial and postcolonial Papua New Guinea, I was struck by the lack of correspondence between the discursive representations of incarceration found there and those provided by prisoners at Bomana.[6]

His standard of punishment is solely corporeal, and it is measured by the power of might and the degree of brutality inherent in the particular person inflicting the punishment. The result of the punishment is death. (*Papua Annual Report 1912–1913:* 70)

When the Territory of British New Guinea was first annexed in 1889 (its administration taken over by the Australian government in 1906 and renamed as the Territory of Papua), colonial officers responsible for implementing the rule of law recognised that they would be punishing a very different kind of offending subject. Discursive attention was directed to the 'savage'. Up until the outbreak of the Second World War, this subject figured whenever annual reports discussed penal administration or the exercise of punishment. The Savage was presented as male, Black and Other, at times characterised as childlike and at other times as animal (see Reed 1997). He was said to be innocent, without a sense of individual responsibility, and honest, but also wild, impulsive, cruel and indifferent to the sight of suffering. The Savage was driven by sensual motivations, such as a 'lust for blood' (*Papua Annual Report 1906–1907*: 11) and the 'eye for an eye' (*New Guinea Annual Report 1921–1922*: 50) principle of payback or revenge. He sought compensation through casual and brutal attacks upon the body. By comparison, or so those writing in the annual reports inferred, the importation of incarceration appeared both humane and fair.

But this attempt to draw distinctions on the basis of punitive cultures, between the Savage and the civilised White coloniser, ran into difficulties. Officers submitting dispatches to the annual reports worried over how to present the corporeal side of government punishment. Most of all they feared that native subjects would mistake the administration's justice for their own. For while the annual reports stressed the differences between a standard of punishment directed to the body and one directed to the mind or self of the offender, this distinction did not seem to coincide with the punitive powers that officers actually exercised. Right up until the Second World War prison ordinances included provisions for flogging and pack drill (in the Territory of New Guinea, which was taken over from German administration in 1914 when Australian troops invaded, planters themselves, under government officer supervision, were permitted to punish their labour force with detentions and whippings [*New Guinea Annual Report 1914–1915*: 13]). However, it was the exercise of the death penalty that caused most concern. Those writing in the annual reports expressed fears that this punishment might be misconstrued as an act of retribution or vengeance. What is notable in the listing of court judgments, with the exception of those offenders convicted of killing or raping members of the colonising population (*Papua Annual Report 1914–1915*: 10–12; and cf. Inglis 1974, 1982), is the frequency with which magistrates commuted death sentences to terms of imprisonment. By the First World War those hangings that were carried out tended to be staged behind closed doors (*Papua Annual Report 1914–1915*: 98). If corporal punishment took place, it was not to be made a spectacle.

The Barugi attacked Mr Monckton and party some 18 months ago, at night, whilst he was camped on the sea beach close to the river. Mr Monckton beat them off and then proceeded to their principal village and captured several of them, including the chief of the tribe. The full name of the chief is Oyogoba Sara, but he is usually called Oyogoba. After being kept prisoner for some months at Cape Nelson, Oyogoba and his companions were sent home. Since then the Barugi have been on friendly terms with the Government (*British New Guinea Annual Report 1902–1903:* 14)

The patrol officer brought his prisoners across country into Port [Moresby], a distance of 250 miles, over mountains and across rivers, and delivered them safely at Port Moresby gaol. They were tried by Mr Justice Gore, some were sent back to their village with a warning that they must sin no more, and others were sentenced to 12 months imprisonment with hard labour (*Papua Annual Report 1933–1934:* 22)

Imprisonment played a vital role in the colonial government's pacification programme. By sending patrols across the country, the territories were explored, contact made with different peoples and fighting between them put down (see Schieffelin and Crittenden 1991). Should any resistance to the patrol officer or his party be shown along the way then those hamlets or villages would be raided and punitive arrests made (Figure 7). Those men taken by the patrol would be led back to the government station, brought before the magistrate and sentenced. Some would be released and sent back home with instructions to tell people to end resistance, while others would be given cautionary prison terms and so be forced to remain. Annual reports presented these patrols as heroic adventures and the kidnappings as pedagogic exercises in good government and the rule of law. Imprisonment was important in this process because it provided a reason for keeping the captives at the government station for longer periods. It was said that in these civilised surroundings the Savage learnt to respect the administration's justice and also to cooperate with members of hostile tribes (*British New Guinea Annual Report 1901–1902*: 24).

Figure 7 *Arrested murderers from the interior (Aitape District)*

But this education was held to be a fragile procedure, requiring that prisoners be handled carefully and given a gradual
introduction to the strictures of incarceration. An officer reporting from the Western Division of British New Guinea in the
second year of its annexation recorded the cautious way in which
he began to punish his subjects, at first only detaining them for
hourly periods until they learnt the nature of this punishment

(*British New Guinea Annual Report 1890–1891*: 19). Indeed, annual reports mentioned the excitement that initial acts of confinement caused among local populations, men and women said to visit the government station just in order to sit and watch the first prisoners (*Papua Annual Report 1911–1912*: 73). These reports described both the inmates and their observers possessing childlike wonder at the situation. One officer at Ramu station in the Territory of New Guinea warned of the need for patience, declaring that 'in spite of the fact that they like to crawl in and out and interfere with office work, they (the visitors) are welcome', and that in the end the example set by watching prisoners in a well-maintained station would prove 'beneficial to their minds' (*New Guinea Annual Report 1933–1934*: 28). Reports extended this image of the crawling, troublesome but innocent child by providing anecdotal stories of the Savage's capacity for mimicry. One account spoke of a man dismissed from the Armed Constabulary (government police force that was responsible for both arresting offenders and guarding them during their incarceration) who proceeded to visit a village and there handcuff a 'prisoner' and open his own 'court' (*British New Guinea Annual Report 1902–1903*: 25). Another account spoke of some village councillors who acted as judges, tried and convicted a man on a spurious charge and then sentenced him to be flogged, to have his hair cut short, his armlets removed and to serve a three-month prison term (*Papua Annual Report 1932–1933*: 25). The stories are related in the annual reports in a tone of good humour and forgiving tolerance. Even the fugitive is treated lightly, one dispatch describing the frightened and helpless behaviour of a prisoner who tried to run away and who was 'brought back to the station crying like a child' (*Papua Annual Report 1924–1925*: 33). It was said that the Savage, unlike 'white races', had no conception of an offence against Society (*British New Guinea Annual Report 1899–1900*: 38). Officers approvingly recorded that prisoners suffered no stigma from their conviction or imprisonment and so were able to return home without disgrace.

A scene of the wildest confusion followed – canoes darting right and left, some crews throwing up water with their paddles as a sign for us to go away, others impelled by curiosity to come nearer, and the majority taken aback, and at a loss what to do. All the time the returned prisoners kept calling out 'do not be afraid; we are Government men now. There is no more fighting,' and soon the general consternation changed to expressions of surprise and delight as the released prisoners were recognised by their friends... the scenes as these men were taken

to their Ravi, or men's house, were really touching — old men welcoming sons,
and brothers and friends crowding round and embracing the returned captives,
whom they evidently expected never to see again — and the pleasure they felt
manifested itself as a display of gratitude towards us, so that it was with a boat-
load of gifts.. that we returned to our camp at Baimuru. (*Papua Annual Report
1908–1909:* 88)

The prisoner, Awari, after vainly hailing his people, disappeared, and I had given
him up for lost, when he returned late in the evening with all the Katapia
people, who had run away at our coming, and with him came his wife [in
widow's weeds] and chief Deta with over fifty people altogether. Their excitement at the unlooked for 'resurrection' of Awari was intense. I informed them
His Excellency had decided to give Awari back to his people, and that they must
now become good friends of the Government... I gathered that the people had
fully believed that he had been killed and eaten by the Government long ago,
as he had been captured in 'warfare'. (*Papua Annual Report 1925–1926:* 15)

In drawing these scenes of panic, of a wild and confused reception, those writing the annual reports sought to further the
contrast between Savage and Civilised forms of punishment. The
local people are presented as shocked and surprised by the return
of prisoners, believing them taken in warfare and therefore killed
or eaten long ago. Their unexpected 'resurrection' is said to be
the cue for a mass conversion to the side of Government, a realisation of the administration's benevolence and its superior
powers of protection. The enlightened Savage, now gushing with
gratitude, covers the redeeming party with gifts and swears
friendship. Annual reports were keen to portray the Government
as above communal disputes and tribal fighting. Imprisonment
stood out as the discursive antithesis of these corporeal conflicts,
as a properly parental response to brutal, untamed impulses. One
dispatch gloried in the colonial subject's acknowledgement of
this relationship. It described the death of two prisoners in 1916,
who ran away during their transfer between prisons in the Territory of Papua and were killed days later in the bush by local
people. Just before their demise it is said that the fugitives called
out for support to their 'most trusted protectors', not, as was
previously 'instinctive', to their father or village, but instead to
the gaoler and his constabulary guards (*Papua Annual Report
1916–1917:* 6). Imprisonment, it appeared, taught the Savage to
regard Government as his true father.

There are probably no institutions in a colony upon which the moral force and
tone of the administration will be found more clearly stamped than on penal
establishments. (*British New Guinea Annual Report 1900–1901:* xxxvi)

Annual reports represented the colonial prison as an 'educational and civilising institution' (*British New Guinea Annual Report 1891–1892*: 45). There, it was claimed, prisoners learnt not only to respect the rule of law but also the value of disciplined, well-managed lives. Prison ordinances reproduced in annual reports laid out in minute detail the list of rules that inmates must follow, to which guards and the gaoler must ensure compliance through close observation. Thus the 1919 Prisons Ordinance for the Territory of Papua included among its legislated offences behaviour such as 'singing or laughing', 'talking loudly', 'quarrelling', 'showing disrespect', 'omitting or refusing to walk in file', 'answering untruthfully', 'refusing to keep the clothes given to him', 'making groundless complaints' and 'refusing to eat the food prescribed' (*Papua Prisons Ordinance 1919*: section 197). Individual progress was monitored in a raft of journals, and the Ordinance also laid down terms for classification and the spatial distance to be kept between classes. It was held that through regular work, regular hours and 'strict adherence to routine' (*Papua Annual Report 1919–1920*: 48) the Savage might be transformed. Indeed, the very wild and raw state of 'his' being meant that in some ways the Savage was deemed more 'tractable' (*British New Guinea Annual Report 1897–1898*: 46) and so easier to mould. Reports stressed that the prison was as much a moral education as a form of punishment.

After puzzling early failures, the unexpected death of men in custody (see Prologue), those writing in the annual reports stated that inmate bodies were now the healthiest in the colony. Time and again reference was made to the remarkable changes in physical appearance that prisoners underwent, from the 'miserable, starved-looking individual' who first entered prison to the now 'sturdy, plump' convict (*Papua Annual Report 1908–1909*: 118). This transformation was put down to good diet, discipline and employment, but also to intensive instruction in how best to look after the body. The main difference, officers submitted, was that prisoners 'are compelled to take care of themselves until they are well' (*British New Guinea Annual Report 1894–1895*: 25). The reproduced prison routine included hygiene measures such as regular hours for airing blankets, the inspection of sores, sweeping cells, washing clothes and soaping bodies (*Papua Annual Report 1912–1913*: 69). In fact the annual reports described all sorts of extra medical interventions. These included twice daily syringes of permanganate of potash in order to cure mouth disease (*Papua Annual Report 1917–1918*: 21), venereal and hook-worm treatments (*Papua Annual Report 1924–1925*: 68), sulphur fumigation baths for skin blights (*British New Guinea Annual Report 1902–1903*: 44), vaccinations (*Papua Prisons Ordinance 1919*: section 169), shaved heads rubbed with lime in order to get rid of lice (*Papua Prisons Ordinance 1919*: section 172), isolations for infectious diseases (*Papua Annual Report 1913–1914*: 108) and rectal swab tests for dysentery (*New Guinea Annual Report 1932–1933*: 50). Reports stated that prisoners were encouraged to examine themselves for signs of illness, to be constantly aware of the body as a site of inspection. As a result of all these disciplinary measures, the inmate was said to gain in both physical and mental condition (*British New Guinea Annual Report 1900–1901*: 101).

While the discipline of work was held to transform the Savage mind and body, annual reports also acknowledged that this labour played a crucial role in the maintenance of the colony. Up until the Second World War, prison labour was often responsible for building and sustaining the services of townships and government stations. Both Samarai Island[7] and Port Moresby settlements relied upon inmates for their expansion. Reports stated that between 1893 and 1895 prisoners filled and drained the swamp at Samarai, thus reclaiming 9.5 acres of land (*British New Guinea Annual Report 1892–1893/1893–1894*: 43). It is recorded that they went on to construct a road around the island, to lay out the township's streets, to build the local court house, hospital, post office and customs house, to sink wells, clear undergrowth and plant ornamental trees (*British New Guinea Annual Report 1902–1903*: 29). At Port Moresby most public services seemed to operate with prison labour. The annual report for 1912–1913 listed among their civic tasks the discharging and handling of cargo, road making, weeding, coaling steamers, digging graves, shoring up sea walls, maintaining the town's sanitation works and collecting waste, tending government nurseries and plantations, running messages and clearing drains. Long-term inmates even acted as assistant prison guards. Indeed, officers in annual reports regularly mentioned the vital role of this penal workforce and expressed fears that falling numbers of prisoners might restrict the colony's expansion (*British New Guinea Annual Report 1899–1900*: 37; and *Papua Annual Report*

1906–1907: 114). On many patrols prisoners acted as carriers. During times of crisis prison labour was viewed as especially important. Civilian employers who were short of workers could sometimes hire prisoners (*Papua Annual Report 1911–1912*: 118), and during the Depression years of 1929 to 1934 reports asserted that no public work at all would have been carried out in their absence (*Papua Annual Report 1932–1933*: 8). Prisoners, then, appeared at the heart of the colonial regime.

Their role often continued after release. Described in one report 'as the agent conveying the results of the object-lesson' (*Papua Annual Report 1929–1930*: 20), the discharged prisoner was believed to have important knowledge to impart back home – not just as embodied evidence of the administration's benevolence and refusal to engage in corporeal attacks, but even more importantly as a demonstration of what a disciplined and well-ordered regime might produce. The released prisoner was held to be both spy and ambassador for colonial government. Reports claimed that these men acted on their own initiative to stop and arrest fugitives, to mediate in their village and other areas on behalf of the patrol officer and to generally maintain good order (*British New Guinea Annual Report 1902–1903*: 45). Sometimes this assistance was formalised by appointing the discharged prisoner as a village constable, responsible for reporting offences to the local magistrate, or as an interpreter and patrol guide (*British New Guinea Annual Report 1900–1901*: 41). But not all released convicts returned home. The annual reports also portrayed these men as ideal employees. As a result of their imprisonment, which acquainted them with Government practice, taught them to speak English, Motu or Tok Pisin, to be schooled in the discipline of work and drill, and equipped to use tools, they were said to be uniquely skilled (*British New Guinea Annual Report 1902–1903*: 43; *Papua Annual Report 1908–1909*: 121). Officers in the reports stated that many discharged prisoners entered private, mission or government service as free labourers, and that some joined the Armed Constabulary or served as warders (*Papua Annual Report 1908–1909*: 123) (Figure 8). The future, it was often inferred, lay with those who could match the standard of discipline, industriousness and good conduct shown by prisoners.

There is really not much criminality in many of these homicides. Loss of temper, or a belief in the justice, in certain cases, of taking the law into their own hands, was that which in most cases led the culprits to break the law. (*British New Guinea Annual Report 1901–1902*: 8)

| A non-commis-
sioned officer of
native police. | A native police
constable. | A native prison
warder. | A native senior
prison warder. |

Figure 8 *Native officials-natives permanently employed in the*
Administration for a term of years

Early annual reports played down the wilfulness of native
offences. It was repeatedly stated that the Savage was *not* a Criminal, that he did not yet possess the devious and cunning mind
of the professional offender (*Papua Annual Report 1911–1912*:
125). Officers pointed to the low rates of recidivism and the
exemplary behaviour of discharged prisoners (*Papua Annual
Report 1929–1930*: 22). They praised the Savage as honest, good-
tempered and respectful, as not yet 'over-civilised' or burdened
with deceit (*British New Guinea Annual Report 1900–1901*: 75).
One report stated that while 'violence is the badge of barbarism,
dishonesty (is) that of civilisation' (*Papua Annual Report
1906–1907*: 13). Indeed, officers in the annual reports expressed
much regret at what they saw as the inevitable decline into criminality following the Savage's introduction to civilised ways. At
times these reports seemed to anticipate a nostalgia for the innocence of Savagery, for the man who would stand up in court and
confess 'without shame and even with complacency' to a killing

that revolted the civilised mind (*Papua Annual Report 1928–1929*: 9). The legal task, as presented, was to teach the Savage the idea of individual criminal responsibility (*Papua Annual Report 1926–1927*: 124), as opposed to punishment being randomly exacted from a community, but once achieved it was said that honesty and non criminality would depart.

By 1907 officers in the Territory of Papua were already declaring that some native subjects, those closest to government stations and townships, had entered a 'semi-savage' state (*Papua Annual Report 1907–1908*: 62). This development was held to require a legal distinction, between Savage and Semi-Savage, one that would recognise a sliding scale of mitigating circumstances (see Fitzpatrick 1992). The annual reports noted that judges were now making sentencing decisions on the basis of the convicted person's degree of contact with Government and Civilisation. Those prosecuted from 'tribes' which had long and constant contact with the administration were to be treated with the same severity as Whites, while those from 'backward' tribes with intermediate or very limited levels of contact were to be treated far more lightly (*Papua Annual Report 1929–1930*: 22). Murray, the governor of the Territory from 1906 to 1940, was quoted as stating that the prisoner's length of term should be determined on this basis, 'that is to say, he gets a heavier sentence according as he ought to have known better' (*Papua Annual Report 1914–1915*: 12). Often this argument placed the less contacted peoples in the perceived position of children who have yet to be socialised. One report acknowledged that such an offender 'cannot receive punishment for following his natural bent when nothing has been effectively provided to supplant it' (*Papua Annual Report 1929–1930*: 21). In this rhetoric attachment to customary practice and belief was presented in the same naturalistic tone, the convicted person said to be 'mentally incapable of resisting the impulse of his tribal creed', so that it too became a measure of relief from criminal responsibility (ibid). Custom was presented as part of the sensuous, wild and violent aspect of the Savage.

The annual reports expressed anger and upset when someone long associated with Government did break the law. Indeed, these offences were read as the first signs of an indigenous criminality. In 1931 one particular case drew much attention in that year's report for the Territory of Papua. Four men, each with a long history of service for the colonial administration, were convicted of murdering three villagers from the interior mountains behind Port Moresby. One of them had served as a lance-corporal in the Armed Constabulary, another had been educated at a mission school, one had been employed as a government clerk and interpreter and the last had worked as a houseboy to a white settler. Murray, who expressed in the report his bitter disappointment that such men 'so long under European influence' should commit this act, announced that they deserved full punishment as criminals (*Papua Annual Report 1930–1931*: 10). He wished the two ringleaders to be hung, to receive the same standard of penalty as white people could expect. But in the end their sentence was commuted to life imprisonment, while the other two men involved were given ten-year sentences. It seemed that colonial government was not yet ready to forgo the mitigating circumstances of Savagery or admit full criminal parity between the races.

The prison system will aim particularly at the rehabilitation of prisoners and their education and instruction in useful technical trades and agriculture. (*New Guinea Annual Report 1954–1955*: 83)

After the Second World War the Territories of New Guinea and Papua came under joint administration, although they continued to produce separate annual reports. From 1952 it was announced that these reports would be submitted in conformity with Article 88 of the United Nations Charter. This meant that the form of submission on penal administration was standardised and directed to answering a systematic set of questions. As a consequence the annual reports lost their previously anecdotal character, with individual submissions by regional gaolers and observations by government officials substituted for a clean, and usually anonymous layout and text. The United Nations questionnaire, to which the reports conformed, required consistent information on prison 'conditions' (the classification system, diet, education, medical care, sanitation, female prisoners, spatial dimensions of cells), on the 'nature of juvenile delinquency', 'types of prison labour' (kind, location, level of remuneration), 'kinds of corporal punishment', 'prison legislation and reform', 'methods of prison discipline', 'remission and probation details', as well as statistical reports on prison numbers and dietary scales (*New Guinea Annual Report 1963–1964*: title page). In response to this review the language and tone of the reports changed greatly. Suddenly the criminality of prisoners was assumed and for the first time 'rehabilitation' became the stated purpose of incarceration.

This discursive move culminated in the proclamation of the 1957 Corrective Institutions Ordinance, which announced the formal separation of the prison service from the police force (*Papua New Guinea Corrective Institutions Ordinance 1957*; and see Sikani 1994). It stipulated that the prison regime should be focused on educating inmates so that 'they will return to the community as citizens with a social and economic contribution to make to society' (*Papua Annual Report 1957–1958*: 68). As Criminals, prisoners now needed to recover their citizenship, to be corrected so that they could take up a full role in Society (a relationship that reports suggested now meant something to the colonial subject). The designated problem was therefore how inmates could be successfully reintegrated into that body, safely released outside. Whereas previously discharged prisoners were considered as potential agents of Government, now they were perceived as a danger to that good order (those released from prison were no longer eligible to join the police force or become warders). The Ordinance put forward 'after-care' measures to assist in reintegration and help them find employment. It stated that just before their due date of release prisoners were to be transferred to a prison nearer home, with the intention of helping them to 're-establish their family relationships and assist them in their rehabilitation' (*Papua Annual Report 1959–1960*: 80–81). If prisoners agreed to this return then they could expect the prison service to pay their transport and sustenance costs (*Papua Annual Report 1960–1961*: 112). At the same time it became important that prisoners be properly segregated, in order to prevent what reports now saw as the spread of criminality. Types of inmate were gradually siphoned off from the Corrective Institution. In 1950 the first forensic asylum was established for 'criminal lunatics' (see Goddard 1992a) and in1961 the Child Welfare Ordinance laid down that juvenile inmates should not come under prison jurisdiction, but rather be placed in government or mission-run reformatories (*Papua Annual Report 1959–1960*: 81; and *Papua Annual Report 1960–1961*: 112). Specialisation of treatment for the Criminal was now advocated.

In order to carry out this rehabilitation programme it was announced that prisons would be relocated, taken out of settlement areas and rebuilt on the outskirts of town. This development required a huge increase in government expenditure. In 1960 the gaol at Port Moresby was demolished and removed to Bomana, some fifteen kilometres away. There, reports claimed, proper space was provided for establishing agricultural and industrial facilities, and to mark out playing fields for recreation (*New Guinea Annual Report 1961–1962*: 132). Annual reports stated that the focus of correction programmes would be labour schemes. But instead of public works, prisoners were to remain inside the Corrective Institution and learn valuable trade skills. Not just at Bomana, but also across the colony male prisoners would be taught brick making (Figure 9), carpentry, motor mechanics, plumbing, welding, forestry, crop management and animal husbandry. Women prisoners, who were said to be small in number and not regarded as a threat to public order, would be taught sewing and handicrafts. Reports stated that long-term prisoners were to be remunerated as an incentive for rehabilitation and that work itself was to lose its exploitative nature and become 'training' (*New Guinea Annual Report 1960–1961*: 129). Alongside these labour schemes, annual reports presented recreational activities such as football, cricket and basketball, watching

Figure 9 *Prisoners making stabilized earth bricks at Bomana gaol*

films, reading books and magazines as corrective measures. Adult education courses were also introduced on these terms (*New Guinea Annual Report 1964–1965*: 111). The Corrective Institution was to be a self-sustaining rehabilitation centre. There would be no need for prisoners to leave its confines, to be seen in public: the concealed status that reports inferred was more appropriate for a new criminal class.

Specialisation also meant training for staff. From the late 1960s, annual reports stated that new recruits to the prison service underwent programmes of instruction in the management of inmates. A national Staff Training College was established at Bomana, which ran six to nine month induction courses and also refresher courses for senior officers (*Annual Report of Papua New Guinea Correctional Services 1991*: 29). The syllabus included lessons in management skills, security, discipline, supervision, leadership, counselling, use of firearms, basic law, foot drills, unarmed combat, physical training, communication skills and report writing. The warder now had a new discursive position as specialised technician. Annual reports also announced the expansion of after-care projects. Community Development Officers were appointed to visit prisons and discuss with inmates any concerns they might have about their family outside (*Papua New Guinea Annual Report 1972–1973*: 187). In 1970 an amendment to the criminal code introduced powers of 'release on licence', the discretion to set free well-behaved inmates ahead of their due date of discharge (*Papua New Guinea Annual Report 1970–1971*: 191). Reports observed that warders should not only manage prisoners and assess their conduct for classification, but also that they should weigh up whether or not the individual was safe for release.

There has been a substantial increase in crime, especially in urban areas. This needs to be seen against the background of rapid social changes. As a result of these changes, traditional social controls have begun to break down. In these circumstances it is considered necessary to ensure that the forces of law and order can act firmly until society itself begins to introduce new social controls and these new controls are accepted by the people. (*Papua New Guinea Annual Report 1970–1971*: 188)

Towards the end of colonial government and into the postcolonial period annual reports were written against what was presented as a rocketing crime rate. The recorded population of prisoners rose dramatically, from 8,000 bodies committed nationally during 1953 to over 22,000 bodies on the eve of independence (1975). Instead of the old discursive arguments, which regarded criminality as an inevitable side-effect of advancing Civilisation, the rising crime rate was now explained as the result of a failure to come to terms with that civilising process. Custom, which had previously been treated as a source of impulsive, violent behaviour, was now a 'traditional social control', whose loss left urban male youth without direction and so turning to crime. Until new social controls were found to replace it, the reports asserted that agents of law and order such as the Corrective Institution must act robustly. In these apparently rapidly changing social times the prison service presented itself as 'a vital aspect of social development', properly responsible for ensuring that prisoners transformed themselves into 'productive and safe members of the community' (*Papua New Guinea Annual Report 1971–1972*: 216). This language, which articulated rising crime and the fear of social collapse, only intensified in post-independence reports. By 1990 officials presented the Institution as a 'social defence system' (*Annual Report of Papua New Guinea Correctional Services 1991*: 27), leading the then Commissioner of the service, Pious Kerepia, to warn his staff that 'traditional and cultural values are eroding away and are being replaced by western concepts and modes of behaviour... Papua New Guinea stands at the crossroads of prosperous development and social anarchy' (*Korek Nius: newsletter of the Correctional Services 1990*: 5). And this despite the fact that prison population statistics actually showed marked fluctuations or even a decline in numbers (in 1983 the national committal rate was 19,000, five years later it was down to 12,500 and by 1991 it was 11,000; the total population recorded on any given day at Bomana, however, rose, from around 330 bodies in 1983, to 440 in 1988, 460 in 1991 and 670 in 1995 [*Prison Statistics of Papua New Guinea 1983–1988*]). Crisis became the discursive background for writing reports – not just the perceived crisis in law and order, but also the crisis of overcrowding and the financial crisis of diminished funds for dealing with that expansion.

This tone was exacerbated by the fact that in 1985 the prison service, for the first time, became an independent government department (previously it was under the umbrella of the Department of Justice), and so had to stake a direct claim for the distribution of State funds and resources. Named as the

Department of Correctional Services, it was now responsible for producing its own annual reports. As a result these took on the form of self-advertisement and the language of justification. The department was presented in a struggle for survival, with strains on expenditure leading to staff and housing shortages, a reduction in trade training programmes, high escape rates and low staff morale. Four years after gaining department status, the Correctional Service decided to appoint a Director of Public and Community Relations to develop further its profile. In his first statement, this official called for a nation-wide publicity drive (*Korek Nius: newsletter of the Correctional Services 1990*: 3). Annual reports also reproduced what was termed the department's 'mission statement' and list of 'objectives'. These included a commitment to 'strengthen the protection and well being of society' by ensuring 'secure, efficient and humane containment and treatment of individuals', to respect 'moral, religious and cultural values', to provide 'comprehensive training for staff', to 'foster community involvement' and to recognise that the department should not 'aggravate the suffering' of its prisoners (*Annual Report of Papua New Guinea Correctional Services 1991*: 7). In 1990 a series of new welfare projects was announced as a response to those commitments. Prisoners were to be sent out to visit schools and give public talks in order to dissuade pupils from becoming involved in crime, a literacy and educational correspondence course was to be set up and made available, newspapers were to be provided so that inmates could develop an interest in national issues, and mid-weekly Christian services established, to be known as Dedication Days, and run by visiting church groups (*Annual Report of Papua New Guinea Correctional Services 1990*: 16; *Annual Report of Papua New Guinea Correctional Services 1991*: 32–33). The idea was that Community should assist in the rehabilitation of its own offenders.

The duties of a member are to respect and protect human dignity and maintain and uphold the human rights of all persons in the performance of the member's duties. (*Papua New Guinea Draft Correctional Service Bill 1995:* section 37c)

In part inspired by the rhetoric of the Papua New Guinea Constitution, annual reports began to adopt the language of rights. The back page of one report printed in bold, large type the message: 'Lest we forget... Prisoners are Human Beings' (*Annual Report of Papua New Guinea Correctional Services 1991*:

100). Indeed, penal regulations started to read like a negotiation between the human rights of competing parties, with both the prisoner and the warder presented as rights-bearing sets of individuals. In 1995, under the editorial and financial guidance of the Australian government's aid agency, a draft version of a new Correctional Service Bill was proposed. This document, tabled in accordance with a wider funding package, outlined a series of obligations that warders and the Correctional Service would owe to their detained charges. These included the recognition of the prisoner's 'right' to reasonable medical care and attention (*Papua New Guinea Draft Correctional Services Bill 1995*: section 141 [1]), to the practice of religion of choice (section 143[1]) and to the adequate supply of food rations (section 123 [1]). Prisoners would also have the right of access to a lawyer, visiting judge or magistrate, and to a government watchdog body known as the Ombudsman Commission (sections 73, 74 and 75). Warders in turn had a right to use reasonable force to assure compliance (section 112 [1]), to search prisoners and confiscate what they found (section 85), to take fingerprints or photographs as a means of identification (section 86 [1]), and to extract blood, urine or saliva so as to test for drug abuse (section 91). Such rights carried with them prescriptive expectations – that prisoners, for instance, should keep themselves clean and healthy, that they should attend regular worship and follow the scale of diet provided. Sometimes rights and commands were explicitly intertwined, producing contorted statements of the kind: 'Adequate bathing and shower installations shall be provided so that a detainee may be enabled and required to have a bath or shower, at a temperature suitable to the climate, as frequently as necessary to the general hygiene according to the season, but at least once a week' (section 122 [4]). This draft bill appeared to contribute a new discursive position for representing prisons and prisoners. The preservation of human rights seemed to demand more, rather than less, supervision.

During my fieldwork at Bomana (1994–5), the prison appeared as a ghost of the institution described in colonial and postcolonial annual reports. Only traces of that representation seemed to surface in the prison that I knew. Sprawled across the unbrushed floor of the now abandoned workshop office lay old, trade assessment forms. The warrant covers filled out at reception were

similarly incomplete. Black and white identification photographs, with a broken camera, fell out of cardboard boxes in a
dusty corner of the welfare office. I remembered only one visit
by an inspecting judge and no regular medical examinations.[8]
Watchtowers were infrequently used, industrial and agricultural
facilities understaffed and often with only a skeleton inmate crew
(the vast majority of convicts were without work). The electricity supply failed on many occasions and for the fourteen-month
duration of my stay the gas cookers in the mess of A Compound
remained out of service (prisoners usually cooked in the yard,
burning wood or coal fuel to heat the large metal bowls of rice).
Cells were damp and often plagued with blocked toilets and
dripping taps. There were weeks of food shortages when inmates
received only half rations. The segregation of male convicts from
those on remand was easily circumvented. Some warders lived in
condemned housing and there were not enough uniforms, for
either staff or inmates, to go around. Correctional Service vehicles, used to drive remand prisoners to and from court in Port
Moresby, regularly broke down. One had the feeling of an institution in decline, its buildings and schema harking back to
another time.

The discursive subjects in the annual reports also elided the
presence of women and their experience of prison life. Both the
Savage and the Criminal were presented as archetypal male
figures and the prison as a male domain. Yet from the earliest
reports women featured in the statistics for prison populations.
In 1890, for instance, there were two women recorded as locked
up at the prison in Port Moresby, ten years later there were
eleven and by 1908 the figure was twenty-five. After that the
numbers dropped back and fluctuated, but they remained a
significant, if small, proportion. After the Second World War, the
national figures for women prisoners slowly rose, from a total of
eighty in 1957 to about 280 by 1970. The increase slowed and
dipped during the postcolonial period (in 1995 there was a registered total of 140). But despite this presence they never really
became subjects of report rhetoric, remaining marginal to
discussions about rehabilitation or the threat to social order from
the rising crime rate. Indeed, it was not until 1980 that female
warders were appointed to guard these prisoners (see Borrey
1992). Before that the women were supervised by male warders
and their wives, often left to their own devices and sometimes

housed with staff families. The prison was not held to be a natural or appropriate place for women.

However, despite all these noncorrespondences, the discursive terrain of the annual reports occasionally does echo with the rhetoric of prisoners. Sloop (1996: 61) makes the point that past representations do not disappear, but rather figure as rhetorical boundaries for what supersedes them. They retain a residual presence, resurfacing in undetermined and original ways. While the texts of the annual reports were never the public rhetoric of Sloop's popular magazines and journals, nor I believe a direct part of the genealogy of inmate discussions, I sometimes thought I could hear whispers of those discursive subjects. The Savage, the Semi-Savage, the Criminal, the Human Being, might all be read at the edges of prisoners' conversations about themselves, their offending behaviour and the transformations they imagined themselves to undergo. But then they might not. These were ephemera, ghosts, just like the architecture at Bomana. I hope that in the chapters to come this rhetoric will continue periodically to suggest itself.

'Quasi-ethnography'

Sociologists who have conducted prison studies often reflect upon the peculiar limits of their research practice (see Moczydlowski 1992). Owen (1998: 20), who worked in the Central California Women's Facility, adopts, after Inciardi (Inciardi et al. 1993), the term 'quasi-ethnography' to describe that experience. The term is intended to suggest a deviation from normative ethnographic practice and the relative capacity to immerse oneself in a social world. She states that while aspects of her methodology matched that standard (in-depth interviews, detailed observation of everyday life and analysis), there always remained structural barriers to a full immersion in prisoner life (Owen 1998: 21). She did not gain access to all parts of the prison and some forms of behaviour, those that contravened prison rules, were not available for observation. But most of all, Owen states, her participation was limited by the simple fact of her freedom and their confinement (1998: 22). This disparity meant she could never *really* experience incarceration.

While this position perhaps overplays the possibility of a normative ethnographic engagement, of parity of experience ever being achieved between researcher and subjects (after all the fieldworker is ultimately going to *leave*), it does highlight some of the problems of conducting research in prison. During my own study I remained painfully aware of what I couldn't see. Restricted from visiting Bomana at night, and during the day usually required to have a staff escort before entering cells, prohibited from access to the maximum-security institution of B Division,[9] I relied heavily on inmate descriptions of events in these places and at those times. Indeed, the in-depth interview was a vital part of my research (Tables 1 and 2), not just for the discursive information it provided, but as a form of introduction and the basis for a growing network (I conducted a total of 372 formal interviews, each between an hour and three hours long. This included 216 interviews with convicts, ninety-five with those on remand and sixty-one with warders). Casual conversations and general 'hanging around' worked best in those areas where security was more relaxed (the female wing, the juvenile wing, work parties, especially those at the industrial workshops and agricultural sections, and anywhere outside A Compound but within the high perimeter fence). But I usually felt a degree removed from the events around me, frequently dependent on the company of others for reports on what was going on.

There were also language barriers. Papua New Guinea is well known to have over 700 languages and at any one time Bomana had representatives of well over a hundred different language groups, taken from all the provinces in the country. There were no prison statistics on this linguistic breakdown, but a survey by province of those inmates and warders I interviewed goes some way to demonstrating that diversity (Table 3). The official prison languages were English and the two national languages Tok Pisin and Motu; it was forbidden for either prisoners or warders to use their local language (*tok ples*). Tok Pisin was the most commonly heard, understood by everyone or, like me, quickly learnt. However, there were occasions when prisoners and warders from the Papuan region spoke Motu (which I never learned) or when others broke into local language. So again not all conversations could be overheard.

Table 1 *Length of sentence of those convicts interviewed*

Sentence	0–6 months	6–12 months	1–3 years	3–5 years	5–10 years	10–15 years	life
Number	31	9	47	46	57	17	11

Table 2 *Charges and convictions of remand prisoners and convicts interviewed*

Charges	Male convict	Male remand	Female convict	Female remand
Murder	64	13	10	2
Attempted murder	5	8		
Manslaughter and unlawful killing	9	1		
Assault: grievous bodily harm	9			
Rape and attempted rape	34	9		
Incest	1			
Carnal knowledge	1			
Breaking and entering	10	20		
Armed robbery	26	17		
Stealing	43	28	1	
Attempted robbery	2	3		
Misappropriation	8		1	
Conspiracy to defraud	4			
Unlawful use of motor vehicle	8	9		
Malicious damage and arson	1	1		
Escape from legal custody	1			
Harbouring fugitive		1		
Use of threatening behaviour	1			
Abduction	8			
Possession of unlicensed firearms	4	4		
Possession of drugs	7	1	1	
Possession of stolen property			2	
Drunk and disorderly	1			
Loitering		1		
Breach of court order	1		6	

Table 3 *Province of origin or identity of those interviewed*

Province	Convict	Remand	Warder
Western	5		2
Gulf	24	12	6
Central	74	27	5
Milne Bay	5	1	5
Oro	7	1	7
Morobe	7	4	5
Madang	5	2	2
East Sepik	9	3	7
West Sepik			2
Western Highlands	18	2	2
Eastern Highlands	14	8	2
Southern Highlands	10	8	1
Simbu	15	11	2
Enga	16	13	2
West New Britain	2		1
East New Britain	2	1	6
New Ireland	1		2
Manus	1	2	2
North Solomons	1		

Warders at the welfare office introduced the first prisoners I interviewed. But after a couple of weeks I began to develop my own channels of communication. At the end of each interview I would ask the prisoner to provide the names of others who he thought might be willing to talk with me. This system usually worked well, allowing prospective interviewees time to be told about my presence and what to expect from the requested meeting. I would wander down to the guardhouse next to A Compound and inform the warder on duty of the convict or remand inmate with whom I wished to speak. Depending on his mood, the guard would either assign another prisoner to go and find the person or shout instructions for the selected inmate to come to the compound gate himself. These meetings were always voluntary and usually straightforward, the called prisoner either accepting or refusing the offer of conversation. But on one afternoon I received a very different response. Standing in the middle of his convict cell yard, in full view of everyone who cared to watch or listen, the named man angrily shouted back his refusal, 'I am not the prisoner of the fucking arsehole white man'! Shaken and red-faced at this suggestion of my coercion, I made to withdraw, at the same time beseeching the guard standing next to me not to carry out a threatened beating.

Such situations highlighted what was an ongoing issue: the best way in which to negotiate a balance in relationships between prisoners and warders. In the end I decided to distance myself from the staff (a gradual decision that made them sometimes suspicious and less open to conversation) and so try to better gain the trust of inmates. Jacobs (1977: 215–16), who conducted research at Stateville Penitentiary, Illinois, speaks of this negotiation as a constant struggle to gain legitimacy. He describes the prison as a place where rumour, doubt and factionalism abound, one in which the researcher's behaviour lacks clear meaning to either prisoners or staff and is therefore the subject of scepticism and distrust on both sides. Jacobs speaks of the exhausting need to constantly prove who one is and how that position might relate to the wider hierarchy (217). At Bomana prisoners generally agreed to talk with me because they were tremendously bored, but also as a stranger and a 'white man' (*waitman*) I was something of a prison curiosity (there are usually one or two white expatriate prisoners in E Division, but they generally keep to themselves). The interviews also provided them with a welcome opportunity to get out of their compound and with the promise of a small reward of toothpaste and soap as gifts (not in itself a great incentive). But those inmates, who got to know and trust me, still found it hard to define my status. If the interview questions I asked did not quite correspond with the interrogatory questions of police and warders (I was careful never to ask directly about prisoners' offences), neither did they match the inquiries of the other regular visitors to Bomana, missionaries and lawyers. While many knew and recognised the role of anthropologist (after all Papua New Guinea has been saturated with them over the years), it was something they associated with village life (*ples*) or custom (*kastom*). Few could understand what one was doing in prison! At the same time my presence sometimes sparked hope of a more serious intervention, that my research was part of a new administrative reform programme, the precursor to things getting better. When I played down such expectations they were disappointed; nevertheless most remained keen to talk. They generally liked the idea that someone was going to record their lives and sufferings.

I often found the prison research experience numbing. Any level of intimacy risked being spoiled by my effort to concentrate and jot down everything I was being told. Accounts of violent or disturbing events after a while left me completely unmoved. I quickly found myself emotionally immune to stories of sexual abuse, physical and mental aggression, and even indifferent to the sight and sound of warders handing out beatings (though staff were usually quite careful to hide these activities from me).[10] When I heard about the stabbing and death of a prisoner with whom I had worked closely I was surprised that I felt nothing. When men joked about the inmates they had raped I was able to join in their laughter. The chapters that follow, then, are in part an attempt to recover that missing emotion, to convey the fears, the shock and the pain of these encounters and express what I couldn't feel at the time.

And yet, despite the trauma (not mine, theirs) of incarceration, there remained a good deal of humour in what I was told. I hope that the book also conveys that – the comedy as well as the gravity of what prisoners took from violence and distress. Hence my choice to illustrate the chapters with cartoons. This art form is a strange hybrid, borrowing its frames of reference from cinematography and drawing, showing plasticity that I believe is uniquely able to make a situation appear both funny and poignant. Prisoners themselves are very familiar with the genre, as cartoon strips are regular features in comic books and local newspapers (and the local 'criminal' [*raskal*] is a favourite subject[11]). These strips share the contrast editing qualities of film and dreams, again both media to which prisoners make reference. The cartoonist must draw in a hurry, to a deadline, and must make his or her illustrations capture the distracted attention of those waiting for a bus ride, taking a coffee break or standing in a queue (cf. Rubenstein 1998). In this book the illustrator is Jada Wilson, a cartoonist who draws for the Tok Pisin weekly newspaper *Wantok*, and who himself lives and works in

Port Moresby. I sent Jada written ideas for sketches and then left him to elaborate them as he wished. The results fill these pages and should be judged on their own terms as provocative extensions of what I describe.

The book also privileges prisoners' own forms of animation, in particular their songs, poems and dream stories (related to me in Tok Pisin, English or a mix of Tok Pisin and English)[12]. At Bomana cellmates often sit around and discuss the dreaming experiences they have had during the night. These are taken to have both present and future significance. They also write poems and strum guitar strings to accompany their latest song compositions, which are often expressions of the pains of separation and confinement. These three media are reproduced as narrative evocation, whose style informs and seeps over into the text I provide. They are taken as inspiration, poetic accounts of the constraint of living in the last place.

Notes

1   Juveniles are meant to be detained in separate detention centres known as Boys Towns, which are usually run by church missions (in Wewak town by the Roman Catholic Church and at Ihu station and Sogeri town by the Salvation Army). However, due to the government's financial difficulties, many juveniles are serving their sentences in adult correctional facilities such as Bomana.

2   Bergendorff (1996: 241–42) reports that among the Mekeo people of Central province an analogy is drawn between imprisonment and human burial underground. He states that one man threatened another with death by announcing his imminent incarceration. The man explained: 'I don't mean Moresby jail. But he will go to jail for good, six feet underground, put there by sorcery. The place will be forsaken'. This link between prison and burial is intended to evoke an image not only of death, but also of isolation.

3   The description of B Division as 'underground' and of the prison more generally as a 'dark place' may have a long genealogy. Andrew Strathern (1994: 55) records the claims of Melpa people in the Western Highlands, who stated that early colonial officers in the region used to arrest offenders and detain them in large, deep holes, dug within the grounds of the government station. It appears that offenders were actually kept in these holes until more conventional prisons could be built.

4   Rew (1974: 98–99) describes a similar plan of sleeping spaces in the barrack-room accommodation of the labour compound in Port Moresby where he conducted fieldwork.

5　Ignatieff (1978) points out that the ideals of modern penology evolved from a strong nonconformist Christian tradition of self-discipline. Early penal reformers such as Howard, Fothergill, Franklin and the Philadelphia Quakers were concerned to initiate reforms in order to achieve a Christian disciplinary society. The term 'penitentiary' was actually invented by Howard, Blackstone and Eden in 1778 to describe the institution based upon the disciplinary ideals of 'industry', 'contrition' and 'penance' (47).

6　Errington and Gewertz (1995: 25–27) note the significance of documentation in the work of colonial officers. Their village inspections were recorded in a 'village book' and in a 'patrol report'. Both documents claimed to assess the degree of order in the village and the performance of indigenous officials and police. The patrol report went on to form a crucial part of the annual report of the Territory. Errington and Gewertz point out that the patrol report itself was used to assess the conduct of the patrol officer, and in turn the efficiency of the local government office. They argue that patrols, and the documents produced from them, exemplify the culture of surveillance that existed in the colonial administration (30).

7　The port town of Samarai Island was the administrative base for the south-eastern part of the Territory of British New Guinea. Samarai was the second largest centre in the Territory (after Port Moresby) and the coastal areas around it had one of the fastest growing European populations (Wetherell 1977: 244–45).

8　Probation and parole initiatives have had limited impact. Although legislation was passed in 1979 to set up a probation programme, the service did not become operational until 1985. Three years later the service supervised 2,062 probationers (Banks 1993: 37), who were required to maintain a good standard of behaviour and report regularly to their respective probation officers (38). However, the probation service only remains operational in certain regions and as a result of funding difficulties has failed to develop. A parole programme was also established by the Justice Department but to even less effect. During my time at Bomana prisoners were interviewed and assessed for parole, but without any consequence. Again, the programme is hampered by restrictions on government budgets and a shortage of parole officers able to supervise those released.

9　Although I was not granted permission to visit B Division, I have viewed photographs of the facility. Many inmates got the opportunity to visit B Division when in 1994 the Laloki River burst its banks and flooded A Compound; prison staff removed inmates to the higher ground of B Division where they stayed for three days.

10　Sim (1990: 178) criticises Foucault for ignoring the continuing importance, at least in British prisons and one suspects elsewhere, of violent measures. He states that by emphasising a shift from punishment of the body to reform of the mind Foucault marginalises the role of physical coercion in managing inmates.

11 Kulick (1993: 10) reports that the Sepik villagers he worked with actually regarded the raskal as gaining his strength and power from the reading of cartoon comic books.

12 The songs and poems presented in the text are given in the author's language of choice and in my translation. The dream stories are only given in translation.

CHAPTER 2

Bus Stop

'Jailbird'

Incarceration imposes an obvious constraint upon movement.
Prisoners at Bomana often complain that they are confined in one
place, forced to remain still and view the same landscape day after
day. Winnie, a convict from Wapenamanda in the Highlands,
equated this experience with the effects of personal injury. He
explained that the prisoner is like someone shot and wounded
during tribal fighting. The arrow lodged in the injured man's
body is said to cause him pain and compel his retreat back to his
house. There, alone and immobile, he is restricted like a prisoner,
unable to go outside, to visit his gardens or see his kin and
friends. As a consequence, Winnie stated, the injured man would
feel abandoned and start to worry. This analogy evokes the sense
of curtailment that prisoners experience upon their detention.
They constantly express feelings of impairment, view themselves
as wounded and thus prevented from normal activity.

Human Zoo

Oh! Oh! Oh!
PNG's major human zoo.
Bomana Bomana Bomana.
What are jailbirds in cages.
Freedom is just behind the wires.
Oh my Lord,
Overcrowded with birds from Kerema, Goilala, Gaire,
Simbu, Hagen, Madang, Sepik and Pops.
Different colour skins, hairs and languages.
Sweet Bombex.

(Maurice Mak)

This sense of obstructed movement, of capture, is reinforced by appeals to an avian aesthetic. Prisoners, including the male juvenile convict who wrote the song above, regard themselves as 'jailbirds', as caged or broken in flight. The prison 'wires' are said to hold inmates from across the country (Kerema, Goilala, Gaire, Simbu etc[1]), who display different physical appearances and speak a variety of languages. Around A Compound, small black and white fantails dart back and forth across the fences and between cell yards. Male inmates often catch and raise these birds from chicks. They like to watch the fantails fly away and then return (*flai na go kam*); the pets are given individual names but known generically as jailbirds, just like them. The designation is ironic, for unlike these pet birds, which may fly away at any time, the male prisoner is held back by the security of the perimeter fence. He is frustrated in flight, unable to leave Bomana and visit the people and places that he left behind.

Such a state of seizure renders prisoners stationary and bored. They itch for the movement that they believe they have lost, for the world outside the jailbird's cage. That state of freedom or wished-for mobility seems always out of reach, something enjoyed by others. As a result prisoners tend to review their lives before imprisonment as travel stories and valorise memories of unimpeded passage.[2] They also articulate a more general relationship between movement and its constraint.

Cowboy

Patrick, a remand inmate who stole for a living, told me that he was a 'cowboy'. Although his parents came from East Kerema in Gulf province, he was born and raised in Port Moresby. Among his fellow 'steal men' (*stilman*) Patrick had the nickname Desert. Outside the gaol he roamed the city streets dressed in denim jeans, checked shirt, stockman boots and a wide-brimmed hat. Tied to his waist, Patrick said, he carried a water bottle and around his neck he wore a red polka-dot nose-rag. While other residents of Port Moresby worked, he dozed or hung around the markets and shopping centres, smoking cigarettes and chatting. At night, while residents slept, he and other steal men ranged across the city, on foot or in stolen cars, looking to break into private or commercial property. Sometimes they carried guns.

Indeed, the cowboy is a popular image among many steal men at Bomana. On television sets outside, set up beside trade stores in city settlements or in the houses of parents or kin, young men watch videos from American cinema. They prefer action hero adventures or violent thrillers. Sometimes steal men decide to adopt the name of leading characters or criminal organisations portrayed on film, either as personal or as group designations. Prisoners told me that they stole under names such as Mafia, 007 and Lost Commando. One convict related how the stealing name Heltex came into being. He and his neighbourhood friends were watching a cowboy film set in Texas, which featured gunfights, bandits and bank robberies. At its conclusion they decided to steal under the name Hell Texas, or Heltex for short, since they wished to be known as real troublemakers, just like the cowboys they had seen on film.

Tatum (1997: 41–42), who describes the changing response of the American public to representations of outlaw figures such as Billy the Kid, perceives the dramatisation of the Western in books and films as a debate about the opposing forces of civilisation and wilderness. While attitudes to the depiction of that frontier environment varied, sometimes pictured as a threat to civilisation and at other times a reprieve, it was nevertheless always situated against the urban industrial landscape of the East and later of contemporary America itself (1997: 188). In Papua New Guinea that frontier is popularly imagined to be the city and in particular Port Moresby. Across the country, Mosbi, as it is known in Tok Pisin, is linked with wild, dangerous and noncustomary behaviour (see Battaglia 1992, 1994; Hirsch 1995a; Bergendorff 1996; Clark 1997).[3] Stories circulate of the outrages committed there, of sexual promiscuity, rape, intoxication, theft and casual violence. Popular songs played on the radio portray the capital as a city out of control, where almost anything can happen.[4] Indeed, steal men themselves equate Mosbi with the arid lands of the Western landscape, calling it a 'desert' (contrasts are drawn with other urban centres such as Hagen town in the Highlands, whose fertile land earns it the popular name Beverly Hills). The designation refers not just to the climate and soil quality – dry, hot and dusty – but also to the role of money in that environment. Prisoners say that in Mosbi money talks (*moni tok*). Unlike the village or hamlet, everything has a price and must be purchased. They joke that in the city the only garden is the supermarket. Without money no one can eat or move around, so they need to steal. Mosbi, it is said, makes young men 'fools' for crime.

Accompanying the demands of this frontier location, steal men at Bomana espouse the excitement of touring (*raun raun*). They represent themselves not just as thieves, but also as extraordinary travellers. Whether journeying across the city, between suburbs, or across the country, along highways and between townships, the exercise of mobility is seen to be crucial. Steal men describe themselves as 'local tourists', keen to visit every province and talk about their encounters with scenery and different peoples. They state that their desire for movement requires money and that their desire for money requires theft. As a result crime and travel are inextricably linked.

Friend Adam, here then is my life story:

I was born in 1969, February 23, in the place of my mother: Manus Island; and in 1976 we went to Bulolo town and I started grade one at school. I ran away from my parents and family in 1984 and went around the provinces having fun acting as a *raskal* with my friends. In 1987 I went to prison in Lae, Morobe province, for breaking and entering in Bulolo police station and stealing guns. I stayed two years in jail and I was released. I went to Madang province and the police held me for armed robbery in 1989, the court gave me five years and I escaped and came to Port Moresby in 1990 and they caught me, but I escaped again and went to Goroka in Eastern Highlands province. In 1992 I went to Lae province and the police arrested me again and sent me back to Madang. In 1993, May 30, I escaped again and I went to Simbu province. I was with a friend who has an 18–year sentence. We did not take a car because the police were making patrols and roadblocks, so we walked around for three weeks in the big bush. We arrived in Simbu and I was very sick. After the illness had finished the police caught us at a roadblock in Goroka, three hours drive from Simbu. They sent me by plane to Port Moresby, Bomana jail, to stand trial for all my charges. This is the end of my story.

Jeffrey. H. malepo.
Free bird in exile.
Bombex wire city
Last place.

This story, related by a convict with a life sentence, presents the hazards and thrills of criminal adventure; journeys that are constantly interrupted by arrest and detention. In fact in his account travel seems to take the form of escape, so that movement is always a version of running away. The cowboy is such a popular image among steal men precisely because he is usually depicted as a drifter, someone who moves on the edges of society and is often being hunted. He is also a figure who is associated with speed and urgent movement across the territory. Duncan (1996: 84), who writes about popular images of the romantic outlaw in Europe and America, suggests a common identification between the outlaw and swiftness. Whether the highwayman of the eighteenth century, the cowboy or the American outlaws of the 1930s, figures such as Bonnie Parker and Clyde Barrow who sped in cars away from robberies, she argues that fast travel is crucial to the illustrious image they project (1996: 86). Among steal men at Bomana speed is highly valued. Prisoners talk constantly of their adventures in stolen cars. They relate stories of car chases with police, through the city or along the highways, of drunken celebrations after a successful robbery, driving through the streets and banging the door panels as they pass the houses of rival steal men, of doughnuts, skids, dramatic turnovers and crashes. In fact steal men claim that no one moves around quite like them – not the 'working class', those in waged and salaried employment, who are constrained by work schedules,[5] nor those in the village or hamlet, the 'place people' (*pleslain*), who are rooted to their gardens and ground. Two male convicts laughed and asked me to consider the figure of the village man in Port Moresby. They asserted that he would not know how to move in the city, on the bus or in the car he would feel dizzy and throw up, unused to the pace of nonpedestrian travel.

Jack looks over and sees his Papuan steal mate driving the car. They stop outside the supermarket and run in waving their pistols. 'Hands up everyone, this is a robbery!' But the police quickly surround the store. Jack takes a policeman hostage and threatens to kill him unless the others back away. They retreat. The hostage trembles and agrees to turn a blind eye if the two men escape. Just then Jack sees his mother by the checkout counter. He talks to her in Wabag language and drops his gun inside her string bag. The hostage shouts at them to run, and so Jack runs out of the store into pouring rain. He stops to shake the water from his dreadlocks and catches sight of a woman giving him the eye. Jack winks back and goes over to talk. As they chat, he sees the hostage, his mother and father walk past. Jack tells them to go on without him.

This dream (see Figure 10), related to me by a convict from Enga province, evokes the sense of fast-paced action which steal men are said to enjoy outside: driving round the city, running into a supermarket and announcing a hold-up, taking a hostage and then getting away. It also describes the image steal men have of themselves as daring, reckless, tough and sexually attractive young men. Tatum (1997: 100) states that at certain times the American public ascribed the same characteristics to cowboys. Figures such as Billy the Kid were presented in film and cheap novels as woman charmers, attracting both ladies and whores, and as desperados with a devil-may-care attitude to personal safety and the future. It was this mixture of youthful innocence and violent skills that Tatum says intrigued American audiences (1997: 190). Steal men at Bomana frequently make declarations

Figure 10 *Jack's dream*

of their desire to take part in dramatic criminal exploits. A successful theft is not just about the amount of money stolen, but also about the style and boldness of the operation. A bank robbery, for example, should be carried out in a direct and original way. If opposition is met then steal men should confront the threat bravely and without thought of sneaking away (gunfights with police are particularly admired). It is also important how the money from robberies is spent. Saving is looked down upon, youth preferring to consume their cash in rash buying sprees or carousing (whoring, dancing and drinking) with fellow steal men. There is no discussion of planning for life after crime.

Tatum (1997: 44) states that in the frontier culture of the Western right and justice are often measured by might and the exercise of extralegal violence. The barren landscape in which Billy the Kid is sometimes portrayed is an anarchic environment, an 'upside-down world' (1997: 45). Cowboys, he claims, are presented as the outcome of this border civilisation (1997: 56). In particular, Westerns blur the distinction between outlaw and lawman, between good and evil. Greedy cattle merchants or rail-road bosses are seen to run towns, supported by bribed judges and mayors who sponsor vigilantes. Justice is seen to be arbi-trary, its agents as often the cowboy as the sheriff (1997: 96). Steal men at Bomana present Port Moresby, and the politics of Papua New Guinea, in the same manner. They represent them-selves as existing in a city and nation run by foreign and local commercial interests, corrupt politicians and civil servants, who are defended by the police and an army of private security guards. There are no jobs for those who leave school and even if work is advertised, recruitment is made on a partisan basis. Steal men claim that they target the businessman (*bisnis man*) and his cronies (in prison they etch tattoos on their arms with phrases such as 'hunt darich' or 'kokia' [Motu for 'steal it']); or that these wealthy figures and national politicians are actually the sponsors and architects of their criminal activities. They do not regard their crimes as offences against Society or good Order, but rather as confrontations with an equivalent aggressor, the police. In fact the arrest procedure is often presented as a game, with each side, steal man and policeman, trying to outwit the other. One pris-oner explained that 'we play our part, they play their part' (*mipela wokim wok blong mipela, old wokim wok blong ol*). During interro-gations, it is said that the steal man must hide the names of his accomplices, while the police officers must try and extract them. In court the steal man must attempt to trick the judge by 'sneak-ing bail', swapping places with another defendant on a smaller charge, paying his bond and thus gaining release. The act of one side is seen to affect the morale of the other. A successful bank robbery, for instance, may shame the police, while the foiling of a heist or the capture of its protagonists may embarrass steal men. This ongoing transaction, rather than a distinction between the forces of right and wrong, is how steal men understand the legal process.

The cowboy of Hollywood movies is often a loner, orphaned like Billy the Kid or rejecting the support of kinship. Drifting across the desert of the Western landscape, he seems to be escaping the obligations (and responsibilities) of civilisation (Tatum 1997: 47). In the life story quoted earlier, the first stage of the steal man's journey is presented as an evasion of kin ('I ran away from my parents and family in 1984 and went round the provinces...'). Indeed, from Bomana, steal men regard their lives outside as a struggle to overcome a series of constraints imposed on their movement. Not just kin, but school, custom (*kastom*), employment and 'place work' (*pleswok*) in the village garden, are all perceived to prevent the travels of youth. Prisoners say that those who live at home in Port Moresby or other towns can only wander the streets and steal after first eluding the gaze of parents. They must either play truant from school or try and sneak out after dark from the family house. Steal men describe the nicknames and whistles they invent in order to call out to someone without risk of his parents' hearing. But the ultimate threat to youthful wanderings is held to be the act of marriage. The prospect of being coerced into that commitment, with the affinal obligations that accompany it, is seen as the most serious constraint on the movement of men. Rather than bow to parental pressure, many male prisoners claim to have run away from the village or hamlet, to have left their family home in town, and set off on a stealing tour of the country. Steal men are said to insist that they are not ready for marriage, that they wish to travel around until they grow tired and want to settle down (*mi go raun inap na bihain mv marit*). 'Freedom' is their watchword.

Western movies usually represent the frontier as a place where individuals are in control of their own fortunes (Tatum 1997: 60). At times American audiences read this border area as a 'spiritual landscape of freedom' (1997: 188), one where they might project themselves when the restrictions of urban civilisation seemed too claustrophobic. For steal men that confining civilisation is not urban, but village or hamlet based, of the 'place' (*ples*). Port Moresby and the other urban centres of Papua New Guinea are the frontier they desire, the site of heroic confrontations and new myths. This is also the site where place people are said to feel out of context. Just as they are left bewildered by the city, so, steal men claim, those who enter Bomana are confused and shocked. It is commonly acknowledged among prisoners that 'place men' (*plesman*) and 'place women' (*plesmeri*) break the law by mistake. They don't look for trouble, instead trouble is said to find them (*ol i no painim trable, trable painim ol*). In these claims responsibility for criminal acts is displaced. Their offences are seen to be the outcome of relational histories and not of individual agency. The place man and place woman are drawn into crime through the obligations they owe to others or through sorcery and pay-back, where the cause of action is perceived to be separated from its effect (much in the same way that prisoners' dreams and sneezes are said to be coerced by the thoughts of kin [see Prologue]). If those from the village or hamlet commit offences in Port Moresby then they are held to be led into trouble by the city itself, which is said to overwhelm them with its events. By contrast, the steal man is said to be accustomed to city and prison life. He lives between those places, drawn from one to the other. Indeed, steal men assert that they break the law deliberately. Unlike the place people, they hunt out trouble themselves (*mipela yet painim trable*), are the sole cause of their criminal actions. And this claim to steal on purpose, without coerced causality, is a radical statement, intended as a critique of what steal men regard as conventional Papua New Guinea living.

Like the steal men, women prisoners at Bomana often portray their lives outside as struggles to resist capture by kin obligations. Female youth also wish to travel around the country and visit the provinces. In fact they present their movements as under heavier constraint than male youth. Marriage is rejected not just because it draws them into ties with affines, but also because it places their actions under the direction of men (*meri stap aninit long man*). A wife, women prisoners told me, cannot move around as she likes, or if she does, she will be punished with beatings. Similarly, the restrictions imposed by parents on the movement of daughters are said to be stricter. Helen, a convict who grew up in Wabag in the Highlands, saw incarceration as equivalent to the confining attitude of her parents. She explained that as a teenager she was prevented from ever wandering far from the family house. Like the parents of other girls in the village, Helen's mother and father kept her under close observation, imprisoning the young woman (*banisim yangpela meri*) and preventing contact with men, until she was ready to marry. As a result Helen ran away to Port Moresby. But this ambition to travel is not linked with the tours of steal men.

Indeed, the valorisation of crime with travel is specific to male prisoners. Women at Bomana, while also complaining of the constraints imposed on their movement by incarceration, regard the prospect of criminal adventure with some ambivalence. Their offences are usually the outcome of individual household tensions (a high number are convicted or charged with assaults on husbands after hearing of their infidelity, or with the murder of their spouse's mistress) and not the deliberate acts of trouble-making that steal men claim. Like the place people, these women regard themselves as coerced into wrong action. The popular figures of criminal movement, such as the cowboy, are centred on the journeys of young men or, if focused on female youth, around the loitering of the prostitute or 'road woman' (*rot meri*). None of the women prisoners I spoke with wished to associate themselves with that figure, another wanderer of the urban frontier, but one whose travel involves constant interruptions from male customers and the risk of frequent beatings (every Christmas the sex workers of Port Moresby are rounded up and some are detained in the female wing, but I never met a woman prisoner who admitted to that identity). Steal men at Bomana also mention the presence in Port Moresby of the 'disco woman' (*disko meri*), a character who is supposed to hang around the city nightclubs and hotel bars, enjoying the company of men, dancing and drinking, and choosing her own sexual partners. She is said to be on the edge of criminal activity, sometimes assisting the plans of steal men. But again women prisoners do not identify themselves with that figure of deliberate offending action.

While women prisoners and steal men who represent themselves as cowboys often portray their travels as forms of escape from the constraint of kinship, they also acknowledge the ways in which their journeys are dependent on those ties. Helen, for instance, ran away to Port Moresby because she knew that a cousin-brother lived there. This assumption of far-away hospitality regularly fosters the imagination to tour. A steal man seeking refuge from the police in Port Moresby may consider travelling to Rabaul, a town in the far northern archipelago of the New Guinea Islands, because he knows he can stay with his aunt. Those youth in the village or hamlet who dream of touring the country eagerly wait or anticipate invitations from distant kin as an excuse to set off. Thus a male youth may be asked by his maternal uncle to come to town and help run a trade store or a young woman invited by the wife of her brother to come and assist with child minding and household chores. Crime too may be introduced through kin ties. If a sibling steals his brothers may follow. These pathways to crime and travel somewhat undermine the representation of steal men as Western outlaws, as existing on the edges of conventional modes of support.

The cowboy image also glamorises the miserable outcomes of drifting without kin. In particular I am thinking of the presence in Port Moresby and other urban centres of those youth without homes who are forced to live on the street and scavenge around for basic provisions. Their urban wanderings are not styled to a movie aesthetic; indeed, film, until the closure of city cinemas several years ago, was valued more for the shelter and unguarded sleep its theatres provided than for the images it projected. Oka-Charlie, a convict who described himself as a 'bad luck kid', told me about his street life outside. Born and raised in Lae town, where his father found work, Oka-Charlie said that he never knew his parents' village in Gulf province. At the age of ten he and his family left Lae and moved to Port Moresby. There Oka-Charlie started school, but only weeks later his mother died. Soon his father found a new wife, but grew tired of looking after four small children and so abandoned them. Without money to pay his school fees or buy food, Oka-Charlie roamed the city collecting empty beer and soft drink bottles for resale. With the coins saved, he brought flour from the trade store (he couldn't afford rice or tinned fish meat) and made greasy scones to eat. He explained that although he was not a steal man, he did on occasion pick pockets in the crowds at markets and shopping centres (steal men deride the pickpocket for sneaking around and avoiding direct confrontation). As a result Oka-Charlie was periodically arrested and sometimes found himself at Bomana. His own experience of travel and crime left him wishing for kin support.

Newspapers in Papua New Guinea, in response to public anxieties about crime, regularly call for steal men to be 'sent home', by which they mean that these youth should be forcibly returned to their village or hamlet. Male prisoners point out, however, that steal men would not necessarily be welcomed back. In fact some of them, those born or raised in town, have never been to the 'place' of their parents nor spoken its language. Others, with parents from separate language groups or provinces, have even fewer links and less incentive to 'return'. Prisoners relate stories of those steal men who have tried to settle in an ancestral village or hamlet and been forced out, their claims on garden land rejected as the prospecting of strangers. Indeed, place people sometimes call these intruders 'last minute men' (*las minut man*), criticising them for not showing prior interest in the clan yet expecting to have their demand for residence recognised. The steal men are told, in no uncertain terms, to go back to the city.

Raskal

While steal men at Bomana may wish to represent themselves as cowboys, they are more popularly described, among the public of Papua New Guinea, as 'raskals'. The term derives from the English word 'rascal', which suggests a paternal attitude to their offending behaviour or naughtiness (the word took hold after a colonial judge in the 1960s labelled the man he sentenced as a rascal). It implies male youthfulness and incorrigibility, but perhaps also a certain fondness or reluctant attraction. The raskal is a national discursive figure, constantly represented in newspapers and media and appropriated by many interests. 'He' is the ultimate image of illicit movement.

Kulick (1993: 10) describes the proliferation of stories about the raskal among the place people of the lower Sepik basin in the late 1980s, at a time before they had experienced the criminal activities associated with that figure. In particular, he observes the attraction of those stories for male youth in the village where he worked. No longer able to afford to travel as their fathers once did through taking labour contracts on distant plantations, these boys are said to resent their immobility (1993: 13). To them, the raskal stands as a great adventurer, journeying to far-away towns and leading an exciting life. Kulick outlines the typical form of these stories. They begin, he states, with a robbery of some sort, a group of raskals stealing money from a trade store or guns from a police station. There is then a confrontation with the police, a gunfight, which the raskals eventually win. More robberies and murders follow, before the individual members of the gang are either shot or arrested and sent to prison. But those incarcerated quickly escape and start to steal and kill again (1993: 10). The figure of the raskal, despite or because of his refusal to conform to the moral rules of ordinary people, is held up as an admirable character. He is viewed as exotic, leading an intense and passionate existence, which contrasts with the dull routine of life for the place man. The raskal attracts precisely because he embodies a denial of the present, of the world as it is (1993: 9; and cf. Duncan 1996). For the people of this Sepik basin village there is greatness in the danger of that attitude.

The raskal, as portrayed by these place people, shares a number of characteristics with the cowboy figure that steal men favour. Both conjoin travel with crime and treat their enemy, the police, as equal aggressors in a drawn-out series of shootouts. Indeed in the account that Kulick provides the raskal is accepted by villagers as a possible alternative agent of justice. When a trade store is robbed, it is said to be the fault of the shopkeeper, whose high prices demonstrate greed and a lack of regard for his obligations (1993: 11). Similarly, raskal attacks on government or church property are met with silent approval, seen as fair retribution for the perceived corruption of politicians and Christian clergy. In fact Kulick suggests that talk about raskals provides the place people with a counter-discourse, one that allows them to express their dissatisfactions with their current socioeconomic position (1993: 12–13; but cf. Sykes 2000). The raskal is said to carry their own subversive aspirations.

In Port Moresby, when I conducted fieldwork in the mid-1990s, the raskal had lost much of his popular appeal. Instead of attraction, the figure inspired public anxiety, a fear of clandestine travel. Periodic States of Emergency, announced by government in response to particularly brutal spates of crime, closed the city at night, throwing lock gates across its highways and imposing curfews on the population. The raskal was presented as being everywhere, an impression reinforced by newspaper reports of the latest atrocity. These gruesome incidents became the focus of urban conversation. 'Did you hear about the hold-up in town? That murder? The terrible gang rape? Another bank robbery?' Each event seemed to alter the city map, to mark a raskal journey. Getting closer, then drawing further away, these assaults were terrifying because they appeared so random. The hidden presence of raskals seemed confirmed by the graffiti sprawled across the walls and corrugated fences of the city; stealing names that left menacing traces: Skinheads, Brutes, Nazi Spiders, Devils, Bad Boys, Scorpions, Dirty. But public insecurity reached its height whenever a large number of prisoners escaped from Bomana. Upon running away, these men were said to compensate for their time in prison by launching an orgy of illicit movement: robberies, rapes, kidnappings; fugitive journeys once again recorded by media headlines. When finally recaptured, police displayed the 'raskals' for newspaper and television consumption. The photographic images usually showed policemen, with blue shirts and rifles, standing next to a cowering figure (Figure 11). The prisoner, having run away and now returned, looked dirty and exhausted from what were assumed to be his savage exertions.

Bail denied for suspect

A 21-year-old Oro man about to head off to Bomana jail yesterday after a magistrate rejected bail on a charge of illegal car use. Police intend to interview the man about the death of former radio man Jon-Bill Tokome and the stabbing of lawyer Camilus Narokobi. *More on Page 2.*

Figure 11 *'Bail denied for suspect'*

Taussig (1992) talks of the indeterminacy of terror and situations where violence seems normative (for him 1980s Columbia). He states that in these situations criminal agency is popularly perceived as a terrifyingly ill-defined, vague and threatening force (1992: 19). The raskal seems to embody that danger. At the same time such dreadful formlessness is accompanied by desires to locate hidden structure, to articulate organisation and underground order (1992: 25). In Papua New Guinea an academic enterprise has arisen around such concerns. Social scientists wish to uncover the nature of raskal organisation, its formal rules of association (cf. Schiltz 1985; Morauta 1986; Harris 1988; Goddard 1992b). Indeed, there is considerable public comfort in these designs. I remember conversations with residents in Port Moresby, at first panic and ill ease, but then tremendous relief when a plausible explanation for casual violence is suggested. The criminal incident becomes lost in specificity: revenge, bride wealth disputes or sexual jealousy, and the raskal is no longer a stranger. Savagery is thus transformed, rendered nonthreatening. But the moment is short, nervousness (and indeterminacy) soon returns.

Mosbi is a city associated with the night. Its reputation as a wild and dangerous place centres round events that are said to occur after dark. Schlör (1998: 125), who has written a history of three cities at night (Berlin, Paris and London), comments on the links between criminality and urban night drawn in public discourse. In these discussions, he states, there is a sense of another city, of unknown size, existing alongside the familiar daytime metropolis. Schlör notes the presence of popular anxiety about journeys made from well-lit streets into dark corners, from the accessible town centre to the hidden and unlit poorer districts. He notes the fascination and fear aroused by thoughts of being in the city at night (1998: 9). The idea of 'night life', which emerged with the introduction of gas and then electric street lighting, joined these two emotions together: the nocturnal city as a site of entertainment but also of terror and danger (1998: 10). With nightfall the residents of Port Moresby descend into nervousness. Buses stop running and the streets quickly clear; only bands of young men and road women are left to wander around and visit the bars. Those who can afford to, retreat behind security fences and the protection of hired watchmen. If they go out they do so in cars, driving to various safe entertainment venues: hotels, nightclubs and restaurants. The rest of the nocturnal city is taken over by raskals, a ghoulish presence, who are perceived to emerge from the dark and unlit streets of the squatter settlements. Police are said to lose control of this city, which suddenly becomes unfamiliar and threatening. In the morning residents awake and ask themselves what happened during the night.

'Help me! Raskals! Help me! Help me!' I gulped. This was the first week of my stay in Port Moresby. The cry came from outside my window, a voice that tailed off, leaving just the sounds of receding, running footsteps. I remember sensations of awful panic as I climbed out of bed and checked my door. It was locked, the windows safely barred. Then I felt trapped. The room was too small to hide. I slumped to the floor and waited. Raskals, surely they would come? But they didn't. Every night the same fears returned. The image, despite what I knew, continued to haunt my imagination.

Where do you want to go?	*yu laik go we*
I am asking you, where do you want to go?	*mi askim yu yu laik go we*
You say you don't like me.	*yu tok olsem yu lese long mi*
You say that I am a raskal man.	*yu tok olsem mi raskal man*
Well that's okay; it's your problem.	*a sori em i orait laik blong yu*
	(Henry Kausi)

Steal men sometimes claim to act like raskals. They recognise and play upon the fear and respect that figure engenders. Nicknames such as Night Falcon and stealing names such as Koboni (Motu for 'ghost') are intended to evoke the spectral flight and night-time activities of the popularly conceived criminal. Henry Kausi, the convict who wrote the song above, told me that people outside are afraid of him. 'Watch out', he says they warn, 'watch out for the raskal man'. Yet prisoners themselves are unsettled by this discursive figure. They often advised me how to avoid trouble: 'You shouldn't walk along the road alone. Lock your doors'. Those with families living beside the highways leading out of Port Moresby worry about their safety. They tell parents not to visit them too often for fear that their kin might become casualties of roadside hold-ups and robberies. Male prisoners believe that steal

men outside are becoming trigger-happy and unpredictable, too
high on marijuana and alcohol to control their actions. As a result
they tend to distance themselves from the raskal figure, to almost
share the anxieties of popular imagination.

Catch him and lock him up.	*kisim em na lokim em*
Raskal man is unemployed.	*raskal man i no gat wok blong em*
Let him remain in prison,	*larim em i stap long kalabus*
With a long sentence,	*wantaim bikpela taim*
Until he changes his ways.	*bai sensim laip*

(Henry Kausi)

In fact the figure haunts steal men at Bomana, its power threatens them. They observe that people hate the raskal, they want to
lock him up, to make him disappear. So police arrest and throw
steal men in prison, shoot them down, maim and disfigure;
actions designed to prevent the raskal from moving again. Prisoners point out that the savagery of the figure seems to justify
any counter-measure. Engaging the raskal becomes the basis for
government, for making Order visible (see Taussig 1992: 17–18).
The raskal image locates terror in one place and excuses the
extralegal actions of others. A convict I knew at Bomana hops
around A Compound on one leg, reliant on wooden crutches.
The other limb was removed in hospital after police shot and
wounded him during interrogation. He told me that they wanted
to make sure he wouldn't make any more stealing tours.

Steal men therefore regard the police as an agent of equivalent terror. They arrive at Bomana with terrible stories of
custodial aggression. Swollen faces, black and bruised from
interrogation beatings, ripped fingernails, close-range bullet
wounds, shattered bones and maimed limbs (warders do not
contest these stories, since they have to treat the injuries in the
prison clinic). Reports of post-arrest executions are common.
Steal men reject the raskal image when it hides the diffuse nature
of terror, making these unlawful acts disappear. They observe
that the figure, shapeless and spectral, has a capacity to absorb
a great deal of abuse. It seems to anticipate their own deaths
(since I left Papua New Guinea at least twelve prisoners I knew
have been killed in gunfights with the police). Indeed, steal men
expect to die sooner rather than later. The legend not just of the
raskal, but also of the cowboy, requires the outlaw to ultimately

fail, his life ending in a shower of bullets (cf. Tatum 1997: 195). The difference is that the cowboy dies a hero, while the raskal dies in anonymity and sinks without trace.

Bus stop

In a well-known experiment designed to demonstrate the systemic problems of incarceration, psychologists at Stanford University assigned a randomly selected group of male college students to undergo a simulated experience of detention (Haney et al. 1973). Separated into 'guards' and 'prisoners', the students were placed in the basement of a campus building, reconstructed for the purposes of the experiment in order to resemble a prison. Those chosen to live as prisoners were to remain in their cells, partitioned rooms of six foot by nine foot, both day and night. This 'mock prison' was held to provide a functional representation of gaol life, combining what the organisers regarded as psychological equivalents of the regime with aspects of *physical constraint* (1973: 71). Indeed, despite changing approaches to the study of incarceration, this one property, physical constraint, has remained an unchallenged (if nontheorised) constant. Prison existence, we are expected to understand, involves an experience of coerced dwelling, of restrictions upon movement (think of the total environments described by Sykes, Goffman and Foucault). Any metaphor chosen to describe detention must convey this sense of fixity, boundary and residence. Whether talking about confinement or penal routine, the assumed condition is spatial coherence.

But at Bomana the experience of physical constraint, explored in the sections above, is combined with inmates' recognition of the transient, nonstable nature of prison existence. Metaphors of enclosure and residence are sometimes substituted by language that emphasises the gaol as a site of continuous dispersal. Prisoners are keen to point out the arrivals and departures, the comings and goings of fellow inmates, in particular, the fact that these movements are often unanticipated. No one can be quite sure who might be arriving tomorrow and who might be released. While convicts receive a due date of discharge, the allotment of parole and release on licence can be announced quite suddenly (releases on licence are occasional events, but usually coordinated as group discharges on public holidays, such as

Christmas, New Year, Queen's Birthday and Independence Day). Similarly, those on remand may go to court and not return or find their bail fee unexpectedly paid. The popular nickname for the prison is Bombex, short for Bombexity or Bomana City. This is a very different analogy to the one offered at the beginning of the chapter, of a wounded man forced to retreat to his house after tribal fighting. If the prison is like a city it must share some of the qualities of mobility and intersection that are popularly assigned to Port Moresby.

Jerai, a convict with the charisma and turn of phrase to be known by other inmates as a spokesman (*mausman*), sighed, clearly exasperated, but persisted with his explanation. 'Look Adam', he told me, 'this is how I see Bomana. It is like a bus stop, with people from different cultures, languages and places brought together. Do you understand? This place is like a bus stop.' This image, a queue of people waiting for a bus in the city, evokes the transience of penal meetings, people from different backgrounds thrown together and then scattered (Figure 12). When a bus arrives some passengers get off, while others climb on board and still more stand aside in order to await a different numbered vehicle. As people join or leave, the queue changes its composition. Jerai's image also recalls the manner of arrival and departure at Bomana; the secure police vans, blue and windowless, which

Figure 12 *Bus stop*

roar down to the gates and dump their load, or the yellow prison wagon, which collects those due for court or transports discharged convicts and leaves them in the city. In this metaphor it is hard to locate an idiom of residence. Notions of stability and coherence drop away when attention rests on brief intersections. Imagined as an urban queue, which disintegrates even as it forms, Bomana loses its spatial continuity.

For prisoners the mobility of encounters at Bomana is sometimes disorienting. They express sensations of lost footing, having the ground underneath constantly swept away. In particular, this is a dilemma for long-term convicts, those who are left to try and negotiate residence. Indeed, the designation of Bomana as the last place in Papua New Guinea privileges residence in an ironic manner. It draws attention to a location where dwelling is precisely the problem. If home is constituted through disremembering (see Prologue), losing thoughts of those left outside the gaol, then the constant arrival and departure of inmates can only be disturbing. Long-termers, who claim to convert Bomana into their own origin place (*asples*), complain about these movements, back and forth to prison, back and forth to court. Newcomers, they say, bring news from outside – unwelcome sparks to memory – while those released leave behind envious feelings. Short-term convicts and those on remand are sometimes dismissed as 'tourists' or 'uninvited guests', said to come to Bomana only for a visit, to taste the food, view the scene and then depart. Their good humour and casual conversation about events outside the gaol are seen to demonstrate insensitivity, to risk unsettling long-term convicts and thus ruining attempts to edit memory and construct a sense of abode. This anti-constraint, returning a sense of mobility to experiences of physical confinement, unravels whatever forgetting might have achieved.

The dilemma for long-term convicts, who must try and create a sense of place while those around them appear to treat travel as normative and dwelling as a form of constraint, is intriguing; not least because it reverses the direction of representational strategies found in anthropology and prison studies. As anthropologists have in recent years themselves begun to point out, their own pervasive metaphors of residence need situating (cf. Clifford 1988; Rosaldo 1989; Taussig 1992; Tsing 1993;

Stewart 1996; Clifford 1997). Indeed, claims have been made that conventional understandings are too easily informed by dwelling-like idioms: boundary, continuity, integrity and unit. Authenticity tends to be linked to territory, to a delimited spatial site, or to language, so that the subject is localised, only as resident or language speaker seen as entitled to stand for Culture or Society. As a result travel histories can be relegated to a supplement (Clifford 1997: 3), and encounters, which embody those histories, written out of representations (Stewart 1996: 7). The stable resident patterns which village-based ethnographies and studies of incarceration teach one to expect do not always account for the emphases that subjects provide when describing the nature of their existence.

Clifford (1997: 3) is concerned to make these unrecorded journeys visible, to foreground travel and thus release its representational creativity. He does not wish to replace idioms of dwelling with those of transience, but rather to examine the nature of their mediation (1997: 24). Culture, he states, is not just a place, but also a site of encounter (Clifford adopts the analogy of a hotel lobby [1997: 25]). By foregrounding travel, he believes that residence itself may be reconceptualised, seen not just as a natural state but also as a set of restrictions upon movement (1997: 43–44). If a prison, perhaps the most bounded site of residence conceivable, can draw attention to intersections as well as its constitution as a place of custody, then how might the idiom of travel be considered elsewhere? Bomana, extreme in its problemisation of dwelling, I suggest may provide an alternative route for understanding the limits of these still orienting metaphors.

The anthropology of Melanesia has remained strangely immune to recent debates about travel and encounter. In fact it might not unreasonably be considered one of the primary targets of those wishing to displace the privileging of residence.[6] The region of Melanesia, and in particular Papua New Guinea, with its many language groups, seems to invite a reading of diversity, of plural societies that are unitary and self-contained in character. This impression is reinforced by the sheer number of ethnographies, themselves artefacts of that perceived diversity, that are produced. Each one tends to open with a description of what distinguishes the people under study, usually an account of the territory they inhabit, the language they speak and their separate history. Anthropologists present reinterpretations of previous studies of those people, so that a sense of internal complexity but external coherence is achieved. As a result it becomes harder and harder to conceive intersections across those units, practices and narratives that involve people from different language groups and areas (Kulick [1993: 9] asks why the raskal has received so little attention from anthropologists when it is one of the most talked-about figures in Papua New Guinea; the answer perhaps lies in its nonterritorial and nonlanguage group specific status, also in its travelling reputation). The level of complexity seems nonnegotiable and so anthropologists working in the region tend to remove these histories of travel and encounter from their representations.

Indeed, it is hard to find a village-based ethnography in Melanesia that does not give the impression of autonomous, consistent communities, cleansed of any intruding presence and without alien residents.[7] The appeal to language, as a marker of that specificity and coherence, is particularly baffling, since most anthropologists working in Papua New Guinea communicate at least in part, if not primarily, in either Tok Pisin or Motu. Both are national languages that emerged out of encounters between peoples from different language groups while away on colonial plantations, mission stations, prisons, schools or police barracks. The same perception of diversity has, I believe, hindered the development of urban studies in the region. There are still very few ethnographies of Port Moresby and other towns, or of institutions (schools, mines, plantations, factories, seminaries, hospitals, civil service etc.) that bring together people from different language groups and places (by my count only one [Rew 1974]). Those that do exist tend to follow a language group from their hamlets or villages and focus on that migration (cf. Strathern 1975; May 1977; Gewertz & Errington 1991; Battaglia 1995; Errington and Gewertz 1995); they do not consider urban experiences that involve other relationships, between those who do not share the same local language. Again the perceived problem is too much complexity. If the language or territorial groups of Melanesia are provided with unitary bodies then they become Individuals and, as such, all encounters assume that corporate form.[8] Difference is taken for granted because anthropologists have written ethnographies of what they regard as separately dwelling peoples. From this perspective, urban sites, including the prison, are always an afterthought; places that already formed peoples visit. They are too complex because they appear to require an appreciation of plural Cultures and Societies, before any single urban action can be understood.

Strathern (1988, 1991) has worked to challenge this assumption of Culture or Society as a totality or unit. Instead of the commodity logic of diversity, which treats them as abstract 'things', she suggests viewing the societies of Melanesia as outgrowths or versions of each other (1988: 341–42). They cannot be counted separately, as numerical units, for they are all instances of a single form. This alternative arithmetic is intended to disturb notions of authenticity. Melanesian cultures are to be treated as neither essentially different, nor identical. They are connected, but at the same time other (1991: 38), or rather their difference is negotiated through prior connection. In part this arithmetic is based on a principle of travel, on Strathern's argument that contact has always existed between peoples in the region. The issue is therefore not how societies establish relationships between each other, but rather how differences or local forms develop (1991: 94). Here encounter is an act of separation, a connection broken as well as formed, which constitutes cultures and societies as extensions of one another (1991: 38). Because travel can be considered normative, these forms remain forever connected yet separating.

To return to the metaphor of Bomana as a bus stop, one can now consider some of the parameters of that idiom. If the prison can be regarded as a meeting place and site of dispersal, then encounter and mobility become features of incarceration. However, these intersections do not simply establish relationships between Individuals (persons who stand for the unitary bodies of Cultures or Societies), they elicit differences, act to separate prisoners from each other. By assuming a state of travel prisoners also assume the capacity to recognise connections everywhere. Entering Bomana, just like entering the city, is not a straightforward confrontation with diversity; differences still have to be achieved and drawn out. The description of the prison as an urban queue is part of that effort. At the same time its collapse is anticipated in images of physical constraint. These images recover a state of connection between prisoners (and an impression of spatial coherence), even as they highlight an experience of separation from those outside.

Jerai offered me another analogy for understanding Bomana. Instead of a bus stop, he compared the prison to a ritual action from his own home region, the Goilala area of Central province.

He explained that just as a sponsoring clan sometimes invites men and women to a specially constructed village in order to attend dance and feast celebrations, so the police arrest male and female offenders and escort them to Bomana. Those attracted to the feast come from hamlets across the region or even from as far away as Port Moresby (some 100 km northwest), while those led to gaol come from the capital, the coastal towns of Papua and by transfer from the prisons of the Highlands and New Guinea coast. At the village ceremony the sponsoring clan provides guests with accommodation, firewood and food provisions, and in the same way, Jerai told me, warders feed and house arriving prisoners. This hospitality lasts until the dancing and feasting ends and guests depart, abandoning the ritual village and returning to their homes, scattered across the region. Prisoners enjoy the same support from hosting warders until they too gain release and disperse back to the city and provinces.

This analogy evokes the same movement as an urban queue, drawing people together and then disbanding them. However, it emphasises the coercive nature of these meetings. According to Jerai, both the sponsoring clan and the agents of law and order share a capacity to direct the journeys of others. By hosting these events they coerce participation and determine the moment of dispersal. Indeed, Hirsch (1995a, 1995b, 1995c), who has conducted fieldwork in the Goilala region, argues that the preparatory activity of the sponsoring clan is perceived to align intentions, obliging guests to travel and thus drawing them towards the ritual village. In bringing these guests to a single location, the clan, and in particular its senior men, is said to demonstrate a 'holding-together capacity' (1995b: 218). This then is also the power of government (*gavman*), as exercised through its police and warders. Jerai, who was himself once a steal man, is suggesting that stealing tours are not without alignment. They may appear random and wilful, but ultimately these travellers will find themselves locked in prison, heading in the same direction. In this way the presence of Bomana, and its hosting facilities, can be seen to anticipate (direct) the movement of youth.

Jerai sees this ritual process replicated in the prison routine. He presents everyday life at Bomana as a series of alternations between assembly and dispersal. When warders shout 'Fall in!' male prisoners must leave what they are doing and run from across A Compound to the parade ground. There they form into lines of review. As the roll call is taken, warders walk up and down the channels between men, inspecting their uniform and hair length. Once this examination is over, selected convicts are sent off on work parties, while those on remand due for court are herded into vans for transport to Port Moresby. The rest are dismissed; they return to their separate cell yards and await the next call to inspection (there are at least four roll calls a day). Coming together and breaking apart is one of the identified rhythms of prison life. But here it loses its quality of mobility and becomes instead another form of physical constraint.

Notes

1 Rew (1974: 220–21) states that many of these group names emerged as a response to the colonial regime's habit of developing a principal town or station in each province. Those people living in urban centres tended to call themselves and others by the name of the town or station in their province. Hence those from Gulf province became known as 'Kerema', after the administrative centre there. Rew suggests that these names first came into common usage when people from different places were gathered together: i.e. on plantations, gold fields, labour barracks, mission stations, markets and schools.

2 The moment of seizure or physical constraint is sometimes taken back to the time of arrest. Police handcuffs may be imagined as a version of the perimeter fence at Bomana. Indeed, A. Strathern (1994: 55) notes that among the Melpa people of the Western Highlands the local word for 'fence' or 'prison' is *kan ngui*. This means 'to give a binding': i.e. to handcuff.

3 Battaglia (1994) suggests that Port Moresby is regarded by Trobriand Islanders as a place that inverts the usual direction of social relations. She argues that the presence of gangs in the city, who spend their time stealing and making trouble, is represented as a release of 'illicit' power (4). However, for Trobriand Islanders (at least those from the chiefly subclans) the frontier culture of Port Moresby is best epitomised by the fact that the most successful migrants to the city are from the Bau subclan. In the Trobriand Islands the Bau are regarded as dangerous users of sorcery, but as relatively worthless, weak-minded people. Their success in the city (Bau migrants tend to occupy prestigious positions in government and business) is seen to demonstrate the tricky, lawless nature of that place.

4 During my stay in Port Moresby I heard one song everywhere. Entitled 'Kantri blong yumi' (Our Country), it describes a young man's journey across the country from his village on the New Guinea coast at Finnschafen to the provincial town of Lae, up the highway to the Highlands, back down to the sea at Madang and then by aeroplane to Port Moresby. When the youth arrives in the capital his enthusiasm for travel ends, since he is scared by the crazy behavior of those in the city. Below are two verses from the song:

Go to Moresby, your life will change.	*go long mosbi laip is senis*
I don't think I want to stay.	*mi no ting bai mi stap long hia*
Men and women behave in weird ways,	*ol man na meri wokim kain kain stail*
I must go back to Finnschafen.	*mi mas go bek long finnschafen*

I return home, no longer got any worries.	*mi stap long ples i no gat wari*
Life is okay, but nothing more.	*laip is orait, i orait tasol*
I will never go back to the city.	*mi no tingting long go bek long taun*
Life in the city is far too hard.	*laip long taun i hat tumas*

'Kantri blong yumi', written and sung by the Reks band; produced by Patti Doi and Greg C. Seeto, and recorded in June 1994 at Pacific Gold Studios, Port Moresby.

5 Strathern (1975: 368) reports a similar attitude among some male migrants from the Western Highlands who came to Port Moresby in the 1970s. She states that the migrant population drew a distinction between those men who worked in disciplined institutions such as the police force or in other permanent employment, and so lived in labour compound barracks, and those men who lived in houses in the city and took casual employment. The latter were known as 'outsiders' and were distinguished by the frequency with which they switched jobs. Strathern states that these men sometimes earned the scorn of those in long-term employment, but at the same time the freedom they enjoyed evoked a certain admiration. While these men did not steal, their position as outsiders connects them to the kind of mobility that steal men claim.

6 Foster (1995a) has attempted to redefine the anthropology of Papua New Guinea in light of these criticisms. He advocates a 'New Melanesian Anthropology' that combines the insights of Strathern and those ethnographers of localised practices and beliefs with an historical approach to global processes such as colonialism, capitalism and Christianity (5). In this way he hopes to make social change reappear to readers of Melanesian anthropology. However Foster's approach denies the people of Papua New Guinea any creativity beyond the local context. By relegating disciplined institutions such as prisons, schools and hospitals to the global environment, he risks privileging the anthropologist's own interpretation of what those institutions should look like and do. Ultimately, it seems, local meanings are encompassed by global meanings (over which local people have no control). His New Melanesian Anthropology does, however, promise more interesting ethnography. Foster helps demonstrate that studies in Papua New Guinea should not necessarily start with a set of subjects who speak the same local language, dwell together or come from the same origin place.

7 When village-based ethnographies do present alien figures the effect can be disarming. Tuzin (1997) includes the local expatriate missionary and a woman from the Western Highlands who married a villager among the subjects of his ethnography of the Arapesh of the Sepik region. Bergendorff (1996) finds that among the Mekeo of Central province clan mates sometimes fashion their villages as a 'city'.

8 Wagner (1974: 112) argues that colonial officers and early missionaries first
   exported the vision of Papua New Guinea as a country containing a plurality of distinct, coherent culture groups. He states that their 'strong obligation
   to discover groups', to concern themselves with issues of group definition,
   belonging and participation set the tone for the anthropology of that region.

CHAPTER 3

Jeffrey's Flight

— ❧ —

Die slowly
Jail man you have no freedom.
When the sun rises, when it sets.
Why me, 'Oh bad luck boy'.
I am just going to die slowly.
A-ha A-ha.

dai isi isi
kalabus man yu no gat fridom
taim san i up taim san i go paul
wai na mi O mero madi
mi gonna dai isi isi tasol
a-ha a-ha

Another day will be over.
The months will come and go.
Lie down, sleep and turn, turn.
I am just going to die slowly.
A-ha A-ha.

narapela de bai go pinis
mun bai up na mun bai go paul
sindaun slip na tainim tainim
mi gonna dai isi isi tasol
a-ha a-ha

At nine p.m. the bell is rung,
Warders will go round the cell.
Jail men must be quiet and go
to sleep.
I am just going to die slowly.
A-ha A-ha.

nine long nait belo bai karai
woda man bai raunim sel
kalabus i passim maus na go
long slip
mi gonna dai isi isi tasol
a-ha a-ha

I have been in the jailhouse a
long time.
I gather up my language group mates,
I am sorry for them.
Who is wrong?
It's okay,
I can face the mistakes I made
outside.
A-ha A-ha.

mi bin stap long haus kalabus
mi kisim ol wantok
mi sori long ol
husat i rong
em i orait
mi kan pesim ol rong mi bin
mekim autsait
a-ha a-ha

Ma, what shall I do?
Ma, it is very hard.
Ma, how will I ever get out?
I am just going to die slowly.
A-ha A-ha.

ma bai mi olsem wanem
ma em i hat tumas
ma how bai mi out
mi gonna dai isi isi tasol
a-ha a-ha

(Antony Ume)

Despite the sense of mobility produced by the constant arrival and release of prisoners, men and women often complain that at Bomana they 'die slowly' (*dai isi isi*). The song above, written and performed by a convict from Bereina in Central province, evokes the despair that accompanies those feelings – not just the pain caused by issues of separation from kin outside the gaol (the song's narrator calls out to his mother), but also the experience of being made to accommodate oneself to the pace and rhythm of a prison routine, marked out by the chimes of a bell. The song describes the boredom of life at Bomana, the lack of qualitative change from day to day, month to month. Prisoners complain that every morning they wake to view the same cells, the same yards and the same land-scape beyond the prison fence. They are forced to eat the same food, to wear the same clothes and perform the same duties. This repetitiveness is experienced as a slowing down, a lack of spatial and temporal movement. It is the outcome of a repeating culture whose routine continually returns inmates to what appears the same moment as yesterday and the day before. Steal men in partic-ular contrast this existence with life outside the gaol: the 'live fast, die young' philosophy that they profess to follow is seen to be the antithesis of the slowed-down living that Bomana provides.

Prison studies in Europe and North America have pointed out that those who suffer incarceration tend to adopt a concept of time as a concrete and objectified presence, thus granting it an almost tangible quality (Heffernan 1972: 134). This impression is said to be encouraged by sentencing procedures that present time as an entity that is given whole in punishment, handed down by Society to the offending Individual (Giallombardo 1966: 133). The abstraction of the courts leaves prisoners feeling that time is a problem; instead of a resource that is used, it becomes an object to contemplate and serve (Cohen and Taylor 1981: 99). Prison time is something imposed upon them; it appears to be beyond their control. That sensation is reinforced by the regime of time-disci-pline (Foucault 1977) and by the sense of time lost – all the things one could be doing if time was still free to spend (Wahidin 2002). Prison studies emphasise that incarceration teaches inmates to differentiate between the nature of time inside and outside of gaol.

Prisoners at Bomana say that they live in a place where 'time' (*taim*) is made visible. Every event is attributed with a designated interval. There is a time for eating, for waking, for sleeping and working. No one can afford to ignore this schedule; if inmates are late for roll call they risk beatings or punishment exercises

(push-ups and laps around the compound) and if they miss meal
times they will remain hungry for the rest of the day. Prisoners
contrast this situation with life outside the gaol, where they claim
to be able to act when and as they like (while waged employment
and schooling are acknowledged to be also oriented around
timetables, there is not held to be the same level of coercion; an

Figure 13 *Clock time*

employee can always swap lunch breaks, sneak out for a cigarette
or resign, a school student can always play truant). I was told
that normally 'time does not boss you, rather you boss time' (*taim
em i no bosim yu, yu yet bosim taim*). For prisoners, incarceration
marks a reversal of that order; at Bomana time bosses them, it
appears not just as an object but also as a subject that has the
capacity to direct their action.

One convict, a woman from the Western Highlands named
Clara, told me that she could only remember one instance when
she followed time in the manner of the routine at Bomana. She
explained that long ago she had organised to secretly meet a
boyfriend from her local school. They arranged to rendezvous in
Hagen town at a specific hour. Clara remembered leaving her
village and without telling anyone taking a bus into town. When
she got there she checked the exact time on the clock in the post
office and then headed to the agreed meeting place, where she met
the waiting boy (Figure 13). This example of being bossed by time
is intended to highlight the capacities of the prison routine to coordinate the movement of many people. Just as Clara managed to
meet up with a boyfriend in town by both agreeing to follow the
clock, so prisoners are brought together for roll calls and meal times
by each obeying the sound of the prison bell. The difference is that
while time coerced Clara's rendezvous, it did so as a form of assistance; prisoners do not have the same control over the striking bell.
Indeed, there are few technologies that prisoners can call upon to
coordinate their own movements and gain a sense of temporal
progression. Clocks are few in number at Bomana and access to
them is heavily restricted; inmates are not allowed to wear wristwatches (warders fear another kind of illicit assignation, between
those in and out of Bomana who wish to coordinate escape plans).
As a result they complain about not knowing the hour or minute
of the day. The snatched sight of a warder's timepiece or the clock
on the wall of the general office is a cause for minor celebration.
Its information excites, seems liberating or even dangerous.[1]

If time becomes a visible constraint, then prisoners need to
learn how to accommodate it. Just like the pain of separation
from loved ones outside the gaol, so the length of prison time is
said to require habits of forgetting. Thoughts about those left
behind are believed to exacerbate the experience of dying slowly.
When female cellmates observe a prisoner sitting alone, with
head bowed and back turned, they immediately know that 'time
has got her' (*taim kisim em*). Her cellmates gather around, often

for days on end, telling stories and cracking jokes in order to try and make these worries about the length of her sentence disappear. Indeed, for this reason the art of storytelling is highly valued; a good story or joke is held able to distract even the most depressed individual. Male cellmates will sit in circles and exchange tales, inhaling deeply on rolls of tobacco or marijuana in order to make these words turn 'sweet'. Swapping back and forth, they challenge each other to keep the circle entertained. The task, as prisoners describe it, is to 'shorten time' (*sotim taim*), to make the days go quicker.

Sociologists of incarceration observe similar concerns among inmates in North American and British prisons. Prisoners are said to be concerned to achieve what is sometimes called 'easy time' (cf. Giallombardo 1966: 134; Heffernan 1972: 108; Cohen and Taylor 1981: 100). The trick, so they report, is to keep busy, to focus on events and activities that occur in gaol. These include official programmes such as labour assignments, religious services, education courses and group therapy, which as a consequence take on a quality of 'play' (Heffernan 1972: 135, 141). The same ambitions are expressed by prisoners at Bomana, but with the added frustration that fewer programmes exist to occupy their attention. Most of the time inmates are locked in their cell yards, bored and agitated. The weekly tournaments of soccer and touch rugby, as well as Christian services on the weekend, are well attended precisely because they are viewed as good ways to 'waste time' (*westim taim*). Work parties are also highly favoured, even if access is hard to gain (out of a total population of about 700 male prisoners only sixty men are selected on average to work each day; by contrast, female inmates work more regularly). Indeed, male prisoners are constantly petitioning warders to be selected for work:

Dear Sir,

Subject: Lift the ban to allow convicted life detainee to attend work parties.

Your attention is drawn to the above subject on behalf of the 13 convicted life prisoners at Bomana. We wish that the ban to attend work parties that was imposed in 1990 be lifted to allow us to work again. The boredom of having to spend the entire time of our term living in the compound quarters virtually during the week doing nothing is very unfair and unconstructive. We believe that being engaged in working parties will break the monotonous of staying in the compound all year round. We further believe that whilst engaged in work we will be able to leave our minds occupied and to keep ourselves physical alert.

We as a group earnestly appeal for your utmost concern to take remedial action to lift the ban. Here under are our signatures, bringing our notice to your attention.

Jeffrey Airi Eli, Tau Ted Lahui, George Gadina Hetau, Kenneth Baupa, Aia Marai, James Pari, Eland Elia, Anahui Oua, Kawa Tepete, Kungus Kot, Dee Tandap, Lea Aiak, James Baruhoma, James Kama.

The plea above, written by convicts serving a life sentence (lifers at Bomana were banned from work parties after several escapes), presents physical labour as a means of alleviating boredom and shortening time. The irony of petitioning for work is not lost on these convicts, the majority of whom are steal men. But in prison, they explained to me, those activities that outside the gaol slowed them down (see Chapter 2) become instead a source of quickening. In Bomana prisoners become sensitive to the micro-tempo and qualities of distraction that each activity holds.

As well as measuring official events through their capacity to consume time, prisoners attempt to keep themselves occupied in other ways. Female inmates roll wool and knit net-bags, both men and women read books and write letters, they strum guitars and compose songs. Male inmates play endless rounds of cards and invent board games. Some of them jokingly refer to these distractions as their very own work party (*wok pati blong mipela*). Indeed, prisoners devise their own regimes to mark and shorten time (cf. Heffernan 1972: 135; Cohen and Taylor 1981: 104–5; Owen 1998: 97); in this context any activity, however absurd, may be well received. Thus some convicts choose to repeatedly unpick the stitches of their vests and shorts, just in order to be able to re-sew the now separated garments. Others spend hours walking laps round and round their cell yards or tending flowers that they know will be uprooted when discovered. The desire is to move time on, to coerce it into better speed.

However, this project is often said to fail, causing some prisoners to be overwhelmed by the length of time they have left to serve. Male convicts reminded me, in a cautionary tone, of a place man from East Sepik province who was said to have recently lost his mind (*em i go long long*). One morning, they reported, this prisoner awoke, left his cell and with his blanket still hugged close to his chest approached the duty warder. He smiled at the guard and with a firm voice announced, 'Boss, I want to finish'. The duty warder rejected his plea, barring his way and answering him back with the words, 'No, you have fifteen years, you must stay here'. On hearing this, it is said that the convict grew angry; he started hurling abuse and throwing wild punches. Eventually restrained by a group of warders, the place man was escorted to a detention cell and there locked up. Inside he collapsed into a corner and started rocking violently. When the guards came with his evening meal, they found the convict chewing his blanket and swallowing his own excrement. This story, convicts told me, should act as a warning to those who might dwell too long on the burden of prison time.

Waiting

Once arriving male convicts have been registered, they are taken outside of the reception office and told to change out of their clothes. Now wearing standard issue waistcloths or vests and shorts, these men are instructed to fold their civilian clothes and place them inside the canvas bags provided. Each bag, tagged with the convict's name and due date of discharge, is carried to the property room and handed over to the prisoner in charge of storage. The room itself is rectangular and only dimly lit, but from the open door new convicts can see a series of wooden shelves lining the plaster walls. Small cards pinned to their plane surface distinguish the shelves from each other; these inform the store man where to place the received bundles. As the shelves ascend the walls, so the dates on the cards become more distant: 1999, 2000, 2001, 2002, 2003, 2004 and onwards. At the very top he must fully stretch in order to lodge or retrieve the property of those serving life sentences. Convicts know that these bags cannot be collected until the day of their release.

At Bomana prisoners consider the length of their sentences as units that bear weight. Analogies are made to money, which is seen to share the characteristics of number and divisibility, every unit being distinct and separate, yet at the same time internally partible – Kina into Toea (national currency of notes and coins), months into days. One convict told me that she was serving 'six solid years'. Indeed, when prisoners are convicted and returned to Bomana they complain at suddenly feeling 'heavy', weighed down, as many describe it, like someone forced to carry a sack of sweet potatoes on his or her back. Convicts actually regard themselves taking on the characteristics of these units of time, becoming embodiments of the length of sentence they have left to serve. They are distinguished as 'year men' (*yiaman*) or 'year women' (*yiameri*), 'month men' (*munman*) or 'month women' (*munmeri*). The longer the sentence, the heavier the weight they have to bear and the slower their movements become; until one gets to the 'life man' (*laipman*) (there are no women with life sentences), who is said to be so burdened with time that he walks at a snail's pace, like a rickety old man.

Convicts distinguish their existence on the basis of this future expectation; the designated purpose of their lives is to 'wait' (*wet*) for the date of discharge. Similarly, those on remand actually call themselves 'wait courts' (*wetkot*) because that is what they are said to do (to be waiting for their day in court). The year men and year women, who have long sentences to serve, expect others to show sympathy and 'respect' the period of waiting they are forced to observe. In A Compound month men perform small services for the year men, who often control the distribution of tobacco and marijuana. Month men wash down the cells; they collect the meals of year men and fold their blankets in the hope of thus gaining reward or protection. Year men not only control illicit resources, but also the sharing of food rations, the allocation of sleeping space in the cells and the selection of teams for the weekly tournaments of soccer and touch rugby. These discretionary powers are seen to be their right as long-term prisoners. Both year men and year women at Bomana express feelings of resentment towards the 'month people' (*munlain*), who can look forward to imminent release. They complain that these convicts show too much content-ment and upset their composure with loud and boisterous behaviour. Year men and year women are even prepared to report these troublesome convicts to warders or sometimes to exercise their own punishments.

However, the attitude of long-term convicts is restrained by the knowledge that in the future, the final year of their own sentence, they too will take on this status, become in turn month men or month women. Those with less than a year left to serve are said to noticeably change their demeanour. Their manner eases, shoulders relax and general activity quickens. For the first time they allow themselves to think about events outside the gaol and about the people they know there, and to lose interest in distracting activi-ties such as card games, correspondence courses or physical exercises. The transformed year man or year woman is said to be only half present, to have divided thoughts, or, in the words of several inmates, to now have one leg standing inside the prison fence but the other one planted firmly on the side of freedom.

Prisoners state that at Bomana they begin to make plans for the future. Indeed, the practice of waiting is said to teach them to consider the future as a set-apart interval of time, that period after their release. This anticipatory disposition is contrasted with their habit before incarceration, when young men and women were said to act without forethought or consideration for the consequences of their behaviour. Before going to sleep remand prisoners claim to think about their court date and convicts about their day of discharge, often asking themselves, 'how will my future pan out?' (*futa blong mi kamap olsem wanem*). During long, tedious hours between meals, cellmates sit around and play 'questions and answers'. They interrogate each other about their future prospects outside, demanding to know what each one intends to do when their confinement is over. Bomana is held to provide the time for 'clear thoughts' (*klia tingting*) and well-constructed plans. Place men and place women talk about returning home and setting up projects such as coffee gardens or trade stores, steal men talk about making that great 'last robbery' or giving the stealing life up and getting married and trying to find work. Everyone has a particular ambition to tell. The separation of that future from the present of Bomana, the term of imprisonment, means that these stories are not seen necessarily to disturb the project of forgetting.[2] What is important about them is their anticipation of a state of change.

Joe, a steal man from the Highlands province of Enga, showed me his journal. There he had written down his future plans. The journal stated that upon his release Joe would first go and visit his member of parliament in Port Moresby and ask him for a loan so that he could return to his village and set up a poultry farm and market garden (members of parliament in Papua New Guinea are allotted State funds to distribute as they wish among their constituents). This proposed project was a radical departure from his life before Bomana, which had been dominated by criminal activity. From the age of ten, so he told me, Joe had been stealing, since then either touring the country with other steal men or locked up in prison. But now, at the age of twenty-four, he looked forward to a different life. Joe said that nearly all of his friends had been arrested or killed by police and that he too feared becoming a target upon his release. At home, his parents were elderly and in need of care and the journal stated that he would return to look after them and find a place woman wife. Joe told me that he had already sent a letter to the village, explaining his future intentions.

These plans for a future which only starts when the prison sentence ends are matched by nostalgia for a past, another set-apart interval of time, which is defined as the period before detention. Prisoners observe that for the first time in their lives they view a realm of events that are characterised by their complete disconnection from the present. Reflections upon that reified past are said to provoke tears and bitter regrets. Prisoners compose songs, poems and life stories that evoke what appears the passion and innocence of those lost days, before forethought and reflection were said to exist. Below is an example written by a year man from Central province:

Iron curtain

As I lay in my cement bed,
The memory flooded through my brain vessels.
Thinking of the past,
The tears rolled down my cheeks.
As I gaze through the iron curtains
I saw a moon shine through the iron glass windows,
And it keeps reminding me of the good olden days,
As I walked down the path of no return, not knowing what's
the journey ahead...

(Boboka Zorro Vele)

Penal confinement, then, provides the constraint of a temporal framework, the technology for imagining time cut into distinctive and impermeable intervals. By viewing the past as that period before confinement, the present as any time during it, and the future as that period after discharge, prisoners are handed the capacity to conceive themselves between altered states. They map a number of transformations upon that temporal series (explored in the next chapters). Despite the pain of nostalgia for a past that seems absolutely lost, the tedium of a present that lacks qualitative distinctions and the frustrations of a future that only begins at someone else's direction, prisoners at Bomana concede some of the orienting value of being bossed by time.

Dreaming

Leaning well forward, his back fully exposed, Jeffrey hesitated again before finally allowing his cellmate to make the first stab. From behind he could hear the convict sharpening the needle, which had once been the key to a tin of fish meat, and shaking the pot of ashes, collected the day before by setting fire to a discarded rubber tyre. This time Jeffrey flinched as the needle truly touched his skin and he recognised, in the first uneven scratches, the nerves of his friend. Clenching his teeth to meet the pain, he wondered at the boldness of his project. Him, Jeffrey H. Malepo, alias Tiger Man or Nomadic Gangster, wanted his dream inscribed into his body, dug across the face of his back. He winced, felt the blood ooze from the wound and begin its slow downward turn. However, the second cut was better, more assured. Jeffrey's thoughts returned to his dream flight, to the health of his parents:

He stands, precariously balanced, on the roof of his own cell, trying to maintain his footing against the narrow ruts of the corrugated iron. No one sees him. To Jeffrey this seems puzzling, since the bird, whose legs he now grasps firmly in his left hand, is making an awful commotion, beating its wings and clearly wishing to escape. But Jeffrey does not dwell on the anomaly for long. The excitement of his own anticipated flight soon takes over. Quickly he finds the courage and leaps without reserve from the rooftop. The air rushes by. Jeffrey flaps his arms and for a moment feels he might indeed be flying. But he isn't. Instead his body falls downwards, heading for the ground. However, the bird, whose legs he still holds fast, intervenes, working its wings furiously and managing to lift them up just in time. Now Jeffrey *is* flying. The pair soar for a while and then head away.

Turning corners did appear to hurt more. When his cellmate changed the angle of incision the skin seemed to rip and the blood run faster. Yet Jeffrey did not mind too much. The sensations, now alternating in quality, allowed him to distinguish the curves and flurries of the figure, to feel its dimensions. This pain also had a rhythm; a phrasing that seemed to echo aerial beats. It accompanied the discomfort he sometimes felt at remembering those he left outside the gaol. Much of the blood that criss-crossed his back had begun to harden and Jeffrey could sense the skin around the larger drops tense in response. His friend's hand, now confident, continued its work, perhaps also enjoying the accent and pulse of this operation. But it seemed a long journey and Jeffrey felt comforted that at least the first circuit was done. His thoughts returned to his dreaming experience:

Ahead of them appears Bulolo town. Jeffrey and the bird fly together until they reach his parents' house, where he says farewell. But the house is empty. Jeffrey wanders its rooms, conscious that if he has indeed escaped warders and policemen will not be far behind. In his sister's room he finds some money, twelve Kina, of which he grabs ten. Suddenly Jeffrey grows scared; he swings around and runs to the front door. Upon opening it, he finds a warder, who wears a puzzled expression and asks him to explain his presence. Jeffrey tells the man that he has come because he fears for the welfare of his parents and wishes to see them once again. The warder, who seems familiar, nods in understanding and presents Jeffrey with a bright yellow ball. He takes the gift with both hands, but the ball is heavy and he needs all his strength just to prevent it from falling. At that moment a car approaches and as it draws closer Jeffrey recognises the faces of his mother, father, two brothers and four sisters. Yet when he sees them, he chooses to hide and let the vehicle pass by. Just then someone shouts his name and Jeffrey turns around.

He felt the needle complete the figure, the last stab acting as a return. His cellmate now reached for the pot of ashes and disturbed the contents with his fingers. Once prepared, this man gathered the flakes in his hands and proceeded to rub them carefully into the burrows etched across Jeffrey's back. The ashes felt dry and heavy against his skin, sealing the wounds. At that moment he lost all sensation of injury. Jeffrey knew that the burnt rubber would provide definition, darkening the lines of his still fresh tattoo. Washed and towelled, the blurred image would appear as a bird, its wings extended, but held back from flight by a grasping hand.

When the tattoo was finished, Jeffrey's back felt tender and sore for several weeks. If he moved too quickly, the dry and crusted outline tore at his skin. The pain shook him, but in a reassuring manner. Now he could never forget his dream or stop pondering its possibilities. What, Jeffrey asked himself, did the dreaming experience denote? His flight, and the stubborn refusal to free the legs of the bird, a figure of movement and freedom for prisoners, promised well. But the taking of money (ten Kina out of twelve), he feared, was bad. Its qualities of number and divisibility suggested a parallel with terms of prison sentence, units of currency matching units of time. On top of his existing term, Jeffrey had a murder charge pending. Did the dream anticipate conviction? Ten years? Ten months? The yellow ball, heavy to hold, also implied a long sentence. Why, Jeffrey speculated, would he hide from his parents and siblings? Again this suggested to him a further conviction. But Jeffrey kept hope with the final dream image. Could the voice that called his name and turned his head perhaps be taken as a sign of eventual reprieve? These questions swirled about him, pulling Jeffrey first one way and then another. But the beauty of his dream flight remained. Its memory left him breathless.

There is a sense among prisoners that during incarceration an aspect of temporality is lost. It is not just that time appears as a constraint, capable of bossing or coercing actions, but that it also changes its nature. The emphasis on time as sets of distinguishable and nonpermeable intervals, solid and heavy units such as years and months, that can be handed down, carried and embodied by individuals is accompanied by strict divisions between past, present and future which now become states to pass through, look forward to or look back on. This is a very different temporal existence, one which prisoners identify almost exclusively with the regime at Bomana. In such an environment the dreaming experience is valued as an interruption, conveying a quality of time that prisoners feel has been taken away. Jeffrey, a convict from Bulolo in Morobe province, appreciates his dream flight as a form of temporal digression.

The nature of what exactly prisoners feel they have lost may be recovered by turning to the definition of temporality originally provided by Bergson. He identifies clock-based time with an experience of simultaneity (1910: 100). The interval on a timepiece is said to foreground the present moment and thus draw attention to multiple, concurrent actions. Each interval – second, minute or hour – is discontinuous and external to the ones before and after. On a clock face one moment ends as soon as the next appears (1910: 227). Time therefore takes on the attribute of number, as units of space laid out side-by-side and juxtaposed (1910: 85, 101). Bergson says that moments lose their distinction, become countable objects and only differ in degree (cf. Deleuze 1988: 31–32). He contrasts this state with his idea of 'duration', a form of temporality that recognises differences in kind. Deleuze, who extends and alters Bergson's theory, calls this latter state a 'non numerical multiplicity', the fusion or synthesis of successive positions (1988: 43; and cf. Bergson 1910: 111). Moments are not available to calculation, for they are heterogeneous and noncomparable. Here there is 'other' but not 'several' (Deleuze 1988: 42). Rather than simultaneity, one experiences a continuity of diffuse moments. Past, present and future interconnect and blend into each other (Bergson 1910: 104). There is no distance or break between these moments. In fact Bergson equates duration with a melody or musical phrase (1910: 106); he evokes a state of succession without measurement.

At first Bergson considered clock-based time, the experience of simultaneity, as an aberration, the modern corruption of ancient temporality. But Deleuze claims that he later came to realise the necessary exchange between simultaneity and succession. Rather than in competition, the two states coexist as a composite form, only separable in principle through reflection (a worthwhile exercise as long as clock-based time remains hegemonic) (1988: 23). It is this kind of separation, which Deleuze regards as only a philosophic strategy, that I want to suggest prisoners experience as an effect of incarceration. The time that bosses them privileges that sense of simultaneity and is the principle behind the coordinating power of the prison bell. The emphasis at Bomana is on the present as a site of multiple experiences in the same units of space. There is little sense of succession, only the repetition of homogenous, like intervals. The past and future exist at a distance, in external relation to this tiresome, weighty now. It is not that prisoners reject experiences of simultaneity (they hark after sights of the clock that would allow them to coordinate their own actions), but that they resent the exclusion of experiences of succession. Incarceration imposes a constraint because it appears to reduce the composite nature of time to pure, uncontrollable simultaneity.

Dreaming experiences such as that described by Jeffrey are a source of liberation because they provide sensations of temporal succession. In his dream flight, Jeffrey escapes the repeating culture of Bomana. From a burdensome present, he flies to Bulolo town and there visits the house of his parents, which he has not seen for many years. This very different landscape, drawn from his past, shares continuity with the prison landscape of cells and high perimeter fence. The nature of dreams, just like the nature of cinema and modern forms of travel, juxtaposes nonsequential images (see Schivelbusch 1979; Kern 1983), transporting Jeffrey from one location to the next.[3] Prisoners compare this negotiation of abrupt contrasts with the experience of flying in aeroplanes, taking off in the cool air of the Highlands and landing on the hot, coastal plain of Port Moresby. Or with the experience of bus travel in the city, speeding between designated stops and thus combining distant shops and suburbs. Jeffrey explained that his dream also implicated a future date, his upcoming trial for murder.[4] Indeed, several months later he was convicted and sentenced to serve a life term, a decision that Jeffrey saw as prefigured in his dreaming experience. In the same way he expected the outcome of his upcoming appeal to be already anticipated. His dream flight, now an event from his past, still had presence in his future. It embodied the synthesis provided by succession, a temporal state that he carried imprinted as tattoo across his back.

While prisoners may fear their portent and be concerned by the disruption of composure and efforts to forget, they nonetheless desire dreaming experiences. These are held to be the best way to recover a sense of lost temporality. Johnson, a convict who used to steal in Port Moresby, told me that at night or during the day, before closing his eyes, he always said to himself, 'I must dream, I must dream' (*mi mas driman mi mas driman*). For in his sleep, Johnson explained, he visited his favourite places, such as Ela Beach in the capital, where pretty high-school girls are known to walk the sands, or the shores of Lake Kutubu in the Southern Highlands, where he was born and his parents remain. This instruction to dream is of course wishful; Johnson, like other prisoners, believes that his dreaming experiences are caused by the thoughts of others: kin, friends or enemies outside the gaol.[5] In that sense the temporal liberation they provide can be viewed as a gift.[6] But Johnson also warns me about the dangers of dreaming. If a prisoner spends too long worrying about what is missing or those outside the jail spend too long worrying about the prisoner, then it is said that his or her dreams will become confused. Dream images will start to contrast at a furious pace, alternating out of control so that none of them remain coherent. One moment, Johnson said, he or she may see a dead man lying in a city street, the next a hamlet in the Highlands, a snake, a runabout boat in water between islands, youth dancing in a night-club, a movie character, a cassowary bird and so on. The dreamer is said to overload with images, an experience that Johnson described as 'going computer' (*em i go komputa*). Here then is the other side of incarceration, a state in which succession exists without simultaneity.

I heard the news of Kenneth's death while conducting interviews in the female wing. The female duty warder told me that he had been stabbed and killed by the convict he was bullying in A Compound. I was shocked. Kenneth, a steal man from Oro province, who was adopted and raised by an Australian missionary couple, had been one of the first convicts to approach me and offer his reflections on prison life. He spoke perfect English and introduced me to convicts from his language group, those he used to steal with outside the gaol and the other members of the Anglican congregation at Bomana. Kenneth was serving a life sentence. In the following weeks, nearly every prisoner I spoke with mentioned the incident and retold the story. The gaol commander announced an official inquiry and national newspapers covered the details of the killing. Kenneth's sudden death seemed to consume attention.

Probe starts into death of prisoner

By Daniel Korimbao

PORT MORESBY: Tensions remained high at the Bomana jail yesterday as police and CIS officials began investigations into the death of a prisoner on Tuesday morning.

CIS Minister Paul Wanjik said yesterday he had directed CIS Commissioner Sam Nuakona to appoint a senior officer to investigate the circumstances surrounding the death of the man (name withheld) in a fight.

Mr Wanjik said the situation was still tense and additional staff had been deployed at the jail as a precautionary measure to carefully monitor the situation in the prison compound.

Mr Wanjik said preliminary inquiries showed that the prisoner was delivered the fatal blow sometime after 8am roll call.

A prison official who did not want to be named said the dead man and his fellow prisoners had attacked the would-be assailant several times since Sunday.

The official said on Tuesday morning the prisoner and his companions went to the assailant's cell after the roll call to hit him.

'When they entered his cell, the assailant ran to his bedside, picked up a 40cm piece of sharp iron he had been preparing and plunged it into the stomach of the prisoner', the official said.

According to the official, the assailant then attacked one of the companions but missed his neck by inches.

'He then used the piece of iron to scare away the rest of the companions and the gathering crowd of prisoners, and ran to the safety of the guardhouse', the official said.

The assailant is now in maximum security waiting to be interviewed by the police.

The National 27/7/95

Kenneth's violent death also sparked dream memories; many of the prisoners I spoke with were convinced that past dreaming experiences foretold this killing.[7] During subsequent interviews, prisoners offered me endless versions of the event in what they regarded as dream form. While some of these reported dreaming experiences happened days before or even on the night prior to Kenneth's death, others occurred weeks or months before the incident. The connections that prisoners identified seemed to suggest extraordinary temporal leaps. It didn't appear to matter whether the dreamer knew Kenneth, across Bomana, from the convict and remand sections of A Compound, to E Division, the juvenile and female wings, inmates wanted to tell me their dreams. Below are just a few recorded examples.

The senior men of his neighbouring clan prepare decorations for a customary dance. They enter his village, and with shouts and screams approach the chief. These men issue a complaint at the death of their kin and then leave.

In his arms he holds two squirming piglets. He laughs as they wriggle and try to escape. Suddenly one starts panting, straining for air, and then its body goes limp and he can tell it has died.

She watches two convicts in the female wing arguing. One woman produces a knife and lunges at the other. She misses and the weapon falls to the ground. Then she herself picks up the knife and with all her strength plunges it into the same woman's chest. The woman screams, folds her hands over the wound and dies.

Flames lick the barred ventilation windows and the breezeblock walls of his cell, which glows red with heat. Screams can be heard inside and men run from the now melted door, their arms and legs alight like torches. When he turns round he only sees corpses, burnt black by the fire.

Prisoners surround and stab an unknown man. The blood spurts everywhere, covering the by-standers, including his own trousers, shirt and face. Then the injured man turns to confront him. He is petrified and tries to run away, but the man, still leaking blood, gives chase and with one outstretched hand pulls him down.

These dreaming experiences, and many others I heard like them, were told in order to highlight the convergence of remote moments. If Kenneth's death brought past dreams to the present, then it also drew the present of the event into multiple pasts. Prisoners are impressed by these temporal contortions, by the links unexpectedly revealed across distances in time. As well as a sense of succession, the continuity of past moments into the present, dreaming emphasises for prisoners the exhilaration of discontinuity. Instead of the tedium of waiting and a regime that privileges repetition, dreams draw their attention to unplanned temporal associations, to the shock and delight of radical synthesis. They provide productive disorders, subversive entanglements of time; also a sense of anticipation, one not directed to a court date or day or release, but rather to an unknown, yet inevitable upcoming occurrence. One of the prisoners, whose dreaming experience is quoted above, explained that when he awoke from his dream he sighed and said to himself, 'now something is going to happen' (*nau wanpela samting bai kamap*). He didn't know what it would be, but he told me that he could feel the event in his body.

Emergency

It is a commonplace observation within prison studies that gaol life is monotonous. Inmates, to quote one observer, often complain that 'in prison there are no surprises' (Morris and Morris 1963: 177). At Bomana this lack of qualitative experience, of something happening, leads prisoners to become absorbed by events such as Kenneth's death (events anticipated in dreams, but not confirmed in their specificity until the moment of actual revelation). This killing, in its very unexpectedness, seemed to provide relief from the tedium of prison existence. What could be more different from the slow death that prisoners describe?

In a very different landscape, the old coal camp communities of the Appalachian hills in West Virginia, Stewart (1996: 37) outlines a culture focused on the creativity of emergency events. There, where unemployment is high and many young people leave to find work in the cities, she states that boredom is over-

come by valorising, and looking for signs to anticipate, any incidents that may interrupt daily lives. Car crashes, drunken
violence, murder and suicide become the centre of conversation
and a stimulus to local narratives. Indeed, Stewart claims that
people stand around and wait for these events to occur (1996: 78).
They forever retell these happenings in their stories, which glory
in digression and image presentation rather than grand explanation (1996: 80). Stewart claims that there is never a conclusion,
just further recollections to be told. At Bomana an equivalent
appreciation for contingent events exists. Not just violent deaths,
but sudden fights, unsuspected escapes, surprise weekend visits,
early releases and unforeseen arrivals, excite attention and spark
inmate conversation. There is a sense in which prisoners too stand
around and wait for something to happen. Although these unexpected events may prove distressing (steal men and language
group mates mourned the death of Kenneth; the composure of
long-term convicts is upset by the comings and going of other
detainees), they are valued for their nonrepetitive and singular
appearance. A feeling of interruption is experienced.

Scenes of contingent events therefore enchant prisoners. When
a mango hits the ground beside the playing field within the high
perimeter fence heads are turned. Those closest jump up and struggle to grab the fruit. The winner peels his prize and sucks deep on
the flesh. Fibres catch and irritate his teeth, and the juice burns his
dry lips. But there is nothing more refreshing in Moresby heat than
mangoes and the modest meal comes as a welcome break from the
dulling taste of brown rice and tinned fish meat. Male prisoners
explain that no one knows when the fruit will drop. 'If you are
lucky', they say, 'one will land at your feet. But only if you are lucky.'

This same good fortune can irritate or cause jealousy. In particular convicts resent the presence of remand inmates at Bomana
because they regard them as embodiments of chance. It is said that
those waiting for court, unlike convicts, have an equal chance of
gaining acquittal or being convicted. They are said to 'live 50–50'
(*stap fifti fifti*). Remand inmates do not share the singular fate of
convicts, and this knowledge that immediate futures are still undetermined is held to be liberating. Not just the opportunity for
acquittal, but the promise of bail or probation allows them to
remain focused on life outside the gaol. Indeed, the very physical
appearance of this group of prisoners is seen to reflect their liminal
state. Unlike convicts, those on remand are permitted to wear civilian shirts or trousers, to keep their hair length long, their beards

and moustaches unshaven. Convicts assert that remand inmates are not 'pure' prisoners; they appeal to this ambiguous status in order to justify their unequal treatment. At Bomana those on remand receive heavily reduced food rations (a spoon of brown rice each rather than a plate full, or one tin of fish meat to share between thirteen instead of six inmates), suffer far greater overcrowding in cells and often go without standard issues of soap, razors and blankets. Both convicts and warders tend to regard the remand inmates as impostors, the proper responsibility of the police force rather than the prison service, and cooperate against them when necessary. If, for instance, a male convict strikes a man on remand, warders will tend to ignore the assault, and if food rations are short, warders will ensure that convicts get first priority. Those living in the remand wing of A Compound bear these circumstances because they too wish to believe in their own liminality, to reject the option of a negative outcome in their upcoming trial.

While convicts do not embody uncertainty in the manner of remand inmates, they can still seek solace in games of chance. Indeed, male prisoners will gamble on almost anything in an attempt to manufacture contingency. Bets are placed on dice games, cards and draughts, on Australian rugby league results, heard on smuggled radios, or on contests of touch rugby played in cell yards. Bars of soap, cigarettes or the next morning's supply of breakfast biscuits are put down as pledges to be won or lost; sometimes inmates set each other challenges, the loser of a card round, for instance, being forced to swallow large containers of water. These games help pass the day and alleviate the routine of prison life. Each moment of indeterminacy is seen to recover a faint version of freedom; demonstrations of contingency exhilarate and relieve. It is no coincidence therefore that male prisoners equate these games of chance with the act of masturbation. The wrist action of self-stimulation is said to mimic the throwing arm for dice. Both provide a peculiar pleasure, which makes them shudder, but like detumescence, the usual aftermath of a wager is disenchantment. Convicts observe that an awareness of slow death can only return.

Nancy, a year woman who left her village in the Kompian district of Enga province in order to follow a boyfriend to Port Moresby, told me that she wasn't worried about the length of her sentence. She sat in the shade provided by the cell wall of the female wing and stared at Bisoke hill. Sweating in her nylon prison frock,

Nancy looked awkward and shy. But when conversation turned to
her belief in the imminence of the Apocalypse, or 'last day' (*las
de*), her confidence suddenly grew. Nancy explained that she was
not concerned about the long wait to her date of discharge, set for
2002 (the discussion took place in 1995), because she expected the
world to end with the new millennium in the year 2000. On this
day, she told me, Jesus would return to judge the people, sending
the faithful to Heaven and condemning the rest to destruction. It
wouldn't matter where she was or what she had done, if she
believed and renounced sin, then her salvation would follow.

Peter looks out on a flat land. He sees waves of people, dressed in all sorts of
costumes, bobbing on the ground. Above, the clouds part to reveal a segment
of blue ceiling and light from the Kingdom of Heaven. Peter turns to the crowd
and announces, 'Hey, it must be the last day!' Suddenly the earth shakes and
from the sky bolts of fire rain down. Around him, men and women stand erect,
and alight like candles, they quietly burn. Peter runs. He dodges the fires until
he reaches his own familiar cell yard. There a warder stops him, shakes his hand
and advises, 'You must worship, the time has come, stay and behave well'.

Those Christian inmates who look forward to the Apocalypse
provide the ultimate rejection of prison temporality. Their
dreams or visions of the last day, such as the one provided above
by a member of the Pentecostal church, summon an emergency
event whose significance eclipses all other concerns. In this
context the slow death of incarceration loses its immediacy. The
promised conflagration of Judgement Day threatens to collapse
any distinction between past, present and future. In this scenario
every event is prefigured and fateful, a sign or indication of the
imminent catastrophe to come. Members of the Pentecostal and
Seven-Day Adventist churches at Bomana believe that past,
present and future events are directed by a divine plan, as set out
in the Book of Revelation and other bible verses. These direct
that in the years before the Apocalypse people will suffer great
tribulation. Some Christian inmates point to the rise of criminal
activity in Papua New Guinea, the increasing cases of murder,
rape and robbery, as evidence for this development. They point
also to the rise in government corruption, tribal fighting and
prostitution. Natural disasters are held to provide more signs of
the last day. Tidal waves, floods, landslides, famines and volcanoes (just before I arrived in the country the Rabaul volcanoes
erupted, destroying the town and leaving many thousands home-
less) are seen to anticipate that event. New technologies, such as
television, computing and radio, are taken as further signs, as are

the introduction of marijuana, pornography and rugby. Christian prisoners call attention to events overseas such as the Gulf War, the AIDS epidemic and the reported loose morals of the British royal family. These circumstances appear to confirm that the Apocalypse is about to happen.[8]

This is what I will do in the last days,
God says:
I will pour out my Spirit on everyone.
Your sons and daughters will proclaim
My message;
Your young men will see visions,
And your old men will have dreams.[9]

Acts 2: 17

Even the event of dreaming is taken as a sign of final catastrophe. Christian inmates reference those bible passages that state that the last day will be preceded by an upsurge of dreaming and visionary experiences. The number and anticipatory capacity of prisoners' dreams are therefore taken as a further marker of approaching doom. In this perspective nothing, except the Apocalypse itself, remains *sui generis*. Life at Bomana is just another manifestation of the general chaos of the final days. Those Christian prisoners who believe the Apocalypse is imminent look forward with excitement to that happening, an event that obviates any other temporal regime.

Notes

1 Baudrillard (1996: 94) states that timepieces like wristwatches and clocks provide not only chronometric precision (a basis for coordinating movements in space and time), but also a means of appropriating time, turning it into an object to be consumed. The sight of a clock face in staff offices or the watch on the wrist of a warder can therefore provide inmates with a sense of progression, an active devouring of the time left to be served, as well as a sense of connection with events outside the gaol.

2 Cohen and Taylor (1981: 102–3) highlight what they regard as the paradox of reflecting upon the future in prison. On the one hand, prisoners wish to resist too much thought on the length of sentence left to serve; dwelling on the future can upset their composure and make time seem to move even slower. On the other hand, they rely upon the promise of a future life after imprisonment to sustain them through the ordeal; without that prospect prisoners have to accept that their life is over or at least restricted to a prison existence.

3   The idea of dreaming as a form of travel or movement is widely reported in
    the societies of Papua New Guinea (see Meggitt 1962; Wagner 1972; Weiner
    1986; Lattas 1993). A belief exists that the soul or spirit of the person leaves
    the body and actually experiences the events seen in dreams. Gillison (1993:
    108) reports the Gimi of the Eastern Highlands as saying:'when you go to sleep
    at night you go outside yourself'. Here the dream is not inside the person, but
    rather the person is inside the dream.

4   Herdt (1987: 63–65) notes that among the Sambia of the Eastern Highlands
    dreams are accorded more significance when people are oriented to a particu-
    lar upcoming event. Before a hunting expedition or the departure of a young
    man to a faraway plantation, Sambia expect to receive dream portents.

5   Dreaming may also be associated with the confining space of Bomana. Weiner
    (1991) notes that among the Foi people of the Southern Highlands the activ-
    ity is associated with the capture of flow or the arrest of movement. In order
    to dream, Foi men seek out locations such as whirlpools or bends in the river.
    Weiner suggests that these places contain a 'potential, a pent-up energy, a possi-
    ble source of power or revelation' (2).

6   Stephen (1996: 465) states that dreams provide a natural critique of that anthro-
    pology which, she argues, presents Melanesian sociality as an inversion of our
    (Euro-American) own. She claims that anthropologists such as Strathern and
    Wagner ignore the subjectivity or sense of selfhood reflected in people's dream
    practice. However, the prisoners at Bomana do not connect dreaming with the
    kind of subjectivity that Stephen favours. To them, dreams are not evidence of
    an unconscious mind or the inner life of a historical self, but rather the outcome
    of other people's thoughts and feelings towards them. As Herdt (1987: 61)
    points out, while persons are not held responsible for their dreaming, they are
    responsible for what they say or communicate about that experience.

7   Anthropologists of Melanesian societies report that people regularly connect
    events to their dreaming. Gillison (1993: 199) states that among the Gimi of
    the Eastern Highlands the first sweet potato is believed to have been seen in a
    dream. Indeed, the Gimi say that women must dream a child before conceiv-
    ing it (209), and that future marriage partners should first view each other in
    dreams (233). People often regard dreams as the source of myth and ritual, as
    the basis for new forms of knowing (see Stephen 1979: 14).

8   A belief in the imminence of the Apocalypse, connected with the year 2000,
    was widely reported by anthropologists working in Papua New Guinea (cf.
    Stewart and Strathern 1997; Robbins 1998a). Robbins (1997: 38–39) notes that
    the Urapmin people of West Sepik province started to look for signs or portents
    of the Apocalypse in everyday events, but also in the news they received of
    global events. The Gulf War was believed to fulfil the prophecies made in the
    Book of Revelation.

9   All bible references will use the Good News Bible version. Many different
    versions are read at Bomana, mostly in English, but this particular one is
    perhaps the most common

CHAPTER 4

Place of Men

Foucault (1977: 297) suggests that the rise of the penitentiary and other disciplined institutions caused what he terms a 'carceral archipelago' to emerge across late eighteenth-century Western Europe and North America. This geographic idiom, which presents disciplined institutions as a chain of islands dotted across a nondisciplinary landscape, is adopted in order to explain his postulated shift from a society of spectacle to one of surveillance (1977: 217). According to Foucault, the modern technologies of selfhood first developed in these isolated 'discipline-blockades' (1977: 209), before detaching themselves and spreading their now subtle mechanisms across the social body. A similar geography might be imagined for colonial and postcolonial Papua New Guinea. Indeed, prisoners recognise the parallels between the disciplinary routine at Bomana and those in the boarding schools they have attended, the hospitals they have visited, the army barracks, plantations and mining compounds where they have been employed. However, the aspect of the disciplined institution that strikes them more immediately is the experience of displacement it can create. From Bomana, these institutions are appreciated as places constituted by what is taken away – they have the capacity to establish a sense of loss or distance from certain sets of relations. Thus prisoners complain at being cut off from parents, siblings, spouse, children, kin and other loved persons. Incarceration is distinguished by the technology of nostalgia it provides.

This sense of something missing or suspended pervades the prison atmosphere at Bomana. Previous chapters have outlined the negative impact of separation, the pain and distress it causes and the requirement for purposeful acts of forgetting. The proportions of the constraint that prisoners suffer have been introduced by colonial administration. But that constraint focuses attention not just on what or who is made absent, but also on what or who is brought into presence as a consequence.

The next chapters explore these forms of prison existence and the manner of transformations that detainees plot against the penal division of time into past, present and future units. The forms are always premised on the fact that something is left behind. Indeed, the nostalgia that prisoners experience is never an evasion of present concerns and responsibilities. It is not the 'synthetic' nostalgia for tradition (see Battaglia 1995 and Strathern 1995b), nor is it an appetite for styles and fashions that have lost their historicity (Jameson 1991), but rather it is a sentiment that remains deeply 'practical' (Battaglia 1995: 77 & 93). This nostalgia is always concerned with the present (and future), with what that loss evinces as well as disallows. Imprisonment appears to foreground loss because that sensibility authorises prisoners to reveal themselves in altered states.

While the temporality of these perceived states of existence is crucial, one state emerges through the coerced disappearance of another state that is taken to belong to the time before incarceration; the geography of penal nostalgia may also render them in spatial proximity. Rather than one state being replaced by another, they may be considered as co-present, existing side by side and mediated by the prison fence. In this cartographic imagination alternating states or sets of relations are seen at once, both sides made visible at the same time. That quality is one of the enduring dilemmas for prisoners. It pushes them to try and restore a sense of temporality, to reveal other forms that can eclipse these now coterminus states and in turn be made hidden or transformed. The problem of incarceration is precisely the fact that prisoners cannot forget that missing persons are contemporaneous, remaining present if separated. Anti-constraints such as dreams, sneezes, weekend visits and the comings and goings of fellow prisoners, remind them of that spatial juxtaposition. They also threaten to collapse the singularity or definition of the altered state that prisoners sometimes claim. This condition makes the forms of prison existence (and of life more generally) that are evinced appear necessarily tenuous or even artificial.

Men's house

Leonard, a convict from the Huli region of the Southern Highlands, drew a parallel between Bomana and the ceremony of the ancestral long house that he used to hear about as a child. In the past, he told me, men from his place would snatch boys from their mothers and lead them into the forest. There older men would ambush them, beating the scared and disoriented boys with sticks until they bled and released what was said to be old and bad blood. The old men then escorted the half-naked boys to the hidden long house, where they fed them and tended their wounds. Several months later, with their scars healed, now muscular and their bellies full, the boys were judged ready to return from the forest. The old men painted the boys' bodies in order to make their skin glow and look smart. When the youth reentered their hamlets, mothers and single women immediately recognised that the boys were now men and so ready to marry.[1]

Similarly, Berry, a steal man whose parents came from East Sepik province, equated Bomana with the ceremonies of the spirit house (*haus tambaran*) in his natal place. He told me that at the age of twelve boys are escorted from the village and led to that house of men. There, protected by a fence and boundary marker beyond which women may not pass, they remain for the next six months. One day the boys are taken to a stream, beaten with switches in order to make them bleed and forced to lie down on their stomachs to receive tattoos. In pain they return to the spirit house, where they are told to rest and gorge themselves on fattening soup. Guarded by senior men, who prescribe meal times and prevent them going outside after dark, the boys are allowed to sleep for long hours. However, they are forbidden to chew betel nut or smoke cigarettes. With their bodies healed and strengthened, the boys are released back into female company.[2]

These are but two of many initiation ceremony analogies I heard male prisoners making. In fact they often describe their cells as 'men's houses' (*hausman*),[3] distinguished as sites of extraordinary exclusion from women. Just like ritual hazing, they explain, upon arrival male inmates are sometimes beaten by warders. At the main gate they receive blows, before being registered and sent down to A Compound, where they are confined and cut off from the women they knew outside the gaol. There they rest and consume the meals provided by warders. Nurtured on brown rice and tins of meat and fish, their bodies are said to grow fat and strong. Forced to shave regularly, young men discover facial hair breaking out across their cheeks and above their mouth. Issued with bars of soap and told to wash, they find that their skin smells good and shines. Male prisoners say that at Bomana boys lose their timidity and fear. They quickly realise that they can no longer depend on mothers or sisters to prepare

their food or wash their clothes. Instead they must learn to look
after themselves, to gather strength and act as men.

In his comparison Leonard emphasised that he had not
himself experienced the ritual he described. He told me that it
was a ceremony of his ancestors, a practice now lost. Indeed, this
idea of the separation of men from women as something belonging to the past, and thus recovered in the act of incarceration, is
common. Male prisoners from the Highlands recall the segregated residence of their childhood or remember stories told by
their parents, in which fathers and teenage sons slept together in
a separate house. Those from the coast of Papua, the Sepik River,
the coast and islands of New Guinea recall the older generation's
sense of dismay at the disappearance of many spirit house ceremonies. But the main focus for reflection on the contemporary
loss of male segregation centres on the city. Prisoners often
suggest that urban migration epitomises this movement away
from separation. Leonard, who himself left his hamlet in the Tari
Basin in 1982 in order to find work in Port Moresby, pointed out
to me the changes in the urban household. He said that upon
arriving in the city he noted with surprise the habit of spousal
cohabitation, in particular the disregard of Huli menstrual
taboos that prevented women with menses preparing food or
sharing eating utensils. In Port Moresby, he explained, men have
extraordinary access to women. Prostitutes or road women sell
themselves for a couple of Kina, while nightclubs and hotel bars
allow dancing in couples and intimate embrace. In this aspect
the city is held to be the antithesis of prison life, which, male
inmates believe, looks back to past acts of single-sex separation.[4]

But very few of the male prisoners who make this parallel have
actually witnessed such an initiation ceremony. Their analogies are
therefore drawn from overheard stories and anecdotes, passed on
by fellow inmates or men outside the gaol. The initiation ceremonies of the past are viewed as something unfamiliar. As a result
accounts of male initiation are usually brief and without long
exegesis. Berry, for instance, said that he had no first-hand experience of village life. As an infant he moved with his parents to
the provincial capital of East Sepik province, Wewak town. After
completing high school, Berry travelled to Lae town in Morobe
province to attend technical college and then on to Port Moresby
to find work. He told me that the evidence for his analogy came
from tales he remembered his father telling him as a child and

from conversation with men from his language group in the city. Berry intended his story to sound exotic. The curious separation of men and women is put forward against the urban environment that he knew best. And if the initiation ritual seemed strange, then by extension so did the regime at Bomana.

In recent years those contributing to the sociology of incarceration have called attention to cultures of masculinity. Sim (1994: 100), for instance, notes that while prison studies tend to assume that male inmates are their proper subjects, they fail to provide a gendered reading of the penal experience. Instead of focusing on prisoners *as* men, they concentrate on men as prisoners (1994: 101). By contrast the anthropology of Melanesian societies is replete with analyses of gendered practices. Indeed, gender is put forward as an orienting aesthetic, a constraining form by which persons and sets of relations are ordered and presented (cf. Mosko 1985; Strathern 1988; Battaglia 1990; Weiner 1991; Gillison 1993). Anthropologists are intrigued by the wide use of gender imagery in the region, the fact that indigenous modes of interaction appear styled through the language of gendered positioning. Melanesians are said to perceive themselves constantly moving between gendered states. This is not a culture of masculinity or femininity, since the aesthetic deployment of gender does not assume a straightforward choice between the elaborations of male or female positions. Rather the single-sex state (and this is the crucial distinction) is a form that must be drawn out, only elicited or activated through a perceived act of transformation, by making something else absent (Strathern 1988: 14). The implication therefore is that single-sex status is a moment in sequence, one that anticipates a prior state, now eclipsed, and a future state, to obviate that present status. Melanesians are said to imagine themselves coming out of and alternating back to states of non-single sex composition. This is the kind of transformation figured by male prisoners at Bomana. Their analogy between incarceration and initiation rituals is intended to highlight a moment of single-sex distinction. In prison they become 'men' (*man*), a position elicited by the suspension or concealment of ties to mothers, sisters, girlfriends and wives.

The vast majority of male prisoners at Bomana incise their foreskins. This operation is forbidden by prison rules, so it must be carried out in secret. Cast in the gloom of a cell corner, a convict or remand inmate removes his waistcloth and lies down naked on the concrete floor. Leaning over this reclining figure, another prisoner, the 'doctor' (*dokta*), spreads the man's legs and grasps his penis in order to pull back the foreskin. He slips a wooden spatula, usually stolen from the prison clinic, under the prepuce and in his other hand lifts a razor blade. Careful to avoid any veins, the doctor rips swiftly through the top of the foreskin. Blood, dark and thick, oozes from the wound and is allowed to flow until it turns red and translucent and the lesion is gripped. When the bleeding stops he releases hand pressure and lets the torn skin drop either side of the penis. There it curls and folds, and is left to hang. Male prisoners associate the operation with rituals of initiation – foreskin incision is said to be performed during the spirit house ceremonies along the Sepik River and the coast and islands of New Guinea[5] – as well as with the medical practice of circumcision. However, very few claim to have witnessed the spirit house surgery; they rely on stories from other prisoners to describe the procedure and effects of this incision. The operation is deemed appropriate because Bomana is a 'place of men' (*peles belong man*). In fact foreskin incision is seen to simulate the act of separation that distinguishes incarceration.

Just as male prisoners perceive women as removed from their presence, so the cutting of the prepuce is said to release blood left over from a period of maternal encompassment. The dark blood that first flows from the wounded penis is believed to derive from the prisoner's prehistory inside his mother's womb. Its removal during the operation of incision therefore expels a female substance (mimics the action of imprisonment), allowing fresh blood to circulate and a singular male form to appear. Single-sex definition is enhanced by what male prisoners take to be the additional removal of sexual fluids, lodged under the foreskin after intercourse with women outside the gaol. This female load is held to be responsible for the bad smell that penises sometimes emit and for the development of sexually transmitted diseases such as gonorrhoea, AIDS and syphilis. The detachment of female substance, of what seems a previously dual gender identity, is seen to contribute to the growth, health and shine of the male body, which is perceived as the outcome of penal isolation.[6]

Strathern (1988: 9) notes that in their ritual moments ethnographic subjects are often depicted representing Society to themselves (a scholarly pretension which she equates with the assumption that characters in a novel can know and anticipate the plot laid out for them). Indeed, ritual is conventionally portrayed as a struggle between the competing claims of Individual and Society. The Individual is taken to be a register of social activity, prescribed certain roles which constitute its connection to a wider social body, but at the same time assumed to be a whole or total entity that through its connection to Nature, as a biological organism, exist outside or before Society (Strathern 1992b: 81). In the same way gender is conventionally considered as a construction upon Nature, an elaboration by Society upon the given sexual status of the Individual. Strathern regards this tension, between what connects and disconnects the analytical domains of Individual and Society, as the bedrock of much anthropological inquiry. Thus practices such as male initiation and ritual confinement are usually presented as tales of socialisation (1988: 3). The boys, who are taken from their mothers, beaten and led into the cult house are assumed to there learn the rules of adult male company. They are described as acquiring new social roles that force them to recognise responsibilities beyond those of the Individual. Manhood is associated with the accomplishment of this ritual passage that is seen to educate the Individual, to leave an imprint of Society on malleable boys. But Strathern claims that the gender imagery used in Melanesia contradicts the assumption that people understand male initiation as an act of Society-making. Rather than the Individual gaining a culture of masculinity and adopting Society norms, the subjects of ritual action regard themselves as the products of separation. In their eyes, initiation does not 'construct' a social world; it 'decomposes' a previous state (Strathern 1992a: 73–74).[7] Ritual is an intervention upon an always already existing social world.

In the same way male prisoners at Bomana regard incarceration, and the act of prepuce incision that accompanies it, as a practice that involves gender reconstitution. Being separated from women means being separated from a part of oneself. The single-sex state is not only an outcome of loss; it is itself transitory and susceptible to decomposition. Male prisoners anticipate an end to segregation, a release from prison and return to female company. Their distinction as men is perceived as an artefact of the constraint imposed upon them *as* prisoners. But that status is not considered a construction of prison Society. There is no 'culture' of masculinity because there is no sense of gender as a design upon a presocial state.

As a consequence of separation from women, male prisoners at Bomana report extreme feelings of desire. They claim to be consumed by a passion for sexual intercourse, which is regarded as a further outcome of their single-sex distinction. It is said that the slightest provocation can stimulate these desires. Weekend visits by wives and girlfriends, the immature features of juvenile male inmates and the occasional sight of women prisoners are all held responsible for setting men's teeth on edge (*kaikai tit*) and their penises erect. Sexual thoughts drive them to masturbate endlessly, to have erotic dreams that cause involuntary emissions and sometimes to seize other men and forcibly penetrate them. The bodies of male prisoners are believed to be full of unreleased semen waiting to be ejaculated. These urges are enhanced by the operation of foreskin incision. The sliced prepuce, which hangs below the penis, is said to form a 'double head' and thus improve sexual performance. Male prisoners boast that this enlargement makes them more desirable. It is believed to make women feel 'sweet', persuading wives to leave their wealthy husbands and even giving pleasure to what men claim is the loose vagina of the worn-out prostitute. Those who cut their foreskins are desperate to 'try them out', even if it means entering the anus of another man. They claim to have never before felt so much desire or be as occupied by sexual thoughts.

But the strength of these passions is also held to be dangerous.[8] Male prisoners warn that too much concern with desiring thoughts can disturb mental composure and lead to loss of control. It is said that some men are so overwhelmed that their prison lives are directed exclusively by sexual thoughts. They will do anything to relieve themselves, including the rape of cellmates and men from their own language group. However, male prisoners claim that the women of the female wing possess the most unguarded desires. Just as incarceration is seen to draw out a singular male form, so inmates of A Compound argue that women prisoners also experience a single-sex distinction. In fact they are regarded as highly sexualised subjects. Male prisoners sit around and debate the carnal habits of these women. They state that, unlike them, female prisoners have no straightforward means to relieve themselves, so they remain always frustrated, without ejaculatory outlets for their extraordinary passions. Men picture these women lying naked together at night in their cell, fingering each other's clitoris, sucking nipples, squeezing breasts, moaning and crying with pleasure. Female prisoners are rumoured to smuggle banana and cassava tubers from the prison gardens or to mould penises out of soap and dough and insert them in their vaginas. It is believed that 'sex has got them' (*sex kisim ol*), that these women are out of control. To prevent them suffering the same fate male prisoners tell each other to keep busy and so dilute the power of their desire.

The boy sits in the corner of the cell. He watches a prisoner approach. This man, muscular and strong, grabs him and demands anal intercourse. The boy refuses. Angry now, the man produces a fork, sharpened as a weapon, and threatens to stab him. The boy is terrified by the blade pressed against the skin of his neck and so nods his head and lowers his trousers. The man fumbles impatiently, unravelling layers of red waistcloth, until a penis, huge and with a double head, appears. He forces him to kneel and inserts the outsize organ into his anus. The boy screams with each lunge. But around him laughter echoes, increasing in volume with the speed of thrusts and the pitch of his own cries. In pain, yet curious, the boy turns his head to locate the direction of this gleeful noise.

A convict related what he regarded as this funny dream experience. He told me that it happened to a young man in his cell. When the boy awoke from the dream he was surprised to find his cellmates laughing and pointing derisively at his still half-sleeping form. Confused, the boy looked down and blushed to discover that his own index finger was inserted in his anus! This story, which I heard several times, is intended to humorously demonstrate the compulsive, and sometimes unconscious, action of desire. Here is a prisoner, isolated from women, whose sexual thoughts of intercourse lead him to unwittingly penetrate his own anus. The image is absurd, but unnerving. It also plays on male prisoners' fears of becoming victims of rape and of the transformation in gendered state that is often perceived to follow. For while those who 'go up the anus' (*goapim as*) are perceived to simply exhibit their single-sex state, becoming 'fit men' in the process, those who submit to this insertion are said to lose that form and instead risk becoming known as 'half women' (*hap meri*). The male form elicited by incarceration and demonstrated by rape is held capable of activating an androgynous form in another. Although the half woman is said to consent to his penetration, that acceptance is only defined by the very act of submission, the failure to struggle or resist in what is considered a proper manner. Fit men assert that victims of rape should do more than just cry and whimper, they are expected to fight back, to reject the assault with shouted slogans such as, 'I am a man, not a woman!' Those who respond with silent resignation are said to make themselves passive, just like consenting women.

Of course the ascription of gender to the distinction made between active and passive sexual partners is widely reported in prison studies (cf. Sykes 1958; Morris and Morris 1963; Carroll 1974; Drumond 1992; Sim 1994; Schifter 1999). Those who penetrate the anus of another prisoner often distinguish their actions from those of the submitting inmate, insisting that the disposition of one is male and the other is female. These studies usually present that definition of active and passive roles as a rhetorical attempt by certain men to resist the dissolution of their masculinity in prison. The withdrawal of heterosexual relations is assumed to threaten that sense of manhood. Yet at Bomana the reverse appears to be true; incarceration, which separates men from women, is held responsible for eliciting the single-sex form. Prisoners appear as men precisely because women are made absent. Those who go up the arse of other male prisoners are confirming that status, one that is demonstrated by the ability to convert other men into women.

The prisoner who 'consents' to being raped at Bomana is typically described as developing female mannerisms. Half women are believed to laugh and giggle uncontrollably, to talk in a high, staccato voice, to refuse to make eye contact, to sit cross-legged and to jump when touched. They are said to have toneless muscles and infant-sized penises. In fact fit men state that over time, with the frequent receipt of other prisoners' semen, the bodies of the half women become transformed.[9] They develop soft, yellow skin and sunken eye sockets. Their limbs become thin and bony, but at the same time their 'anus cunts' (*as kan*) swell and start to bounce. The half woman is said to move with the figure of a female pop star (fit men give them names such as Madonna and Linda Ronstadt). As he waddles across the compound, fit men say that semen drips from his anus, released by the pressure of ever-agitating buttocks.

Since fit men identify half women, the period of this designation can vary greatly. Those who suffer sexual assault may lose the label quickly or be forced to put up with it throughout their prison term. Some men will be raped repeatedly until they settle into a reluctant acquiescence, preferring to accept tobacco and canned food in payment for their submission instead of continually receiving violent blows. The possibility of properly consensual relationships, of long-term couples, is rarely discussed and, if it happens, is disguised by the language of fit men and half women.

I state that on the night of Saturday July 1995 at about 9.30 p.m. I was confronted by detainee Wamu Gamea who commanded that he has been beaten by Eastern Highlanders and Keremas.

Therefore he would retaliate by raping anybody from the two provinces. Having said that he turmoil my hands from my side and said, 'You will be the one'. When he said that another unknown prisoner confronted me and swung a clench fist at my right eye.

I teeter and the contingent took me to their sleeping place surrounded by blankets and detainee Wamu Gamea stripped me naked and forced me to adopt the bending position and continuously raped me until he released his sperm into my anus for the two separate circuits.

After he moved out two inmates approached me. They were masked completely that I could not recognise them, came and forcefully took turns in raping me.

Because I was afraid for my life I surrendered myself to the culprits.

The next morning on Sunday I reported the matter to the 8–4 shift for their assistance.

There is one obvious basis for renegotiating the status of half women. Sexual assault may be redefined as punishment or fighting. A convict from Goroka in the Eastern Highlands sent the letter above to the security officer at Bomana. He claimed to have suffered from gang rape, to be the victim of his own language group's dispute with other prisoners. Indeed, sexual assault is a common form of fighting between enemies. It is also a punitive exercise designed to shame a prisoner who breaks cell rules or informs on others. Fit men warn each other to look out for those they have raped. Even the half woman, it is said, carries the memory of his injury with him. Some day, whether in prison or outside, he may seek retribution.

Women prisoners, despite the fantasies of those men in A Compound, insist that they are little interested in sexual thoughts. Indeed, they state that desire is a feeling reserved for life outside the gaol; it is often identified as the passion responsible for getting them in trouble (a high proportion of long-term female convicts are imprisoned for violent offences issuing from arguments about infidelity among couples). There is no talked-about sexual relationship between these women and certainly no reported cases of rape. Occasionally women joke about those male prisoners they see in passing work parties and discuss which men they find attractive, but the emphasis is usually on the contrast between the desires of men and women in prison. They observe that male prisoners seem to get sexually excited on the slightest pretext; those who pass in work parties sometimes lower their waistcloths or shorts and reveal erect penises. But the women of the female wing say they just laugh. They claim not to share the men's state of easy arousal.

Indeed, female prisoners describe a very different experience of incarceration. Although they are confined together and separated from men they knew in civilian life, women at Bomana often complain at a loss of female form. Ultimately, they state, women prisoners are entering a place of men (there are about thirty women at Bomana as opposed to a population of around 700 men). Any single-sex state elicited as a consequence of their segregation in the female wing is undermined by acknowledgement of this broader encompassment. Roselyn, a remand inmate from Kainantu in the Eastern Highlands, described the impressions of her first day. She told me that she arrived in a police van (male prisoners locked in the back while she sat up front next to the driver), which drove to the main gates of the high perimeter fence. There the men got out and lined up for inspection, but she remained inside the vehicle and waited until it passed through and drove up to reception. Ordered to step down, Roselyn opened the door and looked around her. She said that the first thing she noticed was the extraordinary number of men. Panicked by the sight of so many male prisoners and warders, Roselyn paused and thought to herself, 'I must be the first woman to make trouble and come here!' She remembered the stories she had heard outside about the violent behaviour of men in prison. Much agitated, Roselyn entered the reception office and stood crying before the male interviewing clerk. 'What', she wondered, 'will happen to me? Will I be living with men?'

Despite the subsequent relief of discovering her separate confinement, Roselyn and other women at Bomana regard themselves as experiencing a regime of male custody. The fence of the female wing contains them, but they live under the same rules as men. So, female prisoners point out, when convicts or remand inmates in A Compound misbehave everyone across the prison is punished. An escape, for instance, leads to the uniform suspension of visiting rights. Women prisoners suffer as a consequence of offences committed by men. Indeed, if incarceration is acknowledged to effect anything, it is regarded to diminish signs of female distinction. Those women from the Highlands complain that they are compelled to perform men's work, such as digging ditches or fencing gardens.[10] All of them comment negatively on the prison rules that prohibit them wearing dresses, bras and jewellery, which prevent the application of cosmetics and require them to keep their hair cut short (Figure 14). They complain at feeling unattractive, of looking just like men. There is a sense in which they perceive themselves experiencing the reverse transformation of male prisoners. The constraint of incarceration is seen to draw them away from a single-sex form.

Body of men/family of women

Male prisoners' analogy between the men's house and incarceration highlights the constraint of being separated from women. It identifies what that isolation allows. The analogy also highlights the consequences of other separations, in particular the

Figure 14 *Cutting hair*

absence from kin. Cut off from ties to parents, spouses, oppo-
site-sex siblings and children, male prisoners, like boys in the
men's house, find themselves revealed as bodies of men. This
unitary state, between men, is regarded as the outcome of penal
constraint; it is a form of composition drawn from loss.

Strathern, in an attempt to undermine the anthropological
distinction between Public and Domestic spheres, invents terms
that might apply to these alternating states, labelling the ties
between kin as 'particular' and those within bodies of men as
'collective' (1988: 48–49). Instead of the convention that treats the
Domestic sphere as contained by the Public, or vice versa, she
wishes to put forward two states of relations that appear as transformations of each other. The Collective state distinguishes
persons on the basis of their shared characteristics, portraying
them in homogeneous images like clans, while the Particular state
presents them in complementary opposition, their tie styled on the
basis of difference. Her typical example of the Particular state is
the relation between husband and wife, and its affine extensions;
these are assumed and unmediated ties that present partners as
having direct effects upon each other (1988: 178). The Collective
state, by contrast, unifies and often appears through the transaction or competition of like bodies (1988: 180). Strathern holds that
each state provides its own perspective and requires the absence
of the other in order to make it visible (1988: 208). Thus the clan,
which is a body of men, is revealed by making the work performed
by wives disappear. Recognition of their labour involves a vision
of the clan as a matrix of kin ties, an image that would dissolve
that Collective representation (1988: 189). These observations are
premised on what Strathern identifies as a Melanesian capacity to
make social ties the object of action. In her account persons are
always revealed through their relationships (1988: 274), by what
they hide or forget rather than by what they construct.

This insight turns ritual action such as ceremonies of male
initiation into acts of separation or re-composition. Participants do
not consider themselves as experiencing a form of socialisation; if
Society is about relationships, then it is already supposed (see
Wagner 1981, 1991). Strathern directs this critique towards the
Society-making assumption of much anthropological representation. However, the same insight might be directed against the logic
of prison studies. Too much energy in that discipline has been
spent on debates about the Society-making qualities of penal
regimes. The early argument about whether incarceration

produces its own form of Society (Sykes 1958) or relies on norms transmitted from Society outside (see Giallombardo 1966; Heffernan 1972; Carroll 1974) continues to colour representations of prison life. Recent turns to issues of Identity-making (cf. Bosworth 1999) pursue the same assumption that something must be 'constructed'. At least among prisoners at Bomana these questions seem somewhat irrelevant. The forms of relations that incarceration is seen to elicit do not constitute a Society in the making, whether one drawn from norms inside or outside the prison fence, but rather one that unpacks itself, forever recomposed by taking something away. Male prisoners' discovery of unitary bodies of men is premised on that separation.

The sets of relations drawn out in a Collective state by incarceration tend to be styled through a numerical idiom. At Bomana a body of men is distinguished as being 'one' (*wan*), of plural composition yet singular form. Thus male prisoners are sometimes brought together as 'one fence' (*wanbanis*). The distinction is seen to characterise what they share in common: being locked up and forced to submit to prison rules, and to justify acts of mutual assistance or calls to collective strength (during riots or complaints about harsh treatment). Indeed, recognition of oneness is always also a demand for support and expectation of obligation. Those male prisoners from the same language group are known as 'one language' (*wantok*).[11] They assume responsibility for one another and share what they have. The term itself is elastic in scope, referring not only to men who speak the same local language but also often to those from the same province or region, where many different languages may be spoken. So male prisoners can acknowledge a unitary form as men of Wabag, Kerema, Simbu, Hagen etc. The kind of support provided by language mates is replicated in other sets of relations, once again drawn out through appeals to oneness. Men may associate as 'one church' (*wanlotu*), 'one street' (*wanrot*) (from along the same highway or the same neighbourhood in town[12]), 'one work party' (*wanwok*) or 'one cell' (*wansel*). In fact this idiom may evoke any relation that encompasses other male prisoners. Being 'one' is what men at Bomana aspire to, a state that is elicited as a consequence of having kin taken away.

When new male prisoners arrive they are processed at reception and then sent down to the guardhouse outside A Compound. Warders count and search them, before opening the gate and ushering them into the cell yards. There they stand, usually too frightened to enter the cells, hoping that someone will identify them and offer support. Existing prisoners tend to crowd around these men, inspecting their appearance and making inquiries. Gradually the new prisoners peel off with language mates, or any other men who recognise a shared tie, and enter a cell, where they sit down, share a cigarette and start to exchange stories. Those who associate as 'one' expect assistance from each other.[13] If a man is working in the compound kitchens, he is supposed to provide larger helpings of rice or tinned fish. Should he receive smuggled supplies of tobacco or extra bars of soap and tubes of toothpaste, it is assumed that he will share them. Male convicts are particularly concerned with the welfare of those, among their body, who suffer overcrowding and reduced rations in the remand section of A Compound. They often sit against the dividing fence, offering solace and passing cigarettes and plates of food through the wires. In return remand inmates promise, should they win their court case, to leave the convicts their supplies of blankets, towels and waistcloths. The claim to oneness opens expectations of material assistance, but it also ensures safety. The first piece of advice that a new inmate receives from his language mates, for instance, is not to wander too far from their protection. Bomana, he is told, is a dangerous place, where those from other language groups are only too willing to provoke a fight. If male prisoners identify as a body of men, then they are expected to come to the defence of each other.

While these bodies ensure support and protection, they some-times draw male prisoners into hazardous situations. The requirement to stand up for one another can be at the expense of risking personal injury. Thus, one morning, men from the Sepik provinces presented themselves to the warders on duty. They requested the transfer of a language mate to another prison. This man, a life-sentence convict, had earlier in the year stabbed and killed a prisoner from the Gulf province district of Kerema. As a consequence he had been separated for his own safety and locked in the juvenile wing. But the Sepik prisoners told the warders that recently their language mate had struck again. He had ordered a juvenile from the Central province district of Koari to drop his waistcloth and submit to rape. When the boy refused, the lifer had produced a screwdriver and chased him around the wing. Although the boy managed to escape, the Sepik prisoners remained concerned that their language mate would be attacked in return and that as a result they too would be drawn into fighting. Despite their rejection of his behaviour, they knew that they would feel obliged to protect him (a fact acknowledged by the gaol commander, who soon agreed to grant their transfer request). Claiming oneness can therefore place a coercive demand on the responses of others.

Male prisoners, in particular steal men, also elicit a relation as 'one gang' (*wangang*). Indeed, they often assert that gangs, bodies of men who are said to organise and steal under the same name, are equivalent in form to clans. A remand inmate from Gumine in Simbu province, who used to steal in Port Moresby, told me that just as men in his village raise their clan name by fighting others, burning down houses, destroying coffee gardens and killing pigs, so men in his gang demonstrate strength by stealing money. When clan fighting is over men return to the men's house and there celebrate by shouting news of their victory across the valley; in the same way, he explained, gang mates, after a successful robbery, get drunk and drive around the city streets, thumping car door panels and calling out their gang name. He stated that these taunts make steal men from other gangs jealous, prompting them in turn to plan a bigger robbery. Such provocation is said to be the stimulus to criminal invention.

Other male prisoners take the analogy between gang and clan rivalry further. They observe that clans are concerned not only with fighting, but also with competition in business, ceremonial exchange and bride-wealth payments. Thus a convict from the Motuan village of Barakau on the edge of Port Moresby recalled a ceremony from his childhood. In those days (1970s), he told me, clans used to annually erect high bamboo towers, which they filled with recently harvested yams from gardens, depositing bananas and slaughtered pigs above these piles of tubers. The clan with the best display was said to gain the most in reputation. Although these food competitions have ended, the convict stated that rivalry between clans now continues in other ways. When, for instance, a new church is built contributions are given separately; at the official opening the amounts collected by each clan are publicly announced and their respective strengths therefore measured. The convict explained that just like this clan rivalry, men of different gangs are always driven to try and 'surpass' (*winim*) each other. They exist in mediated competition.

Despite the fact that they are usually drawn together from separate language groups and provinces, gang mates at Bomana

claim to offer the best imitation of clan ethos. They tell new prisoners to forget their language mates and instead live in gangs,
which they describe as the ultimate state of being one. If a man
is ill, it is said that his clan mates will take him to hospital, and
if he wants to build a house or raise bride wealth, they will assist
him. In the same way, it is said that gang mates will always
support each other. When a man is locked up, his family outside
is looked after, if he becomes short of money or tobacco in prison
his gang mates will help him. That expectation emphasises the
state of equivalence between men who live under the same gang
name, the lack of difference and hierarchy. While those steal men
with long and impressive criminal histories are known as 'big
boys' (*bikboi*) by their gang mates, sometimes provided with
small services out of respect and often allotted the privilege of
distributing smuggled items, they do not exercise unchallenged
decision-making powers. Indeed, if a big boy fails to properly
circulate the tobacco in his possession or to organise successful
smuggling operations he will quickly lose any influence he had.[14]
Like other states of oneness, there appears little scope for
displays of asymmetry.

At times male prisoners seem to doubt the permanency of their
constitution as bodies of men. Those in gangs tend to infer that
incarceration itself is responsible for their unitary state. Just as the
constraint of exile is seen to draw out a single-sex distinction, so
gang mates regard their tie as the outcome of a transformation. I
was often told that in Bomana gang mates live together for the
first time. Indeed, until the moment of detention they have
frequently never met. Outside the jail those who steal under the
same gang name in a city live in separate households, streets and
suburbs. Their engagement in crime is said to be occasional and
opportunistic; steal men are just as likely to move around and steal
with boys from their neighbourhood as with those from the same
gang. The experience of coexistence at Bomana, sleeping in the
same cube or corner, sharing property, walking around the cell
yards side by side and refusing to talk with men from other gangs,
is represented as unique. In prison the form of gangs appears in
a coherent state, undiluted by those ties that might cut across it
and therefore make that form disappear.

Part of the process of elicitation is the requirement to trace a
gang history. Male prisoners, and in particular big boys, devote
much energy and time to communicating these narratives of
solidity. Stories link dramatic criminal exploits with a particular

gang name and provide maps for its origin and spread.[15] For instance, the four largest gangs drawn out at Bomana – Mafia, Koboni, 585, Bomai – each have well told genealogies. It is said that men from the coast west of Port Moresby, from Kerema and Kairuku, first started stealing in the city under the gang name Mafia. From there the name is said to have spread to the satellite Motuan villages of Barakau, Tubuseria and Gaire, back along the coast to the townships at Kerema and Yule Island, and up into the Central province hinterland of the Goilala district. The story goes on to tell how the name was taken over the mountains into New Guinea, to the border station at Garaina and then down to the coastal towns of Lae and Madang. At the same time it is said that men began stealing in Port Moresby under the gang name Koboni. This name is said to have been carried by steal men along the Papuan coast, west to the township of Daru and east to Alotau and Popondetta, then up to Lae and Kimbe in the New Guinea Islands. Men in the Highlands started stealing along the highways under the gang name Bomai. It is said that the name spread from Simbu across the region and down the coast to Lae and Port Moresby. Finally, it is said that the gang name 585 first emerged at Tapini and other government stations in the Goilala district. From there men carried the name to Port Moresby and over into Morobe province, to the townships of Wau and Bulolo and then to Lae. The name spread north up the New Guinea coast, arriving at Madang and Wewak, and across the Solomon Sea to Rabaul. These narratives of foundation and gang composition involve considerable invention, not least because they eclipse the fact that many robberies actually took place between steal men from different gangs. This deceit, if persuasive, is itself regarded as evidence of gang advantage. In order to make the name impressive, gang mates must provide not only promise for its future but coherence to its past.

Bodies of men are believed to appear at Bomana as a consequence of separation. This transformation prevents male prisoners from figuring themselves through kin idioms (what Strathern defines as Particular states of relation), but it does allow them to substitute one plural body (what Strathern defines as Collective states of relation) for another. Some gang names actually contain the seeds of this displacement. The name 585, for example, may be turned upside down, converted from numbers to letters, in order to uncover the initials GBG or Goilala Boys Garaina. Similarly, another name for Mafia is

KGK, which is said to stand for Kerema Goilala Kairuku, language groups from which men who steal under that name are drawn. This use of abbreviation in order to accommodate other bodies of men, to make them appear as one, can also open division.[16] Gang mates can be broken into bodies of language mates, language mates into bodies of gangs, or into any other unitary states. Competing claims fall upon male prisoners. They are forever negotiating ties to multiple bodies of men. This politics of oneness remains premised on the exercise of penal constraint.

Female prisoners do not live under gang names. Indeed, they insist that women at Bomana do not recognise unitary divisions. One convict in the female wing, drawing a contrast to the behaviour of men in A Compound, told me, 'we have no group business here'. Even the tie between language mates is played down. Women prisoners claim that this division belongs to their lives before incarceration, to life outside the gaol where they were suspicious of each other and prone to break into factions such as language groups. At times incarceration is presented as a movement away from those divisions, an escape from the political struggles of claiming oneness. For them Bomana does not necessarily elicit a Collective state as a body of women.

In fact female prisoners often choose to describe themselves as a 'family'. It is said that when a new prisoner enters the female wing everyone greets her. They line up to shake her hand and offer assistance. A woman from the Highlands may give her a toothbrush, while a woman from the Papuan coast may hand her a bar of soap. They may introduce themselves as sisters (*sista*) or affines (*tambu*), evoking the kind of tie that Strathern defines as a Particular state of relation. This desire to identify unmediated kin ties, those drawn through complementary opposition rather than collective equivalence, is the result of women being led into a place of men. At Bomana they expect to find ties styled on difference. Thus female prisoners married to men from other provinces recognise connections to those women from their husband's region. If the tendency is for male prisoners to regard penal constraint – the exile from loved ones – as the trigger for their transformation into bodies of men, then the tendency for female prisoners is to identify that separation as a moment of substitution, from one Particular state to another. Women prisoners appear to find kin ties replaced with other kin ties.

A contrast between the organisation of male and female inmates is commonly observed in prison studies. Those working in women's prisons in North America observe the existence of what they call 'play families' and the corresponding lack of the group antagonisms said to characterise men's prisons (cf. Giallombardo 1966; Heffernan 1972; Díaz-Cotto 1996; Owen 1998). Unlike the women at Bomana, these female prisoners sometimes conduct marriages, adopting positions as husband and wife, father and mother, brother and sister. These ties are usually presented as coping mechanisms or normative substitutions for gender roles outside the gaol. They do not seem to share the ambiguous status of ties between women at Bomana. Female prisoners there seem caught between the competing expectations of penal constraint. As subjects of an imposed separation they expect to experience reconstitution, to have a different state of relations appear as a consequence of their loss. But this alternation seems denied by the fact of their custody among men. Either they must imagine a reverse transformation, away from a prior state as a body of women (something which the original act of separation contradicts), or they must accept the confusion of one state being replaced by its copy.

Not just women, but male prisoners too at Bomana regard the forms drawn out by incarceration as fragile. The bodies of men who exist as one gang, one language, one church etc. are always vulnerable to dissolution; dreams, sneezes and weekend visits constantly threaten the coherence of those unitary states. Indeed, big boys complain that their gang mates are unreliable supporters, too often distracted and without a satisfactory sense of being one. But the ultimate threat to the constitution of bodies of men is the inevitable day of release. That 'future' is anticipated as a further act of transformation. Both male and female prisoners assume that they will return to the company of kin and as a consequence expect to experience recomposition.

Resistance?

Sykes (1958: 58) notes one of the paradoxes of what appears the 'total' power exercised by modern penal institutions. He argues that prison staff can only guarantee their authority by first allowing it to be corrupted. Without the sanction of moral duty or excessive violent force, guards are always to a certain extent dependent on the compliance of prisoners. This is achieved by offering concessions, in particular by ignoring selective breaches of prison rules (1958: 56). Sykes argues that obedience is enforced in certain areas only by tolerating disobedience elsewhere (1958: 57). The irony is that forms of resistance are an integral part of the successful operation of a prison regime.

More recently, Bosworth (1999: 126) has described the small-scale ways in which prisoners constantly negotiate power relations. If tolerated insubordination ensures prison authority, then it also provides inmates with a vital sense of their own autonomy. Indeed, Bosworth states that this capacity to demonstrate agency is crucial to the ability to survive imprisonment (1999: 127). Prisoners struggle to recover aspects of self-determination, traits such as freedom of choice and freedom of movement, which are seen to be otherwise restricted (1999: 133). In this account, despite the compromises made by both sides, prison staff and inmates are typically represented as bodies in fixed opposition.

Male prisoners at Bomana are capable of regarding their own custodians in this manner. As a body of men, male warders can be considered a like unit. They are held to embody a Collective form, to exist as the 'enemy' (*birua*) of male prisoners. This claim refuses the hierarchy of prison authority, representing staff and inmates as bodies of equivalent strength, drawn out through competition. The transaction between male prisoners and warders becomes like that between rival gangs or rival language groups. Highlighting the struggle with another agent of government, the police, best elucidates this sense of competing bodies of men. Indeed, male prisoners consider the police as their 'first enemy' (*nambawan birua*), those responsible for their arrest and interrogation, and in whose hands they are often beaten and bullied. Like feuding clans, the police and male offenders are said to be constantly fighting (see Chapter 2). By contrast, inmates of A Compound state that prison staff are only 'little enemies' (*liklik birua*). While male warders may sometimes curse and hit them, they also provide men in custody with accommodation and regular meals. Male prisoners do not recognise the same level of antagonism.

In fact there exists some sympathy between male prisoners and male warders. The latter are fond of complaining that they too are treated like convicts. They resent having to wear uniforms, to shave and keep their hair length short, to be always punctual; but most of all they resent being separated from loved ones. New recruits are forced to leave home and travel to Port Moresby in order to receive induction training. Once the six-month programme is over, these new warders are posted to prisons across the country. There is little choice in transfer selection and very few receive postings in their home province. Warders have to wait two years before gaining leave and thus paying visits to their parents and kin. Just like the prisoners, they worry about the welfare of those left behind. There are also limits on public entry into the prison complex, where staff housing is located. The gaol commander has the power to suspend access and rules forbid visitors from staying overnight. These restrictions are compounded by the fact that accommodation is in short supply, in particular houses for married couples, which often means that warders are forced to send their spouse and children back to live in distant villages or hamlets. As a result, warders perceive themselves as living under similar constraints to their charges.

If male warders can be acknowledged as enemies, then just like the rivalry between gangs, evoking other unitary bodies of men can collapse that opposition. In particular, male warders and male prisoners often recognise a tie as one language (*wantok*). This relation cuts across the division between staff and inmates, demanding unofficial forms of support. Thus male warders are expected to treat prisoners who are language mates with respect, to favour them in their everyday dealings. They might provide them with gifts of soap, toothpaste or writing paper, organise their own families to visit them on the weekend or liaise on their behalf with a lawyer. Sometimes warders smuggle money or tobacco to their language mates in A Compound, carry messages from kin outside or post uncensored letters. Male warders often choose to turn a blind eye when they catch language mates smoking, violating the dress code or listening to contraband radios. They tend to privilege them when making parole or release on licence recommendations. If fighting breaks out between staff and inmates, male warders are careful not to hit their language mates. This network of obligations is commonly known as the 'wantok system'. It favours not only male prisoners, but also male warders. The latter enter cells alone and unarmed, secure in the belief that language mates will protect them. Male warders boast that unlike prison guards in other countries they need never worry about their personal safety.

At Bomana the opposition between male warders and male prisoners anticipates its own dissolution. The capacity to elicit these bodies of men, who compete as enemies, is also the capacity to

undermine them. Resistance, rather than an act of individual assertion, as Bosworth describes it, is just the outcome of that
substitution between bodies of men. Drawing from a warder his
obligation as a language mate may be considered an act of defiance, but it is one that conforms to the shape of relations allowed
by penal constraint. If the separation triggered by incarceration
makes bodies of men visible, then finding language mates among
staff and inmates is not surprising. In these circumstances resistance might better be conceived as those moments when bodies of
men are made to disappear.

Unlike male prisoners, the inmates of the female wing do not
regard themselves as coerced into unitary states. If there are no
bodies of women in competition then female prisoners and
female warders cannot be figured as enemies. Instead women at
Bomana tend to consider their custodians as part of the 'family',
typically representing the tie between them as either that of
parent and child or husband and wife. Female prisoners often
style themselves as children, claiming to live under the authority of female warders, to thus all come from a single parent (*kam
long wanpela mamapapa*). Parallels are drawn between the defer-
ence shown to warders and the submissive manner that
daughters adopt towards their mother and father or wives
towards their husbands. Just as children and wives are abused
and hit when they misbehave, so female prisoners say warders
demand obedience and keep women in the female wing under
close observation. Describing the tie between them in these
terms privileges the asymmetric, nonequivalent nature of that
relation, quite the opposite emphasis from that chosen by male
prisoners. Women at Bomana acknowledge a hierarchy, viewing
themselves in complementary opposition with female warders.
This kind of relation has less capacity for confrontation and
violence; there is far less tension between prison staff and
inmates in the female wing and far more intimacy and affection.
However, this tie styled on Particular or kin-based idioms also
leaves less room for women to show defiance. Female prisoners
are noticeably more compliant, reluctant to disobey or break
prison rules. Perhaps resistance would require them to draw
forth an alternative state of relations, to make bodies of women
for the first time visible and competitive.

Notes

1   There are many accounts by anthropologists of male initiation ceremonies in Papua New Guinea. A common theme is the emphasis given to the shift in company that boys experience when first confined in the ceremonial house. Poole (1982: 116) notes that among the Bimin-Kuskusmin of Telefomin boys begin the ritual cycle as 'people of the women's house' but end it as 'people of the men's house'. That shift is premised on the fact that through entering the ceremonial house, boys make themselves 'hidden' (see Meggitt 1964: 210). Indeed, Biersack (1982: 249) argues that among the Paiela people of the Eastern Highlands growth (including the transformation of boys into men) is premised on the relation between observer and observed first being cut (248).

2   A. Strathern (1994: 56) states that the Melpa people of the Western Highlands came to view the colonial prison as a kind of men's house, where they would be fed on brown rice and corned beef. He reports that upon release those men who went to prison on behalf of their leaders were greeted in the village with dances and general celebrations. Strathern sees these festivities as evidence that there was no stigma attached to imprisonment among the Melpa people.

3   The term 'hausman' is often used in anthropological literature to refer to segregated houses for men in particular regions, most commonly the Highlands; and often in contrast to the 'haus tambaran' of the New Guinea coast (and the long house of the Papuan coast and interior). Prisoners are aware of such distinctions, but they also use the term 'hausman' generically, to refer to all instances of male segregation. By calling the prison cells in A Compound men's houses, they are drawing attention to that generic comparison.

4   The idea that imprisonment mimics past acts of single-sex separation (such as traditional initiation ceremonies) may connect to a general impression that since colonisation men have acted more like women. Clark (1989: 123) reports that the men of the Wiru people of the Southern Highlands believe they are physically shrinking as a consequence of government pacification (120). Missionaries directed the Wiru men to discard their customary clothing and cut their hair short; they encouraged spouses to live together in a single household. At the same time, government agents promoted cash cropping and the production of coffee. These programmes prompted Wiru men to regard 'development' as a process that required them to act like women (127). Garden work, which previously had been considered as women's work, appeared to be gaining increasing recognition at the expense of men's activities such as ceremonial exchange and fighting. To many prisoners, the regime at Bomana seemed to promise a reversal of this process; imprisonment required them to act like men.

5   Male prisoners draw complicated and often contradictory genealogies that describe how the operation of foreskin incision arrived at Bomana. It is often presented as travelling with individuals between prisons or with those who have first-hand experience of spirit house ceremonies. For ethnographic descriptions of foreskin incision and other acts of penile bleeding within male initiation rituals see Panoff (1968), Hogbin (1970), Lewis (1980), Tuzin (1980) and Kempf (1994).

6   Clark (1989) notes that 'notions of the body provide a vivid idiom for percep-
    tions of change' (123), in particular for changes in social relations (cf. Strathern
    1988). So men of the Wiru people of the Southern Highlands claim to shrink
    as a consequence of colonial pacification and increased proximity to women.
    At Bomana, men claim that their bodies grow as a consequence of being sepa-
    rated from women.

7   Strathern and other anthropologists of the region make the argument that
    Melanesian creativity does not lie in the establishment of relationships or the
    ordering of discrete bodies (as it is assumed to in Europe and North America),
    but in defining which of several relations is relevant in a given situation. This
    separation of one from many possibilities is achieved, as Weiner (1993: 292)
    describes it, by placing a limit on other sets of relations. Through these acts
    of separation persons are decomposed and 'individuals' momentarily made
    visible. Wagner (1981: 88) suggests that this mode of action might be
    conceived as an inversion of the colonial agenda, as a kind of 'continual adven-
    ture in "unpredicting" the world'.

8   It is commonly reported in the societies of Melanesia that sexual intercourse
    can exhaust the male body. Meggitt (1964: 210), for instance, records that
    among the Mae Enga people of the Highlands semen loss is perceived to drain
    the strength of men and leave their bodies tired and withered. Prisoners
    acknowledge that incarceration preserves their semen from excessive deple-
    tion.

9   Herdt (1981: 257) records a myth among the Sambia people of the Eastern
    Highlands, which highlights how the actions of one man can affect the
    gendered state of another. The myth tells the origin story of the first two
    Sambia men. One of these men is said to discover a small penis growing on
    his body. He watches the erect organ and decides to ejaculate into the mouth
    of the other man. This act transforms the bodies of the two men. The breasts
    of the inseminator are flattened out and his penis enlarged, while the breasts
    of the semen receiver swell and his belly expands to contain a child. A slit is
    then cut in the pubic area of the pregnant man, to relieve his pain, and the
    child is released. This story emphasises the fact that men can be imagined in
    female form.

10 The gendered division of labour is reported across the Highlands region.
    Gillison (1980: 145–46), for instance, states that among the Gimi people of
    the Eastern Highlands men are held responsible for constructing fences
    within which women are left to nurture children, pigs and sweet potatoes.

11 The term 'wantok' is in common usage outside Bomana; it is regarded as an
    important kind of relation across Papua New Guinea, but especially in urban
    centres (cf. Rew 1974; Levine and Levine 1979; Monsell-Davis 1993).

12 It might be useful here to compare the 'one street' relation between men at
    Bomana with the commonly described homeboy networks of North Ameri-
    can prisons. Díaz-Cotto (1996), for instance, writes about the way Latino
    prisoners in the United States organise themselves not only into racial or
    ethnic groups, but also into cliques, often cross-racial and cross-ethnic, drawn
    from those who knew each other before imprisonment or came from the same
    cities or neighbourhoods. The 'one street' tie at Bomana similarly cuts across
    language group or regional divisions in Papua New Guinea.

13 The principle among those male prisoners who identify as 'one' is not dissimilar to the ethos of classificatory siblingship that anthropologists in the region describe. Weiner (1982: 11) points to occasions among the Foi of the Southern Highlands when men regard each other as brothers despite having no obvious genealogical link. Indeed, he argues that the concept of brotherhood does not assume biological ties; it is an alignment brought together and separated by exchange. Classificatory siblings may not share blood, but they may share and circulate food, and hence constitute themselves as brothers.

14 Goddard (1992b) and Harris (1988) have drawn on the notion of the 'big man' to explain the role of senior gang members (what prisoners call the 'big boys'). Indeed, Goddard (1992b) suggests that rather than a finite group, the gang might be better understood as a network of relations that centre around these men (25). Each big man, he argues, competes to mobilise such relations, and those who organise the biggest and most successful robberies attract more support (29).

15 Wagner (1991: 163) reports that in Melanesia names instantiate relations. Those who share a name (clan, language group, gang etc.) are in that regard congruent. Wagner states that a name is one of many relations that animate a person and at the same time goes beyond that person in its capacity to include others (164). A name provides a reference point in a world of relations; it avoids a merely denominational status (165). Persons are related and unrelated by names. These names may remain constant, while people come and go, instantiating sets of relations through the names that separate and join them (see Biersack 1982; Lindstrom 1985; Harrison 1990).

16 O'Hanlon (1995: 481) suggests that such 'graphical play' may also be connected to the rise of school literacy and the power of advertising in Papua New Guinea. Commercial brand names such as SP for South Pacific Beer are well known and appear everywhere as replicated slogans (482).

CHAPTER 5

Place of God

∿

Conversion

Hell on earth

Prison, there is no better place.	*haus kalabus it ain't no betta peles*
You are going to worry all the time.	*yu gonna wari wari tumas*
Every day and every night,	*every day na olgeta nait*
You are going to suffer headaches.	*yu gonna sindaun slip with headache*
Don't have any freedom of movement,	*no gat fridom of movement*
Don't have love, don't have mercy.	*no gat luv no gat merci*
He who lives inside,	*em i stap insait*
All hopes abandon those who enter.	*all hopes abandon thou art enters*
Oh it has a nice, handsome, quiet outlook,	*oh it gat nais hansome quiet outlook*
But inside it is terribly strange!	*tasol insait em i terribly strange*
Bombex city is a place called Hell on earth.	*bombex siti em i peles called hell on earth*
The first time I came inside,	*pastaim tru mi bin kam insait*
I was close to going mad.	*mi klos tu kisim mental kas*
I looked around,	*mi lukluk all around*
I saw the high fence and watchtowers,	*mi lukim hai banis na towers*
My head swirled with confusion.	*het blong mi em i paul stret*
Don't have any freedom of movement,	*no gat fridom of movement*
Don't have love, don't have mercy.	*no gat luv no gat merci*
He who lives inside,	*em i stap insait*

All hopes abandon those who enter.	*all hopes abandon thou art enters*
Oh it has a nice, handsome, quiet outlook,	*o it gat nais hansome quiet outlook*
But inside it is terribly strange!	*tasol insait em i terribly strange*
Bombex city is a place called Hell on earth.	*bombex siti em i peles called hell on earth*
	(Antony Ume)

Prisoners commonly perceive Bomana as a hellish place. Antony, a steal man from the Papuan coast, described it in his song as a site of worry, where inmates are cut off from the love and mercy shown by people outside the gaol. Distinguished by the pain of separation, Bomana is said to make its detainees suffer. The difference between life outside the gaol and life inside is compared to the difference between heaven and hell. While heaven is said to be a place of joy and happiness, hell is its opposite, a place of misery and regret. Antony observed the contrast between the peaceful setting of the prison and the tortured feelings of those forced to reside there. He evoked a life without hope.

But that despair is never a straightforward negative. The act of separation, which is the principle of penal constraint, is acknowledged to refigure sets of relations. Male prisoners, for example, perceive themselves transformed into unitary states, revealed as one language, one gang etc (see Chapter 4). Christian prisoners argue for a different transformation. They claim that when everything else is taken away, God appears to them. Indeed, that supporting relation is presented as the ultimate consequence of the constraint of living in the last place: it is best revealed at the moment of most desperate isolation.

As I sit here,
Wondering why I'm all alone
—Just me, just I.
These dreary walls,
The awful smell.
It's nothing less than living hell.
The days come quick and then drag on,
You close your eyes and night times gone.

I listen, yet can't hear a thing.
The birds outside,
Why don't they sing?
Everyday I hear the sound,
As again my dreams crash to the ground.
I stand tall and take my breath.
What could be worse than this but death?
All that I have will soon be gone,
But yet I trundle on.
I'll make them see.
The doors are locked,
Yet He can see the tears,
The pain, the misery.
I know in Him I can depend.
It's Him who is my true friend.
He is by my side.
I know Him there,
His strength, His love is everywhere.
And so to Him I give my love.
He is my Lord,
My God above.

(Paul Isikia)

This poem, written by the chairman of the Lutheran congregation of prisoners, displaces the pain of incarceration by locating the presence and love of God. The experience of confinement is held to make prisoners newly appreciate His support. By stripping away familiar sets of relations, imprisonment makes the enduring company of God visible. In fact closeness to Him is often presented as a direct substitute for the loss of closeness to kin. Andrew, a convict from Gulf province, described to me the dream he had on his first night in prison:

He digs a drain. Yet each time his spade hits the ground the water level seems to rise. When it reaches his waist, Andrew runs and scrambles up the nearest tree. Around him waters surge, snapping the trunks of surrounding forest. On the far side of the torrent he sees dry land and standing there his own mother and sister. Andrew calls out for their help, but his mother shouts back that her canoe is a long distance away. 'You must stay and have faith', she advises.

After this dreaming experience, Andrew determined to put aside thoughts of those he left behind and instead to concentrate on God. His faith is a response to his experience of disengagement, a replacement for the faith he previously lodged in kin. No longer hidden from view, God appears as the revelation of exile.

Christian prisoners present their conversion as an act of coercion. Incarceration, being cut off from people outside the gaol, is seen to make them turn to God. This transformation is usually figured through the division of time into past and present units, the period before and after the moment of detention. Prisoners repeatedly told me that conversion is not a matter of choice. Although Bomana may provide favourable circumstances, the event itself cannot be anticipated. Only God determines when an individual shall convert or 'turn emotions' (*tainim bel*), when His spirit shall hit or enter. 'It is not my plan, it is the plan of God' (*i no plen blong mi, i plen blong bikman yet*), is the explanation often given. Both steal men and churchgoers are suspicious of those male prisoners who appear to convert for convenience, in order to please the warders and try and gain preferential treatment. They warn that God cannot be deceived; those who fake conversion are said to risk divine punishment, a premature death in road accidents or fatal gunshot wounds at the hands of police. It is held almost better to continue stealing than to convert without conviction. One steal man at Bomana told me that he couldn't predict the day upon which his emotions would turn, but he would know when it happened. On that day, he disclosed, all thoughts of crime would abruptly leave him. He would drop to his knees, begin to cry and with conviction announce, 'God is here, I must worship'. But until then he would continue to act as a steal man.

Conversions are often public events. On Dedication Days, every second Wednesday afternoon, outside church groups are invited into Bomana in order to lead an interdenominational service. During one of these Crusades, Dii, a place man from Wabag in Enga province, reported that he experienced the intervention of God. The spirit of the Lord first hit him while listening to a Pentecostal preacher. This man's words moved him strangely, making him feel wounded or struck in the heart (*sutim bel*). When the preacher started to speak of the crucifixion and the criminal who died on the cross beside Jesus, following the Saviour into heaven, Dii found himself crying uncontrollably. The preacher continued, describing prisoners as lost children who, when separated from their parents and offered help, are unable to provide a name or address. In the same way, he told the congregation, too many men and women are lost from God. The preacher ended by inviting prisoners to come forward and declare their faith. Inspired, Dii rose and picked his way between the crossed legs of sitting inmates, stepping up to the podium. In total about twenty prisoners came forward, a mixture of men and women (female prisoners are invited to these services); each one was greeted by a member of the visiting church party, who placed supporting hands on their shaking shoulders. Dii said that he stood dazed as he watched himself and his fellow converts raise their arms in praise, break-down and declare their love for Jesus. Since that day his life had changed. Dii told me that he now acted with the perspective of God in mind.

Indeed, prisoners define Christian faith as the recognition of a certain kind of relation. The tie to God is presented as different in kind, marked out in opposition to other states of connection. People are commonly perceived to locate the cause of their actions outside themselves, and at the same time to assume that they in turn can become the cause for someone else's action (Strathern 1988: 272). Just as Christians act with God in mind, so others feel coerced into action by the anticipated presence of kin, of language mates or gang mates. Yet, unlike the Particular and Collective states that Strathern describes, the Christian relation is not reciprocal (see Reed 1999). Prisoners stress that God cannot be forced to act with them in mind. Divine agency is discretionary. In fact Christian prisoners regard the performance of this relationship as a denial of standard sociality.

The revelation of God marks the disappearance of conventional states of relation. This tie not only substitutes for the loss of kin, it eclipses the unitary states that define male prisoners as one language or one gang. Christian prisoners reject these obligations, criticising Collective attachments for obscuring the tie to God. Preachers warn their congregation that there are no divisions in heaven. On Judgement Day, it is said, people will be assessed on their own merits; God will save one person but send his or her kin and language mates to burn in hell. Those chosen to ascend cannot worry about the people they leave behind. This message can be comforting for prisoners, who are trying to deal with their separation from loved ones outside the gaol. The Bible is said to teach them that an infant enters the world without social commitments. It is not until infants start to suck the breast milk of mothers, to grow big enough to wear clothes and get married, that they acquire obligations and earthly concerns. Similarly, when people die these commitments cease. 'We come with nothing', one Christian prisoner explained to me, 'and when we die, we take nothing with us' (*mipela kam nating na taim in dai mipela karim nating*). This denial of unitary and kin-type states of relation is particularly appealing to women prisoners. Finding it hard to sustain the transformation either from Particular to Collective form (as male prisoners figure their altered state) or from Collective to Particular form (an alternation that requires them to deny the fact of their separation from kin), they often present incarceration as self-substitution (one kin form replaced by another) (see Chapter 4). This gives an ill-defined and nebulous form to their experience. By having God appear to them, women prisoners regain a sense of dramatic transformation, a form through which they can conceive the past distinguished from the present. Conversion produces a strange kind of association. Christian prisoners are neither the same (like a body of men) nor different (like kin); instead they share an identical relation to God.

A strip of cardboard, whose handwritten message is decorated with drawings of flowers, hangs above the desk in the rations store. Placed there by the convict in charge of recording supplies, the sign displays a verse from the Bible: 'The Lord listens to those in need. And does not forget his people in Prison' (*Psalms* 69: 33). This verse is often quoted by Christian prisoners and regarded as a source of comfort. While steal men complain that inmates only convert in order to waste time and thus 'make the day go quicker' (*wokim de go hariap hariap*), Christian prisoners counter that this distraction is part of the divine gift. God is held to manage their worries and sexual desires, to have the power to help them forget (*bikman em i rausim dispela kain tingting*). In particular those who pine and sicken for loved ones outside the gaol can make appeal to prayer. Nancy, a convict from the female wing, told me that before her conversion she used to fret about her elderly parents. As a result she lost her appetite and her weight fell to a dangerous level. Only when God appeared to her and she started to pray did Nancy relax and her body began to recover. Similarly, Ned, a convert to the Jehovah Witnesses, contrasted his reaction to the news of his mother's death to that shown by his two brothers, also locked up at Bomana. At first, Ned told me, he withdrew to his cell corner, placed a blanket over his head and broke down in tears; but after a few minutes he began to pray and his composure soon returned. His siblings, however, who remain steal men, found no relief from the pain of mourning and spent a miserable fortnight tearing their hair and crying uncontrollably. For Christian prisoners this necessity to disremember makes the tie to God indispensable.

Haven

During Saturday worship, a deacon of the Seventh-Day Adventist church rose and addressed his congregation. He asked them to imagine a place blanketed by snow, in which even the tops of trees were covered. The birds of this winter landscape had nowhere to perch or feed. Out of sympathy for the birds, a boy and his father laid out nuts and berries on the sheltered balcony of their house. This allowed the birds to land and rest. They stayed there until the snows melted and they could once again fly away. The deacon announced to his congregation that they should regard Bomana as a similar form of refuge. Outside, he told them, steal men eat poorly, they wear tattered clothes and constantly run the risk of being wounded or killed. Bomana provides them with food and safety. The deacon asserted that as a consequence no one should complain about the lack of freedom; God has given them a second chance, the opportunity to live without temptations and thus to change their ways. In this interpretation incarceration becomes a blessing, an experience that might be regarded as noble or even worthwhile.

Duncan (1996: 10), in her review of prison memoirs and literature from North America and Europe, notes a tendency among captives to regard prison as a haven from the superficialities of life outside. She reports that the act of taking away or reduction is often felt as relief. Prisoners contrast the rush and distraction of freedom to the stillness and quiet of prison life (1996: 11). Being locked up is seen to provide an opportunity for thought and reflection, a position from which another perspective on the world might be gained (1996: 13). Duncan records the frequency with which imprisonment is linked to feelings of protection and nurture (1996: 24). The provisioning of food and shelter and the experience of timelessness are commented upon for collectively providing a sense of release from the burdens of usual responsibility (1996: 27). The prison is represented as a sanctuary from unwelcome stimuli.

At Bomana this view of incarceration is tied up with the belief and practices of the new churches; in particular the Adventist

Church, which has gained popularity among inmates precisely because it places value upon the moment of constraint, on the rewards of having things taken away (the Adventists have the largest and most active congregation; typically a service includes thirty five 'full members', twenty 'visitors' and twenty three 'interested members'). Adventist prisoners tend to dwell on the similarities between penal and scriptural restrictions. They point out that the prison service prohibits the same narcotics as the church, policing the consumption of tobacco, alcohol, betel nut and marijuana. Those foods forbidden by the Book of Leviticus are also unavailable at Bomana. Adventists welcome the absence of urban favourites such as fried chicken, chips and soft drinks, but especially the lack of those foods they regard as 'dirty': pork, scale-less fish such as eels, the meat of snakes, flying foxes and crayfish. They claim that both prison and church are concerned with 'body security', the need to live with rules (*stap wantaim lo*) and obey instructions.[1] The separation of men and women, and thus the prevention of prostitution and the spread of sexually transmitted diseases, is met with approval. Members of the Adventist Church appreciate the rituals of inspection and roll call carried out by warders, the requirement to wash regularly, brush teeth, shave, cut hair and fingernails, and look after uniforms. With conversion comes the recognition that the body is a divine gift, the site where God's spirit dwells. By demanding acts of self-grooming, the prison regime is held to be praising God and at the same time drawing attention to the body's inhabited state.[2] Prison rules seem to assist the Adventist's revelation of this relationship; God appears as constraint itself.

Prisoners belonging to the Jehovah's Witnesses, Adventist and Pentecostal churches (under the Pentecostal umbrella there are several churches: the main ones being Assembly of God, Four Square Church and CRC, whose members all worship together) contrast their beliefs and practices with those of Papua New Guinea's more established Christian denominations. The latter, which include the Roman Catholic, Lutheran, United and Anglican churches, go back to British and German colonisation in the late nineteenth century, when the two territories were carved up into agreed spheres of denominational influence (see Wetherell 1977). This meant that each church became associated with specific, well-defined regions and language groups. The Roman Catholics, by far the largest church in Papua New Guinea, have geographical strongholds across the country. So prisoners not only come from a certain area, they are also acknowledged to come from a certain church. Those from the Goilala region of Central province, for example, tend to be Roman Catholic, while those from Oro province tend to be Anglican and those from Morobe tend to be Lutheran. In converting to one of the new churches prisoners are therefore always turning away from the denomination of their birth and often from the sets of relations that accompanied it (between kin and between language mates). Thus Kave, a place man from Ihu in Gulf province, told me that he used to attend the United Church services in his village. When he came to Bomana, he decided to visit all the other congregations and see how they worshipped. Kave decided to join the Jehovah's Witnesses because he felt they more closely followed the truth of the Bible. Unlike the church of his home, he explained, the Jehovah's Witnesses refused to drink beer, chew betel nut, smoke tobacco, draw tattoos or eat unbled meats. Kave said that since his conversion his parents and siblings have stopped writing to him.

If the Vatican is so clever tricking us then wat about Christmas? Could it be a form of white witchcraft? Is it occult?

● the Queen of Babylon (*SemiRamis) ordered the world to celebrate the birth of her son (*Tammus). Was the Sun God Baal representing Satan (she set '25th' for Baal's birthday: her astrologers told her that the Sun set at its farthest point from the earth during the Winter Solstice.

● so they told the people that on the (21st) of December the Sun or Baal dies.

● then on the 24th of December He starts coming back to life, and the 25th is His birthday.

As time past all over the world on the 25th of December the Sun was worshipped by this various names (Tammus, Horus, Osiris, Sol). It was for orgies (sacrificing of babies to Baal. Drunkenness. Merriment. (SemiRamis) ordered trees to be decorated with little Baal representing the Sun.

● when the Mass was first said on the midnight December 24th, around the year 394AD.

● it was the mass of Christ, or Christmas. The religious machine changed it from (Baal's Day) to the birthday of Jesus. The pagan loved it. It became the biggest day of the year for the (Catholic) Roman Catholic insitution.

● God fought this evil holyday by forbidding the Jews to decorate trees as the heathens were doing (Jeremiah 10: 1.4)

● does the Bible instruct us to celebrate the birthday of Christ? 'No' neither
Christ or the Apostles ever taught this. There is no record that the early
believers ever celebrated Christ birthday. Much less, Xmas. This unbiblical
practice was instituted by the Vatican to tie Christ to the Mass. Today Protes-
tants are pressured into observing this (Roman Catholic HolyDay).

This handwritten note, passed between Adventist prisoners at
Bomana, illustrates the tension between members of new and
established churches. The former, in identifying with prison rules
and the act of separation, regard the old churches as part of the
world they left behind and rejected. Among the Adventist prisoners, many of whom come from Catholic areas, the Roman
Catholic Church is connected with freedom or lack of constraint.
They complain that the church at home did not follow Saturday
worship; it did not forbid the consumption of pork, the smoking
of cigarettes, the drinking of alcohol, the playing of cards and
swearing. One Adventist prisoner from Goilala told me that the
Catholic Church lied to them (*Katolic giamman mipela*), instruct-
ing its congregations to worship saints and revere the Pope as
the head of the Christian movement. He complained that priests
only read edited extracts from the Bible and falsely claimed the
right of intercession. The permissiveness of the established
churches is perceived to be responsible for the rise of crime and
violence. Bomana is also presented as a refuge from this damag-
ing (lack of) influence.

God I truly love you.	*God mi laikim yu tru*
You are always sorry for me.	*yu save sori long mi*
You always help me	*yu save helpim mi*
And offer the protection of your fence.	*long strongpela banis tru*
It is the fence of God.	*em i banis blong God*
It is very strong.	*em i strong tumas*
Satan is not able to come inside.	*Satan i no inap kam insait*

During Pentecostal services at Bomana preachers often demand
an answer to the question, 'Who is our real enemy?' Members of
the congregation are expected to shout back the appropriate
response: 'Satan!' In fact Christian prisoners of all denominations represent their lives as a struggle between contrasting
influences; they claim to either act with God or Satan in mind.

The gospel song above is a favourite of most church groups. It styles the influence of God through idioms of protective enclosure, of incarceration. Outside His fence men and women are driven by the presence of Satan to steal, gamble, commit adultery, drink and fight. But inside the fence they are said to be safe, free from Satan's embrace. Members of the new churches extend this image, of God offering the protection of His fence,[3] to explain the experience of imprisonment. They claim that the evil influence of Satan only leaves men and women once they are arrested and detained at Bomana.

Christian prisoners believe that God or Satan can be read as the ultimate cause of every action. In particular, they argue that steal men are coerced into criminal deeds by being made to anticipate Satan's presence. This idea is enforced by steal men, but also by popular representations of the raskal figure. National newspapers carry articles that describe the testimony of men who claim to have given up raskal activities and turned to God. Typically, they present themselves as once having made a 'pact with the devil'.[4] Stories of animal sacrifice and ceremonial consumption of human flesh abound, the support of Satan as a consequence said to be guaranteed (see Kulick 1993: 10). Both the raskal and Satan are viewed as outlaw figures, leading a wandering existence and associated with the night, in particular the night of the city (Port Moresby is held to be the ultimate place of Satan). While steal men reject the ghoulish attributes of the raskal and his more theatrical dispositions, they often concede the influence of Satan in empowering their stealing lives. To them, Satan and God are equivalent forces. Just as they expect one day to find their emotions turned towards God, so they admit that at present Satan must lead their thoughts.

Christian prisoners and steal men accept that the form of the relation to God and of the relation to Satan is parallel. Both ties involve a sense of containment: either God or Satan wraps Himself around the subject or He inhabits that subject's body, is encompassed by it. Both also involve a diminished experience of reciprocity. The worshipper of Satan is no less able to coerce His attention than the Christian prisoner can cause God to act. Similarly, the form of the relation eclipses other states; when God or Satan is elicited, kin and bodies of men or women disappear. Just like the shock of sneezing or receiving weekend visits, it is said that God and Satan constantly interrupt the presence of each other. Christian prisoners claim to have the difficult task of deciphering the origin or stimulus for each event – is it caused by God or by Satan? Naku, a convict from Kerema in Gulf province and member of the United Church congregation, told me about his reaction to a distressing dream. At first he shuddered upon waking and recalling his dream image – the sight of his younger brother laid out dead in a morgue – but then he forced himself to take deep breaths and think again. Naku said that soon he began to smile and addressing himself to Satan rejected the truth of what he had seen: 'You deceive me, my little brother is still alive.' He explained that Satan is always tricking inmates, causing them to worry unnecessarily about events outside the gaol and thus to grow tense, fight or attempt escape. The Christian prisoner must not only act with God in mind; he or she must anticipate and reject the often-disguised prompts of Satan.

Light

As well as dreams, inmates at Bomana claim to experience visions. To Christian prisoners, they represent a more transparent or direct form of divine communication. For these half-waking states are distinguished as visitations, an encounter with God or one of His angelic emissaries. Maria, a convert to a Pentecostal church, told me of her own recent vision. She said that one afternoon she lay down on her bed, exhausted after a long day working in the garden of the female wing. Maria fell quickly into a light sleep.

From far off, she sees a bird with huge wings approaching. The bird flies closer and closer until it breaks the mosquito netting surrounding her bed and hovers above her face. Suddenly, Maria feels herself lifted off the mattress and realises that she is being carried away to a holy place. She addresses the bird, thanking it for selecting her and comments upon what she now sees, 'This place has no humans or noise.' The bird starts to sing.

When Maria woke from her vision she immediately understood that she had been called on by an angel and taken to view heaven. She felt very fortunate, as a sinful woman, to have been given that private experience. Indeed, visions are perceived to isolate the subject, to take her or him momentarily out of earthly relations and into celestial communion,[5] just the vision receiver and God.

The cell bed is held to be a privileged site for that communication.[6] But at Bomana beds are prominent as much by their absence as presence. Male prisoners explain that the cells in A Compound used to be equipped with metal frame beds until the prison riot of 1992, when inmates took them apart in order to use the frame legs as weapons. Since then men have had to sleep on the cement floor, flattening out cardboard boxes and laying them down as rough support. They have chosen to hang blankets and divide the space of the cell into screened corners or cubes, inside which a number of inmates live together (see Chapter 1). By contrast, the cell of the female wing remains furnished with beds. Those nearest the door are metal sprung and, being more comfortable, are usually occupied by long-term convicts. The remainder, at the rear of the cell, are supported by wooden planks and occupied by month women and those on remand, who complain of suffering back pains. There are no cubes, leaving the cell noticeably lighter and more spacious (Figure 15). The presence of beds is held to favour women as vision receivers.

Another site deemed to be suitable for divine visitations is the maximum-security institution at B Division, whose single cells hold men in solitary confinement. There, Alex, a steal man from

Figure 15 *A women's prison cell*

Goilala, experienced a vision that sparked his conversion to the Seventh-Day Adventist Church. During police arrest, Alex told me that he was shot in the eye. After being rushed to the town hospital for emergency treatment, he was driven to Bomana and dumped in the maximum-security institution. Still in pain, Alex said that he curled in the corner of his single cell, falling in and out of restless sleep.

A bright light hits him. Alex sees a man come forward and hand him the reference for a bible passage. The note reads 'Psalms 34: 7'.

When he woke from this vision, he immediately scribbled the verse number on the cell wall. The next morning Alex was allowed out of his cell in order to exercise in the institution yard. There he approached a warder and asked him to find the verse reference that he had written down the previous night. Clutching his bandaged eye, Alex said that he listened carefully to the words that the warder read out from the Bible: 'His angel guards those who obey the Lord and rescues them from danger.' The passage made him realise that God had saved him from death, from an injury that should really have killed him. Alex swore never to make trouble again. He recognised that God had appeared to him.

Christian prisoners associate visions with the 'light' (*lait*) of revelation. Accounts of these states often include descriptions of blinding, joyous luminosity. This harmonious glare links to the spirit of God, which is said to dwell inside the believer like the light of a candle. In fact Christian prisoners revise the prison consensus on the politics of vision (see Chapter 1). Instead of a 'dark place', members of the new churches regard Bomana as a site of comforting light. All Christians tend to value transparency and condemn acts of concealment. They associate darkness with Satanic influence and forbidden acts. Thus the converts of A Compound criticise the construction of those cubes or 'dark rooms' that divide the cell. They reject the activities – assault, rape, smoking, drinking alcohol, gambling, telling rude stories and making plans for future robberies – that screening allows. Those who occupy these concealed places are said to be greedy, unwilling to share things with everyone else. When men worship in these cells, they like to lift up the hanging blankets around them and thus create an open space. Indeed, within A Compound there exist two cells that form a separate section, designated by warders as the site for well-behaved male convicts.

The section is less crowded than the others and dominated by place men and Christian converts. Instead of cubes, the men of these cells live altogether, in what is distinguished as a 'clear place' (*klia peles*). They argue that it is better to live face to face, without screens, since God can see everything anyway. As a consequence, Christian prisoners claim there is far less trouble between cellmates, few fights and no reported cases of sexual assault. Sleeping on the floor side by side, they welcome this clearing for admitting the light of God.

Dear Adam,

Hello over there! Hope you're fine and happy. Almighty God's blessing of love, faith and joy reigns in between us forever. Amen!... As per our conversation I will now give you the story of this prison camp. Firstly when this prison camp was open it was dangerous to live in between the criminals because it was full of murderers in the prison. In the 80s the state of the Government then introduce the word of God Almighty and the Lord Jesus Christ work in between the prisoners. When the word of God started like having Dedication on every Sundays and Wednesdays it was so hard. Pastors or church groups from various denominations came and shared the word of God. In the 90s the word of God broke in the prisoners in which there was a big change. Every prisoner changed and surrenders their lives to the Lord Jesus Christ. Now this year 1996 is a change altogether now. Every night we are singing gospel songs and prophet songs and praising the Lord. Every each individual detainee has turns sharing God's word and giving their life testimony out to friends. It is a big change now and I'm very, very happy... My friend, I have to pen off because it's nearly time for us to sleep. May God bless you and family in love and faith. Goodnight and hope to receive your reply soon. Goodbye! or Bamahuta!

This letter, written by a male convict who is one of the deacons of the Seventh-Day Adventist congregation, describes a dramatic transformation in prison life. From a place of dangerous criminals, Bomana has turned into a site of mass conversion! According to the deacon's account, every prisoner has turned to God, so that nights in the cells are now taken up with singing gospel songs, sharing readings from the Bible and giving witness to past lives of sin. His description reinvents the experience of incarceration and the kind of relation there revealed. But this optimistic portrayal of Christian community denies the ease with which the tie to God can be eclipsed or made to take the form of alternative states of relation.

In A Compound male prisoners complain that denominational congregations too often become opposing bodies of men. Thus Adventist and Catholic prisoners tend to regard each other

as enemies and treat the act of conversion as a form of competition. Within church congregations men develop ties akin to
those between gang mates or language mates. Like those unitary
states, this relation opens obligations between prisoners and staff
of the same church (*wanlotu*). So warders give small gifts such
as pens, writing paper, bars of soap, guitar strings, toothpaste and
envelopes to their church mates and favour them in selection for
work parties. They offer pastoral guidance, supply bibles and
songbooks, and arrange outside church parties to visit on Dedication Day and represent their concerns to the prison chaplain
or visiting pastor. Warders also favour church mates when listing
candidates for parole or release on licence. However, the Collective relation between those in the same congregation is itself
vulnerable to reconstitution. Church mates may be revealed as a
different body of men. It is common for male prisoners to follow
language mates or gang mates into a particular church, making
it sometimes difficult to determine whether the act of conversion is coerced by God or by the example of comrades. Even
those well-behaved prisoners in the cells without cubes tend to
find themselves sleeping next to men of one body.

Christian prisoners express fears for the integrity of their
congregation. They speak of the dangers of relapse or 'backslid-
ing'. The Seventh-Day Adventists, for example, acknowledge the
protection that Bomana provides, but at the same time remain
on guard against the distracting influences of life outside the
gaol. The Adventist chairman, another prisoner from Goilala, is
particularly sensitive to any stimuli that might tempt his
members away. When an outside rock band was invited to play
on New Year's Day, the chairman issued a formal complaint to
the gaol commander and prison chaplain. He told them that he
feared for the spiritual safety of his congregation, warning both
officers that any 'disturbed' lyrics about sex, drugs or violence
might risk reviving his members' previous stealing habit.[7] The
church's ministry, he explained, depended upon the use of 'soft,
clean, pure words' and the absence of corrupting influences.
While the prison service was happy to support the conversion of
steal men, the Adventist chairman complained that little appreciation was given to the fragility of that drawn-out state.

But the anxiety of Christian prisoners is more usually directed
to the future after incarceration. Just as the tie to God is elicited
out of the separation from kin and the concealment of unitary
bodies, so the promise of release seems to anticipate a reversal.

As a refuge, the place of God, Bomana makes conversion easy. The challenge, so Christian prisoners say, is to sustain that tie in the world outside the gaol, where temptations and bad influences pervade. The vast majority of converts, I was told, throw their bible away and forget God as soon as they leave the prison fence. Faith is placed elsewhere, in Satan, kin and money. Freedom is lack of constraint, the inability to have God appear.

Notes

1   Changes in the state of the Christian body, its disciplining and cleansing, are often at the centre of conversion stories in Papua New Guinea. Kempf (1994) reports that initiation ceremonies and ritual circumcision among the Ngaing people of Madang province are considered a form of baptism. The ritual is intended to absolve sin and create a new, stronger man. Indeed, the Ngaing people of Madang province regard the crucifixion of Christ as the ultimate act of ritual bleeding (113). They draw direct comparisons between biblical events and their own ritual sequence. Just as the death of Jesus ensured the redemption of humankind, so the Ngaing perceive circumcision as cleansing the body of sin (117).

2   The idea that the Christian must seek to demonstrate, through ritual action, that the spirit of God inhabits his or her body is widely reported. Robbins (1995: 214) records that the Urapmin people of West Sepik province think of themselves as a Christian society. They are particularly concerned to control desire through 'spirit discos' or dances in which people try and get violently possessed by the Holy Spirit in order to cleanse themselves of sin (217). Robbins (1998b: 311) argues that successful possession in spirit discos provides them with evidence that they have reached a lawful Christian kind of personhood. They aim to achieve a state of desirelessness (313).

3   Whitehouse (1995: 43) presents a different example of the 'fence' as an idiom of religious language in Papua New Guinea. Among the people of the Pomio Kivung spiritual movement in East New Britain, a fence is said to contain the living and separate them from the dead. However, unlike the fence that Christian prisoners at Bomana imagine protects them from Satan, the members of the Pomio Kivung regard their fence as an obstacle to improvement. They look forward to the day when the fence will be broken and the ancestors will return, bringing wealth and new government.

4   This reference is from an article in the weekend magazine of the Post-Courier newspaper (19/5/95), entitled 'A pact with the devil broken'. The article outlines the conversion of a 'once hardened Mount Hagen criminal' to the Assembly of God Church. It describes his life of crime and engagement with the worship of Satan.

5   Stephen (1982: 119) reports that among the Mekeo people of Central province visions are more highly valued than dreams, for they require no interpretation. The Mekeo believe that visions can be ritually induced or caused by God and ghosts. There is a characteristic vividness (a light) to visionary experiences, which distinguishes them from ordinary dreams.

6   Perec (1997) describes the bed as the 'individual space *par excellence*' (16). He says that in French society it is the 'elementary space of the body (bed-monad), the one which even the man crippled by debts has the right to keep; the bailiffs don't have the power to seize *your* bed'. Perec asks us to consider the bed as an ethnographic site.

7   Not just the lyrics, but also the pace and rhythm of rock music is attributed considerable power; it is associated with the speed and frenetic movement of the city (and the steal man lifestyle). Hirsch (1995a: 194) records the reaction of one young man from the Fuyuge region of Central province upon hearing rock music being played on the anthropologist's cassette machine. The man explained that the music evoked a certain feeling inside his body, that it reminded him of his days walking the streets in Port Moresby.

CHAPTER 6

Following White Men

―――――――――― ⌘ ――――――――――

New

One day, I was told, a 'primitive' (*buskanaka*) arrived at Bomana. He could speak neither English nor Tok Pisin; no one understood his language. The policeman who arrested this man and escorted him to prison reported that he came from a remote hamlet, somewhere in the interior of Western province. Since the registration clerk could not question him, it was decided to name the stranger after his arresting officer. Officially recorded as 'Ivan', the man was handed prison clothes and directed to A Compound. There, male inmates crowded round him and attempted to communicate. Using hand signals and exaggerated facial expressions, they offered Ivan a bowl of brown rice and encouraged him to eat. But when he tasted the grains, he vomited. Next they handed him a bar of soap and towel and gestured for him to wash. But when Ivan smelt the cleaning agent, he vomited again (Figure 16). The prisoners did not know what to do; for Ivan, everything, it seemed, was unfamiliar and thus disagreeable.

Three long-term male convicts first gave me this story, one related with derisive snorts and screams of amusement. Ivan's ill ease when faced with even the most banal of everyday consumables was held to be incredible, the stuff of high farce. A man who couldn't swallow rice or realise the uses of soap was ridiculous. However, this laughter was tinged with anxiety, for convicts regarded the anecdote as a tale about their collective past, the way they, through their ancestors, once were. Ivan was revealed and dismissed as a throwback, last echo of First Contact, as a figure whose time had passed. Indeed, the convicts ended their story by pointing out that after a year in Bomana Ivan changed. He learnt to speak Tok Pisin, to eat the prison diet and wash with soap and water. Just like them, Ivan became a 'new' man.

Figure 16 *Ivan*

Up until now the constraint of incarceration has been seen to
reproduce forms that already exist. Rather than a site of socialisation or Society making (see Sykes 1958), Bomana is
understood by prisoners to redraw sets of distinctions and so
elicit previously hidden states of connection. Thus bodies of men
appear because the prison fence separates male inmates from
kin. The same is also true for ties to God. These are perceived
as always there, waiting to be made visible by the simple act of
taking away obscuring sets of relations. Prisoners view the act of
separation as the potential of penal constraint. However, they also
recognise that Bomana sometimes produces new forms, ones that
cannot necessarily be anticipated or assumed as the outcome of

alternation. These attract value precisely because of their claim to be innovative or unprecedented, to break the conventions of usual sociality. They are said to carry critical dimensions.

Among prisoners, to draw a distinction between old (*olpela*) and new (*nupela*) ways is to enter a debate about ethics (either new is good and old is bad or new is bad and old is good). In particular, it is an invitation to consider the nature of social expectation. Towards the end of his life, Foucault became interested in presenting a genealogy of the ethical subject in Europe and America. His project turned on studying discontinuities between certain 'arts of existence' (1985: 11), or what he referred to as the changing nature of the 'kind of relationship you ought to have to yourself' (1984: 352). It is the transformation in these technologies, the formation and performance of varying relations to the self, which he held to be crucial. If one imagines a contemporary aesthetic of existence for the prisoners of Bomana, one that accords with the wider Melanesian ethic suggested by Strathern, then it might lie in the need to demonstrate that someone else always causes one's actions.[1] This assumption of the axiomatic nature of connection might be a suitable reading of the politics of constraint and separation described in previous chapters (even if the experience of incarceration places that aesthetic in an unusual mode, by highlighting the very inability of prisoners to act on behalf of those they left outside the jail).[2] However, while this particular ethical subject offers Strathern (and other anthropologists) valuable critical insight into her own knowledge-making practices, it does not offer the same critical position for prisoners (and Melanesians) themselves. Instead, they are left with orthodoxy, another kind of constraint. This chapter aims to think about what a subversive ethics might look like to the men and women locked up at Bomana.

Loose bodies

There are men who enter A Compound only to discover that no one recognises them. In the cell yard they stand alone, and inside the cell they are ignored. Other prisoners turn their backs on them or just stare. No one comes forward to shake their hand and no one offers these men a blanket, bar of soap, towel or piece of cardboard to use as bedding. Without an invitation to join a body of men, they are left to sleep on the cement floor of the

corridor that separates rows of cell cubes. Male prisoners desig-
nate these men as 'loose bodies' (*lus bodi*), distinguished by the
fact that they appear to have no ties to draw upon. Indeed, loose
bodies are said to 'float' around A Compound, without the
grounding of support from others.[3] As a result they are more
vulnerable to assault and mistreatment. Cellmates may hit and
rape loose bodies without fear of reprisal, bully them into
performing small services such as collecting meals from the mess,
washing uniforms or sweeping the cell floor. Those who resist
may be forced to eat bars of soap. As unknown men, the loose
bodies can never anticipate what will happen to them; male prisoners say they are like detached 'particles' waiting for collision.

However, male prisoners assert that this unrelated state is
manufactured rather than given. Anyone can always recognise a
tie to someone else; the point is that in the example of the loose
body they choose not to. That lack of connection is the outcome
of a deliberate effort to disregard. In fact the negative autonomy
experienced by loose bodies is often intended as a form of
punishment. A recidivist who fails to send his gang mates provisions while outside the gaol or a new inmate suspected of
providing the police with information may both find themselves
constituted as strangers. This state is unwanted not just because
it threatens physical safety, but also because it is perceived to
present a danger to the mind. Since no one recognises them,
loose bodies are said to spend their time alone, worrying exces-
sively about those people they left outside the gaol. Without the
support of language mates, gang mates or other bodies of men,
these thoughts are unchecked. The risk is that loose bodies will
more easily succumb to despair and eventual breakdown. In this
scenario to appear unrelated represents a stage into insanity.

The politics of forgetting or disregard has featured throughout the book as an integral technology of prison survival. In
order to manage the pain of separation from kin, male prisoners
are forced to try and forget them. But this act of disremembering is perceived to have positive consequences, making visible,
for instance, bodies of men. In the case of the loose body forgetting has a negative outcome. Instead of disregarding certain ties
in order to reveal others, male prisoners forget for the sake of it
or in order to render someone out of connection, anonymous.
No one wants to be a loose body.[4] However, this particular practice of forgetting, of making someone else seem independent, is

taken up by both male and female prisoners and extended into an understanding of their capacity to produce new forms.

Friends

Duncan (1996: 13), in her survey of prison memoirs from Europe and North America, notes the frequency with which the quality of friendship among inmates is praised. Forced to live together and share hardship, prisoners are said to develop unusually intense relationships, of a passion and power they have never before experienced. The memoirs describe these friendships in a language of ecstasy (15). In particular, Duncan reports that contrasts are drawn between the loneliness of life outside the gaol, portrayed as an atomised, unfeeling and detached existence, and the warmth of prison sociability, where lasting relationships are formed which are characterised by affection and trust (18–19). The loss of family contact is rewarded by unique receptivity to others, those with whom one endures incarceration.

Prisoners at Bomana also argue that gaol is an especially good place to make 'friends' (*pren*). In fact they regard friendship as one of the 'new' forms that their custody produces, something to be welcomed and valued for the original qualities it brings. These attributes are contrasted not just with those of the form of sociability outside, but also with those of the conventional state of relations in prison. Rather than friendship being distinguished from an alienated, isolating civilian life, it is put forward against the usual expectations of sociability, whether exercised as kin or collective obligation. Claims to friendship carry implicit and explicit critiques of what is regarded as normative ethical life. Prisoners treat the form as unprecedented.

The perceived newness of friendship lies in the rhetoric of difference that accompanies it. For in order to make friends, prisoners must first appear as unrelated, they must demonstrate their independence of each other. This distancing effect abrogates ties in common and emphasises strangeness. In this positive assertion of autonomy existing sets of relations are forgotten so that prisoners can claim to 'create' this relationship. Rather than connection being viewed as axiomatic, they must pretend it requires work. Indeed, prisoners claim that in contrast to other ties they can always refuse the advances of those who want to be friends. This premise, that friendship is *voluntary*, a tie that cannot simply be acknowledged but must be constructed and carefully maintained, is a radical intervention. It allows, for instance, the behaviour between male friends, which in truth is hard to distinguish from that between gang mates or language mates, to appear subversive.

Prisoners typically describe friends as 'partners' (*patna*), a term best held to convey the qualities of that relationship.[5] Thus Johannis, a convict from the Western Highlands, told me that his best friend was a cellmate from the Motuan coast of Central province. As partners, they shared a cube together. If either man was short of tobacco, his friend supplied it. If one of them was unwell, the other fetched his meals and washed his clothes. If one became depressed, started thinking too much about those he left outside the gaol, then the other told stories in order to distract him. Johannis said that he and his friend walked around as a 'pair', cracking jokes together, drawing tattoos on each other's bodies and sharing cigarettes. Friends are represented in a caring relationship, with each partner expected to demonstrate concern for the other. Thus Anasi, a convict from the Goilala region of Central province, told me that she regularly washed the blanket of her friend. When this woman, who came from Marshall Lagoon in the same province, sweated or became dirty, Anasi wiped her face with a towel. In return this friend provided her with supplies of toothpaste and soap, and helped look after her small child (women prisoners are allowed to keep their infants until weaned, then they must hand them to kin outside). Since the woman's family lived in Port Moresby and paid frequent weekend visits, Anasi was invited to join them. Together they consumed the food that was brought and listened to news about life outside the gaol. The visitors played with the child and gave Anasi infant clothes. When they left, the two women sat down and worked together, rolling wool into strands suitable for making net bags.

As partners, friends are also expected to share secrets. Since mistrust among prisoners is rife, this exchange is treated as special; a male inmate may refuse to answer questions about his criminal activities, even if the inquiry comes from language mates or gang mates. In an environment where everyone is suspicious of each other, the claim of friendship to be based on *trust* appears extraordinary. Remand prisoners who are friends discuss the details of their court cases, while convict friends reveal to each other the true story of which crimes they committed. Partners also confide knowledge about the prison rules they break. Women in the female wing, for example, state that they can only safely steal food from the garden work party in front of friends; they fear that other female prisoners may betray them. Friendship is therefore viewed as conspiratorial.

Prisoners at Bomana regard this form as slipping between the orthodox states of relation. Friends are said to be unlike kin and unlike bodies of men or women; in fact they are defined against these ties. The alternation that Strathern describes (see Chapter 4) between Particular and Collective forms cannot capture the critical dimensions of friendship. In the Collective state persons are said to come together and act on the basis of what they hold in common (1988: 93). They perceive themselves in the image of those around them (121). At Bomana, one might think of any relation of sameness, of male prisoners who define themselves as one gang or one language, of female prisoners who define themselves as one church. This Collective tie is presented as nonhierarchical or between equals. When prisoners talk of friends, however, they always stress their independence, an element that separates them. This relationship is only established by making partners appear unrelated. Strathern describes the Particular form as asymmetric (49), between persons held to be separate or unlike. But their distinction is complementary, based upon mutual dependence. The parties hold nothing in common, but the relationship between them. Friendship, while sharing an emphasis on difference, would resist that sense of dependency, any suggestion of a nonequal status. The direct, unmediated effect, which persons in a Particular state of relation are said to have upon each other, contradicts the claims prisoners make, that this is a voluntary, non-coerced acquaintance. Friends are regarded as distinct but equivalent, autonomous and free selecting agents.

Mixmates

During the brief months of the rainy season (usually between December and March) the landscape at Bomana undergoes sudden transformation. What for the rest of the year is a dusty ground, drained of colour, is overtaken with vertiginous green growth. The grass shoots long and wild, and prisoners warn each other to watch out for snakes. Most afternoons the sky thickens, rumbles and releases a fresh downpour. After the rain, the air cools rapidly and around the compound yards water lies in puddles. Coastal prisoners retreat to their cells and wrap themselves in blankets in order to keep warm. Those from the Highlands find relief in this drop in temperature. They become boisterous and active, the lack of heat seeming to end lethargy and set free previously held-back energy.

But with the rains also come mosquitoes. These insects invade Bomana; during the day one can hear the sound of slapped skin as both prisoners and warders try to evade their attention. At night the mosquitoes enter cells. While women in the female wing are equipped with nets, only the long-term male convicts share this form of protection. Others, in particular those on remand, are left to fend for themselves. Some choose to roll up towels and set them alight, in the hope that the smoke from this slow-burning material might repel the insects. Many try to cover their bodies with blankets and enfold their heads in waistcloths. Despite the obvious breathing restrictions, they remain this way, wrapped up like embalmed corpses, throughout the night. But whatever precautions are taken, the buzzing mosquitoes always seem to get through. Those without nets complain that they wake up bitten and sore; too often they develop the shivers that signal the onslaught of malarial fever.

In some cells of A Compound, men turn their predicament into sport. It is said that while mosquitoes fly around at night, injecting and removing blood from cellmates, in the morning these insects rest on cell walls, digesting what they have stolen. As a result of overfeeding, they are often heavy and slow of movement. Gathering the flattened pieces of cardboard that served as bedding, cellmates take the opportunity to strike back. Together they charge the dozing insects, smashing the cardboard against the walls and pressing firmly. When the men pull back, they discover the mosquitoes squashed and extended, like flowers compressed between the pages of a book. What impresses them most is the sight of their own blood, now released from the insects, splattered and smeared across the plaster walls. Prisoners say that the different shades of stain, black, red or pink, reflects the variety of men in the cell. There, in the swirl and confusion of human substance, they believe they are presented with a different portrait, one that confronts their image of themselves.

Cellmates describe these blood-thrown patterns as 'mixed' (*mix mix*). They seduce because they compromise impressions of

singular form; the contrasting shades of blood are said to come
from an unknown number of different men. 'Whose blood is
this?', they ask themselves. But mosquitoes not only draw
substance, they implant it in the bodies of others. Thus, prisoners say, they are themselves mixed. The consequence is
challenging, but also dangerous; after all, these out-of-place
substances carry the risk of spreading sickness.

Male prisoners adopt the idiom of mixed composition to describe
what they regard as a new form of criminal association. 'Mixmates'
are men from different gangs who plan and steal together. Like
friends, they are seen to be unrelated; involved in a discretionary
partnership that privileges their equivalent status as autonomous
agents. Mixmates are seen to provide a critique of bodies of men,
in particular to point out the limits of sociability between gang
mates. It is said, for instance, that too often support is not forth-
coming, those in the same gang are unreliable, quick to run away
at the first sign of trouble and too easily broken during police
interrogation. When someone dies, his gang mates only mourn for
a day and then forget about him, or when a comrade is arrested,
no one remembers to look after his family in the city. Gang mates
are said to have 'open mouths', to be unable to keep a secret or
restrict information. Mixmates, like friends, are valued as confi-
dantes, seen by some steal men as better, more dependable
thieving partners. Again trust is put forward as the artefact of a
relationship premised on independence.

   The introduction of mixmates is attributed to a convict
named Jeffrey, who drew inspiration from his own mixed parent-
age, a mother from Manus Island and a father from Hula, on the
Central province mainland. As a 'mixed blood' (*mix blut*), Jeffrey
told me that he was better able to appreciate the requirements
for such partnerships. He first thought of the idea while serving
a prison sentence in Lae town. Disillusioned with the behaviour
of his gang mates, who only seemed to appear when there was
beer or tobacco to distribute, Jeffrey determined to find more
secure stealing allegiances. With a razor blade, he scratched away
his gang tattoo and then started to seek out what he called
'quality' relationships. Jeffrey approached other prisoners from
competing gangs who he believed he could trust and invited
them to become his accomplices. This tie, he explained, was not
a gang, but rather an association between consenting partners.

At first the invitation drew angry reproaches. Gang big boys in Lae prison and then at Bomana accused him of casually switching his loyalties, attempting to draw steal men into a rival gang. They instructed gang mates to beat and punish Jeffrey. But after a while, some of them began to understand what he was offering them. Jeffrey told me that one big boy in particular, from his cell, acknowledged the value of mixmates. Together they persuaded other prisoners to accept its merits. The strength and attraction of the tie was confirmed some months later when a male convict was stabbed and killed by someone from a competing gang. In the past such an event would have sparked large-scale fighting, but this time many refused to engage. As mixmates, they identified individual partnerships that cut across the gang divide.

In acting as friends or mixmates, prisoners believe themselves to be doing something original. They describe this behaviour as belonging to a 'new generation'. This rhetoric of old and new gives shape to the kinds of forms that prisoners recognise, it provides an aesthetic device for distinguishing sets of relations. Indeed, in many ways the partnerships described between friends or mixmates better reflect the circumstances of criminal activity. Outside the prison, steal men regularly join up with boys in their neighbourhood from competing gangs; they do not tend to operate as bodies of men. It is therefore often hard to see what is new and what is old.

Critique

Prisoners at Bomana claim that loose bodies, friends and mixmates live 'one-one' (*wan wan*), as if people existed independently of each other. They contrast these forms to those that privilege ties between kin and collective bodies such as language mates or gang mates. There people are said to live together or 'one-time' (*wantaim*), to treat sets of relations as if they are axiomatic. This distinction draws together the usual alternating states (what Strathern calls Particular and Collective states), which inform prisoners' understanding of what incarceration achieves (see Chapter 4), and situates them as a single ethical position. We might understand that stance as the dominant aesthetic of existence, defined earlier as a kind of coerced agency: 'the need to demonstrate that one's actions are always caused by someone else'. Indeed, prisoners believe that the experience of detention allows them space to identify a critique of that expectation and the obligations that accompany it. Being exiled from kin is said to cause them to reflect upon not just the pain of separation, but also the constraint of those ties and of normative responsibility. Bomana is perceived to make that ethics explicit, the subject of conscious reflection. Typically, the arts of living together, one-time, are described by prisoners as old or customary and contrasted to the new aesthetic of living independently, as one-one.[6] But that distinction may also be shaped through images of race. Instead of old and new, prisoners can describe themselves as either living like 'black men' or 'white men'. Whichever idiom they choose, the contrast is perceived to open a subversive dialogue.

Appeal to one-one ethics can provide prisoners with a critical basis for making complaints. A convict from Kerema once explained to me how he sent letters without them being censored. After writing his message, he handed the note to a language mate on guard duty, who smuggled it out of Bomana and then took a bus into town. There the warder entered a post office and passed the letter to a language mate who worked behind the counter. This clerk stamped the envelope, without charge, and placed it into a sack post-marked for Kerema town. This example of what is called the 'one-language system' (*wantok sistem*) highlights the benefits of living one-time, but prisoners are also quick to point out the inequalities, especially when they themselves are the victims of negative discrimination.[7] Male prisoners complain, for instance, that warders only tend to select language mates or church mates to join work parties. Those in the remand wing resent the fact that they are prevented from visiting reception, in order to inspect their civilian clothes before upcoming court appearances, unless a language mate is on duty. Convicts complain that a warder may beat and detain one inmate caught smuggling tobacco, but let another one, with whom they recognise an obligation, go unpunished. If a steal man robs someone outside the gaol, they protest, he may be whipped and assaulted by those warders who are language mates of the victim. The implicit basis for these complaints is the alternative ethical position offered by one-one living; in particular, prisoners distinguish a quality of *fairness*, treating everybody the same, which they say is missing from the one-language system and other conventional modes of one-time existence.

It is said that white men judge others as though they are unrelated. Selection is made through assessment of each person's
merits, by forgetting the fact that obligations may already exist.
Prisoners contrast this practice with the typical criteria for
advancement. They complain that release on licence and eligi-
bility for parole is too often determined on the basis of favouring
language mates. Similarly, it is said that outside the gaol it is
impossible to find employment or gain promotion without this
means of support. Prisoners point to the example of gaol staff.
Warders frequently bemoan the expectations of the one-
language system. They state that if a sergeant makes a complaint
about a private who is always late on duty, he or she must be sure
to approach the right senior officer. If that officer happens to be
a language mate of the private, one can be certain no punishment or disciplining will take place. Promotion between ranks is
said to operate on the same basis. Warders assert that it doesn't
matter how hard they work, since decisions about career
advancement are made with different priorities. If a language
mate does not occupy a senior post, there is held to be little point
in demonstrating enthusiasm or proficiency.

These staff appraisals are sometimes accompanied by what
appear fond remembrances of the colonial regime (Papua New
Guinea gained independence in 1975). Warders tell stories about
how Bomana used to be managed when under the authority of
white men. In those days, it is said, they had to be always 'on
their toes'. The gaol commander and other white officers
checked their behaviour closely, paying unannounced visits to
those on duty and requiring them to keep their hair cut short,
their boots polished and their uniforms well ironed. No one
could afford to be late on duty. Warders who served under the
colonial administration remember the prison as a far tidier place,
with freshly painted buildings, mown lawns and neat flowerbeds.
The white officers inspected staff housing to ensure it was properly maintained (one old warder claims to recall an officer
running his finger along window louvres checking for dust), allo-
cated accommodation for married warders and prevented single
men bringing women or beer into the barracks. Most importantly, however, warders claim that the white officers recognised
and rewarded their efforts. If someone worked hard and obeyed
instructions, then it was likely promotion would follow.

Similar observations are made about the behaviour of prisoners. Under the colonial regime, warders assert that discipline was strict, so that no inmate would dare to disobey an order. Staff did not converse with prisoners and never favoured their language mates. The distribution of rations was closely monitored to ensure that each inmate received the same amount and security was said to be far tighter. For every prisoner there were two guards, the watchtowers were always manned and if someone escaped the search party tracked the fugitive thoroughly. Many warders contrast this tradition of penal management to the regime today, which they believe is governed by the one-language system. They describe Bomana as like a 'holiday camp', where prisoners come and go as they like, smoke tobacco and marijuana with impunity, listen to smuggled radios, wear unauthorised clothing, rest and enjoy the food, free water and electricity services. In this account, warders regret that the one-one arts of living belong to the past.

The ethical display of coerced agency is often presented as burdensome. While the support that kin or language mates may provide is highly valued, both prisoners and warders regret the weight of their own obligations. A male convict from the Western Highlands told me that he preferred to share a cell with men from Papua, only visiting his language mates during the daytime. He explained that if he saw them more often, they would start to argue over what each expected from the other. Male prisoners are wary not just of the exhausting requirement to share, but of the threat of being drawn into fights between competing bodies of men (see Chapter 4). Warders complain at the constant demands placed on their urban budgets. Despite access restrictions, they receive frequent visits from kin and language mates, with accompanying requests for hospitality and financial support. Geoffrey, the prison chaplain at Bomana, informed me that like other warders visitors from home overran his household. They would arrive unannounced, expect to be fed, given pocket money and accommodated for weeks or even months on end (Figure 17). Since Geoffrey was mixed blood, his father from Fergusson Island in Milne Bay and his mother from the Telefomin area of Sandaun province, he could expect even greater numbers. In fact he estimated that his house was only free of visitors for three weeks out of any given year. Geoffrey stated that his pastoral work among prison staff and their families

showed that these demands were often responsible for marital
tensions and financial stress. The problem, he explained, was that
warders felt unable to refuse such requests; how else could their
presence be recognised, and others, in turn, be forced to act on
their behalf?

Living one-time can be exhausting. Both prisoners and
warders present themselves as bombarded with sociability,
weighed down by what appear ever-increasing demands for
action.[8] As a consequence, they are often glad of the restrictions
on access that Bomana provides. Warders welcome the fact that
language mates living in Port Moresby are sometimes afraid to
visit the prison complex or that employment rules generally
forbid them from working in their home province. Prisoners can
appreciate the breathing space from obligation that living in the
last place allows and the interruption of inmate sociability
caused by penal routine. In the same way performances such as
those between friends or mixmates can offer relief, an excuse to
temporarily disregard the burden of orthodox ethical commitment. One-one behaviour or 'following white men' (*bihainim ol
waitman*) is perceived to open a distance on conventional expectations, allowing prisoners to come up for air, to evade versions
of themselves.[9]

Figure 17 *'Wantok'*

Counter-critique

In February of 1995 media outlets announced an historic court judgment. For the first time since 1954 a judge had sentenced someone convicted of murder to the death penalty.[10] Reports confirmed that the condemned man was Charles Bongapa Ombusu, a steal man who was arrested and tried in Popondetta, the administrative centre of Oro province. Not long after, Ombusu was transferred to Bomana in order to await his appeal before the Supreme Court. His arrival at B Division sparked meetings among inmates in A Compound and the female wing. Over the ensuing days and months, they debated the appropriateness of this sentence and the general principle of the government's right to take life.

When prisoners first read the newspaper headlines they were deeply shocked. Although the government had reintroduced the death penalty for crimes of wilful murder in 1991, no one at Bomana expected that judges would actually exercise this power. The news caused widespread panic – in particular among those remand inmates charged with a capital offence and those convicts serving life sentences, who feared that this punishment might even be backdated. Anxious prisoners approached me with their concerns. Ebon, a place man from Lufa in the Eastern Highlands, explained that he could think of little else. Like others in his remand cell who were charged with wilful murder, he stopped eating and found it hard to sleep. 'What', Ebon asked himself, 'would happen to my mother and sisters if the government killed me? Now that my father and brother are dead, who would build houses and construct fences for the household gardens?' It seemed to him that his kin would be the ones who suffered. 'Would the government provide for them after I am gone?' Similarly, Dii, a convict from Wabag in Enga province, expressed worries that if the government killed him before he was married or his wife gave birth, then his ancestral line might be extinguished. He told me that he had sent a letter to one of the national newspapers outlining these fears and requesting that the government release selected prisoners in order to act as messengers, spreading news about the death penalty across the country and warning people about the dangers of making trouble.

News of Ombusu's sentence also provoked anger. Male prisoners asserted that the condemned man was just like them and so worthy of their support. Max, a convict from Goilala and gang mate of Ombusu, told me that he felt sorry for his comrade. He warned that if the government did go ahead and execute him, Ombusu's gang mates would be forced to retaliate. They might attack the court witnesses who spoke against him, the sentencing judge, national politicians or civil servants. Max said that Ombusu's kin and language mates would feel the same way. Indeed, many prisoners doubted that the government would have the nerve to carry out the death sentence. Papua New Guinea, they explained, was not like the countries of white people such as Australia and the United States of America. There, people lived independently or one-one, left their parents and kin as soon as they matured and married. In these circumstances a government could put someone to death without fear of repercussions. But in Papua New Guinea, they countered, people lived one-time, they couldn't forget the obligation they owed to others (inmates noted with scorn that the sentencing judge was herself a white woman). Prisoners insisted that State execution would be a disaster, involving the government in an open cycle of injury and revenge.

Inmate rhetoric about the death penalty presents a deep concern with the consequences of individual events. The government's proposed action upon the body of the condemned man is criticised not by appealing to Ombusu's own suffering or humanity, but rather by gauging that deed's effects upon other persons. It is the distress and discomfort that this punishment will cause to kin or bodies of men that is held to be the measure of its injustice. One man's death is significant precisely because it reverberates and coerces responses from others. In this argument prisoners are strategically reversing the point of their critique. One-one behaviour is rejected, presented as foreign and therefore unnatural, out of sympathy with a postulated Papua New Guinea ethics. What is 'new' is suddenly bad. The distinction between one-time and one-one living seems to equip prisoners with a double critique. Either the customary aesthetic of existence – that need to demonstrate that one's actions are always caused by someone else – is revealed as constraining, when contrasted to the alternative arts of living like a white man, or it is liberating, knocking down the pretensions of introduced and unwelcome action. It is this capacity to alternate between ethical states, therefore opening critiques on either, that is truly subversive, the mark of imposing a new constraint or discontinuity in the arts of living.

Prisoners state that warders hark back to the colonial era of penal management not just because the behaviour of white men was perceived as strict or fair, but also because it was far more violent. They point out that treating everybody the same, as if they lived independently of each other, allowed staff to beat inmates without fear of reprisals. Warders themselves acknowledge that this was the case. One warder, who started his commission a couple of years before Independence, told me that he recalled being impressed by a particularly violent white officer. This man used to throw disobedient male inmates against the electric fence that I was told once surrounded B Division or hit and kick them until they became unconscious. The warder explained that when prisoners misbehaved they were automatically beaten. If they broke prison rules, the gaol commander instructed warders to make them break rocks, dig up tree roots or carry heavy logs until their hands bled and blistered. Most warders believe that these corporal punishments should be reintroduced. They resent the fact that they feel restricted in the use of violent measures, not so much by the enactment of legislation, but by the constraints of the one-language system. Warders express nostalgia for the days when they could hit someone without worrying about its effects upon others. Some find hope in the news of Ombusu's death sentence, an event welcomed by nearly all of them. In fact several warders suggested that the condemned man be hung live on television, as a warning to others that may think of making trouble.

The critique that prisoners provide of the death penalty is not their only attack on one-one behaviour. While friendship and the association between mixmates are praised, other performances are contested. In particular, prisoners criticise the actions of 'businessmen' (*bisnis man*), held up as perhaps the most convincing mimics of white people. They state that these men distinguish themselves by their refusal to acknowledge obligations to others. It is this pretence that allows them to accumulate their wealth. As self-styled 'independent men', they can be seen to help others voluntarily, but not to be coerced into actions of giving. So businessmen may reject the petitions of kin or bodies of men such as language mates, while at the same time offering generous contributions to large-scale public celebrations. Prisoners regard this behaviour as foolish. They point out that autonomy is a short-lived performance, that the illusion of unrelatedness cannot be wisely sustained. When businessmen run into trouble, they will have need of the supporting ties they previously failed to recognise. Indeed, male prisoners are frequent witnesses to their downfall. They say that when broken businessmen enter Bomana they do not know how to behave. Many are rendered anonymous, turned by revenging prisoners into loose bodies or made into 'work boys', responsible for washing their cellmates' clothes, sweeping the floor and collecting meals from the mess. Those who refuse are punished by beatings, forced to eat their own excrement or sexually assaulted. They have no ties to call upon.

In 1997, after I left Papua New Guinea, the Supreme Court finally gave its ruling, quashing Ombusu's sentence and ordering a retrial. Although the judges provided legal technicalities for their decision, everyone, it seemed, believed that the government had no real appetite to become a public executioner. As the prisoners predicted, politicians and civil servants feared the kind of response their actions would coerce. An implicit consensus seems to have emerged that the death penalty is inappropriate for Papua New Guinea. For prisoners the victory evinces the strength of one-time thinking, an acknowledgement that the requirement to demonstrate coerced agency remains inevitable. However, this 'Papua New Guinea' arts of existence is still viewed as constraining; prisoners complain of ethical exhaustion, of frustration with the expectations of normative sociability. One-one behaviour will continue to have its appeal as an outlet for that sense of obligation overload. What Bomana teaches them is that they are constrained whichever way they turn. Whether they present themselves living one-time or one-one, prisoners retain a desire to be somewhere else, to take up alternative, unoccupied ethical ground.

Notes

1 Strathern (1992a: 74) advises that 'you cannot look inside the person to discover the true person: you will instead find other (particular) persons'.

2 It is worth noting that the way anthropologists of the region represent indigenous sociality resonates strongly with the way madness is sometimes represented in Europe and North America. Indeed, Bateson (1973), whose work with the Iatmul people of the Sepik River in the 1930s is the inspiration for the later work of Wagner and Strathern, actually goes on to develop a thesis of mental illness. He argues that those people who view analogies where the 'normal' person might see a plurality of things are suffering from (enriched by) what he calls 'trans-contextual syndromes' (243). Bateson claims that in the hands of an artist this capacity might be judged as a gift. In this sense he follows an old European tradition.

Foucault (1973: 49) notes that Classical and Modern conceptions of madness view the sufferer as a 'man of primitive resemblances', as one 'who is alienated in analogy'. He points out that poetry can be perceived as a positive manifestation of this habit of seeing connections. The kind of ethical subject that Strathern describes for Melanesians therefore indulges her own sense of poetry (or madness).

3   Rew (1974: 100–102) reports the existence of a similar figure in another discipline institution: the barracks of labour compounds in Port Moresby. Certain workers were distinguished as alone or *wanpis*. These individuals complained to Rew about the unfriendly regard of their work mates; that they had no one to support them in fights, to borrow things from or to sit and share stories with.

4   Strathern (1975) notes that for Hagen migrants to Port Moresby in the 1970s the experience of being *wanpis* or alone was not straightforwardly negative. Some of the men she interviewed, who had spent time in the city's labour barracks, told her that being without support (and therefore obligation) had value. It meant they could escape any demands that might be made on them (146–47). Indeed, migrants claimed that in a way all those Hageners in the city were *wanpis*. Through the act of leaving home, they had made a decision to cut themselves off from the expectations of kin and those in the village or hamlet (148 and 301).

5   Schwimmer (1974: 58–61), who worked among the Orokaiva people of Papua New Guinea, sets himself the task of finding an indigenous equivalent to our own convention of friendship. Unlike prisoners at Bomana, the Orokaiva, when Schwimmer visited them, did not use the term. The best comparison, he argues, may lie with certain kinds of reciprocating partnerships, known locally as 'otavo'. These involve pairings between men from different clans who may dance, feast or trade together. Schwimmer suggests that this partnership is original, and predicts that it will provide the model for the kinds of relationship that will succeed in disciplined institutions such as plantations and boarding schools (67).

6   Recently anthropologists of the region have become concerned to connect the rise of commodity consumption and a growing sense of nationhood in Papua New Guinea with a shift in indigenous conceptions of personhood. Foster (1995b: 18) argues that nationality is attached to certain commodities and acquired by 'possessive individuals' through acts of consumption. He contrasts this possessive individual, defined by the commodities he or she consumes, to the image of a Melanesian person who is animated by social relations (after Strathern 1988). Foster argues that the latter is displaced by commodity forms of personhood (1995b: 154). However, prisoners' desire to live one-one (*wan wan*) is not necessarily an expression of possessive individualism; they do not identify the achievement of independence with acts of commodity consumption.

7   Monsell-Davis (1993) argues that in Port Moresby and other towns the 'wantok system' is of ambivalent value. On the one hand, it provides access to a series of 'safe' relationships and ensures assistance in times of trouble (49). On the other hand, it leaves those in employment with intolerable

demands on their money and hospitality (56). Indeed, Monsell-Davis states that those earning modest wages in the city sometimes find it easier to leave work (and rely on language mates themselves) than to try and meet the expectations of wantok (57).

8   Strathern (1999: 96) has more recently argued that the perception of intensified sociability, of coerced action, is linked in people's minds to the specific qualities of money. In particular, the divisible nature of currency, its capacity to be broken down into smaller units, to be held back and used for multiple transactions, is said to increase the frequency and therefore expectation of small gift giving (106). Strathern argues that money activates the mind's divisions (97), accelerating obligation and the demands for action.

9   It is worth pointing out that prisoners often present the act of urban migration as a deliberate attempt to flee the expectations of kin (see Chapter 2). Young men and women leave the village or hamlet precisely to avoid the surveillance of parents and the pressure that exists to marry and take up affinal responsibilities (see Strathern 1975).

10 Inglis (1982) provides an account of one criminal sentenced to death by the colonial regime and executed in Port Moresby before the Second World War. Her book includes historical descriptions of the condemned man's last days in prison and subsequent hanging.

Conclusion

Homesickness

A quite wild native was sent into Port Moresby as a prisoner, and although homesick and very frightened, appeared in the very best of health. After a short time, he began to show signs of abdominal pain and to vomit. In the course of a few weeks these got worse and he finally died without any very definite signs and without marked wasting. (*Papua Annual Report 1917–1918:* 53)

It might be expected that when colonial officers diagnosed 'homesickness' as the cause of unexplained prison deaths (see Prologue), they were drawing attention to a feeling of exile from which they too suffered. Themselves far away from familiar faces and land marks, it was perhaps easy, even comforting, to imagine that in equivalent circumstances the less travelled and innocent 'native' might pine, sicken and die. And not just colonial officers and missionaries, but also early anthropologists working in the region. In his fieldwork diary, Malinowski describes his own ongoing struggle to combat a longing for home.

'Homesickness'. I summoned up various figures from the past, T.S., Zenia. I thought of Mother. (Malinowski 1967: 52)

That journal reads as a eulogy for those people left behind when the anthropologist travels abroad. Malinowski laments the 'absent ones' (194). His thoughts of them continually intrude; the arrival of post on the Trobriand Islands disturbs his composure, bringing on what he describes as a 'sudden rush of (their) presence'. At rest the anthropologist thinks about missing persons and places, at night he dreams about them:

Toward the end of the day's work hidden longings come to the surface, and visions as well: yesterday I saw the western end of Albert Street, where the broad boulevard cuts across it towards Lonsdale St... At moments I long violently to go *South* again (175).

At night, sad, plaintive dreams, like childhood feelings. I dreamed about Warsaw, about our apartment in the boarding school, about some apartment with a bathroom (Zenia and Staś) in Warsaw. Everything permeated with Mother... Tiny details recollected: the linen Mother gave me when I left. Continual memories and associations (295).

Indeed, Malinowski frequently depicts his fieldwork as a form of imprisonment (162; and Rapport 1997),[1] an act of self-imposed detention that has him counting the days and months before the 'moment of liberation' (205), his date of departure.

In setting out the principles for ethnographic work, Malinowski insists upon this separation, not just from loved ones back home but also from the company of other 'white men' in the Territory (1922: 6). The kind of contact that scientific fieldwork demands is held to be premised on first cutting oneself off or taking something away, becoming confined in 'native' life and society. While ethnographic work is the cause of homesickness, Malinowski believes it is also the cure: by keeping busy with fieldwork, he can make his worries disappear (1967: 201). That exile is held to be painful but productive, the source of what anthropologists can know.

Those working in Papua New Guinea today still figure their project as a particular kind of displacement. Kahn (1996), who works among the Wamira at the southeastern tip of the country, describes her motivation for travelling to the region – 'I had decided to work in Papua New Guinea precisely because it was the last place in the world in which I could imagine myself being' (168–69). This deliberate uprootedness, the professional requirement to place oneself outside the familiar, is for her the basis of anthropological insight and knowledge. Kahn reports her initial bewilderment when Wamirans took her strategic position as a predicament; they expressed their sorrow for the sense of loss she must feel at being away from her own place (170).[2] For them, the idea of self-exile, purposefully seeking the furthest location from home, was incomprehensible, an act that denied the crucial relationship between people and the land in which they saw themselves reflected.

My own presence at Bomana sometimes drew the sympathy of prisoners, especially on Christmas Day, when many came up to say how sorry they felt that I was such a long way from the people and places I knew. Their reaction to my situation revealed their own predicament; they diagnosed themselves as *sick for home*. The embarrassment I felt at receiving such attention highlighted the difference between our circumstances; for myself (like other anthropologists) spending time out of place was a choice, for them it was a punishment. Among prisoners there remains great anger and bitterness at what has been taken away, the ambitions that are thwarted and the obligations left unfulfilled. These frustrations show themselves in inmates' songs and poems. I remember one in particular, a song written and performed in 'heavy metal' style by a male convict and his band during the prison's annual Independence Day celebrations. The singer delivered his lyrics with a rasping, angry voice, accompanied by the sound of thrashed electric guitars. It was the most popular song of the day:

In the field of dream,
I ain't enjoying one bit of its passing day.
Everyday it is a pain in the arse
And I don't like it all.
O, I miss my home.
Sweet home.

Like the lilies of the field,
I was born wild,
Like the shadows of yesterday.
Yesterday's gone,
And today is another day of pain and isolation.
I was blind to all reasons.

Circumstances don't suit me,
But like it or not circumstances prevail.
Someday they'll be an end to all this anguish and pain.

Bye bye Bombex city.
I had enough of you.
Too much, too little, too late.
Bye bye Bombex city.

(Antony Ume)

Prisoners claim that the act of detention makes 'home' appear to them. The term embodies everything that is missing in gaol; it is an artefact of the constraint of living in the last place. At Bomana prisoners feel cut off or hidden from people outside the gaol, caught in a dark place where home exists in the past and future, but not the present. As the song says, these circumstances may not suit, but they prevail. 'Sweet home' is what prisoners long for, what they spend their time dreaming and worrying about, and what they aspire to eventually recover. And finally, home is what always seems to evade their grasp.

Taussig (1992: 149–50) argues that for anthropologists today the complaint of homesickness is double-edged. Not only do they hark back to what is missing when conducting fieldwork; in their subsequent writing, they display nostalgia for what is familiar. Ethnographic description relies on 'home' metaphors to make fieldwork experiences communicable. Taussig says that anthropologists are both sick for these conventions and sick of them (homesickness motivates Strathern to impose certain constraints on her writing), if not exactly escaping home metaphors, at least making their presence felt.

In her survey of inmate memoirs from North America and Europe, Duncan (1996: 24) reports a general sense of dis-ease with home. Indeed, prison is often depicted as a peaceful and safe place when compared with the dangers and insecurities of life outside the gaol. Those who leave accounts of their incarceration tend to express nostalgia for their period of detention, which is distinguished as a time of suffering, but also of unmatched intensity and comradeship (see Chapter 5). Prison is a place where 'serious things happen' (23). At the same time it is a place of dependence, where inmates are reliant on others to feed, clothe and shelter them and where the need to make ordinary life decisions is taken away. In memoirs, this release from responsibility is usually depicted as a source of satisfaction (27) – no more worries about paying bills, finding or keeping employment, wondering what to eat, what to wear or do. Locked up in gaol, the individual is no longer faced with bewildering choices, with the threat of not meeting his or her life expectations.

To illustrate her point, Duncan quotes from the journal of James Blake (29–30), a convict in Florida prisons during the 1960s. Blake conveys the regard he had for detention, while at the same time criticising the assumption that everyone has a 'home' to which they resolutely wish to return:

> I think it was then I realised I wanted to go back to the tribe, to my people, in the joint. And I said to myself, home is where, when you go there, they can't turn you away. Homesick, how about that? And homesick is where, when you go home, they make you sick. (Blake 1971: 378–79)

If prison provides a refuge, it does so at a high cost. Blake states that gaol is his home, but it also makes him sick. Homesickness is therefore not just a longing; it is also the act of return or home-coming itself. Being at home, whether inside or outside the gaol, has its drawbacks or ill effects. Indeed, for Blake home is a nega-tive, a site of reluctant obligation – the place where 'they can't turn you away'. Homesickness makes him write his memoir and ulti-mately choose to re-offend (Blake was arrested and imprisoned again).

At Bomana prisoners claim that they learn to regard the idea of 'going home' as constraining. If homesickness leads them to worry about the obligations they fail to meet, it also makes them sick of feeling coerced by kinship. Sick for home and *sick of home*, prisoners are radicalised by their experience of detention. Being away from home allows God to appear to them (see Chapter 5); it makes radical forms of social engagement, such as the claim to live one-one (see Chapter 6), seem possible. Their loss has the potential to reconstitute sets of relations through acts of forget-ting; and, by reifying what is lost into the category 'home', to make life outside Bomana seem suddenly open to judgment.

Despite their efforts to forget, home keeps intruding. It makes its presence known through sneezes, dreams, letters, weekend visits or earaches. The idea of homecoming dominates the thoughts of prisoners at Bomana; men and women imagine a return to civilian life. They try to anticipate the kind of recep tion they can expect outside the gaol. Maria, a female convict whose date of discharge was only six months away, related to me the dream she had experienced the night before:

Maria returns to her house in Port Moresby. There she sees her daughter and son-in-law working a garden. The plot is small and yields few crops. She stands at the front door and calls out, 'Lizzie, come here!' The woman keeps on working, but her husband looks up and recognises Maria. He shouts excitedly to his wife, 'Your mother has returned, she must have finished her sentence!' The two of them drop their tools and run towards her. All the people that Maria knows in the city follow them. Men and women, including the kin of her victim, eagerly shake Maria's hand and welcome her home. But Maria feels embarrassed by this greeting because she realises that everyone knows she killed a woman. The people see her shame and offer reassurance. Maria smiles and tells them, 'I thought you were cross with me, but you are happy, so I know we can live together.' She then indicates for them to sit down, to close their eyes and join her in prayer. Afterwards everyone claps hands and sings gospel songs.

In her dreaming, Maria sees herself back in Port Moresby, greeted warmly by her daughter, son-in-law and by others she knows well in the city (she is even welcomed by the kin of the woman she killed). This dream pleased Maria, easing her fears about her own upcoming release.

Other prisoners, however, find the thought of returning home too disturbing to contemplate. Male prisoners are fond of reciting the story of a life-term convict from the Goilala region of Central province. After the conclusion of his twenty-five-year sentence, this man refused to go home. He told warders that his parents were dead and that other people in his hamlet had long ceased to think of him. Instead of returning to that place, the ex-convict preferred to remain locked up at Bomana. Eventually a compromise was found: the man agreed to be released on the promise that he would be given employment as a cook at the staff officers' mess and accommodation within the grounds of the prison complex (where he remained during my time at Bomana). Faced with the prospect of unkind or hostile reception, I was told that some end-term convicts actually lose their minds (go *long long*). This is another kind of homesickness.

Leaving Bomana is an event that affects the composure of many people, not just the soon-to-be-discharged prisoner and those waiting for him or her outside the gaol, but also the state of mind of fellow inmates. A convict's release risks upsetting the feelings of other prisoners, undermining their efforts to live as if home does not exist (when my own time to go came I felt confused – a mixture of relief at finishing my fieldwork and of guilt at leaving everyone behind). Those who are sensitive to this situation try to play down their imminent departure. In the weeks or months before discharge, they begin to consciously withdraw from the company of other prisoners and so attempt to minimise the harm caused by their release. Of course the endeavour is never completely success-ful; those inmates who remain at Bomana must work hard at making the discharged figure disappear, adding him or her to the list of must-be-forgotten persons.

Taussig (1992: 150) believes that for anthropologists one can take the sentiment of homesickness further. He says that when fieldworkers return to the academy, they develop longing for the time spent away and the lost powers their position in the field allowed. A second home emerges, and with its loss, accompanying pathologies. Kahn (1996: 189) observes that on her return to the United States she was surprised to find she still felt uprooted — 'I went home and thought, talked, and wrote about Wamira. As people had predicted, I cried about it, too. I was, as Alice (a Wamiran) had warned, "homesick"'. The anthropologist longs to return or to recover that experience in writing, to make the memories live and there find relief. But she or he discovers there is no final resolution for homesickness, no ultimate homecoming.

Even those discharged prisoners who find a friendly reception outside Bomana may be dismayed to discover that home is not everything they expected. There remains a sense that something or some place is missing. Prisoners told me that those who gain release often think back to their time in gaol, they find themselves surprised at the realisation that discharge does not necessarily bring an end to the sense of constraint. They may be reunited with kin, but at the expense of losing contact with comrades in prison. They may revel in free movement, but regret the loss of the vision of God (and the space for critique) that Bomana provided. It seems that for them too a second home appears, from which they remain displaced. That loss is registered in sneezes, dreams and letters from those left in gaol; also on the bodies of men, whenever they look down at their incised penises or view the tattoos that spread across their arms, legs and torsos. So there is no simple resolution, no return to full Society. The place known as 'home' is not what they remember. Those discharged pine for the home they believe they had before incarceration and for the home forced upon them at Bomana. They do not usually wish to go back, but they sicken for the version of freedom that they first imagined in prison.

Freedom

O freedom! O freedom!
The day goes and I talk about you.
The night comes and I dream about you.
You look beautiful and so pretty.
What time, which month, which day,
Which year, will I come and see you?

And I hears you singing,
Shouting, laughing and crying.
O freedom!
I stand and looks to the east, west, south and north,
But the bars surrounding me.
O freedom! O freedom!
You looks pretty.

(Henry Tiare)

Notes

1 Rapport (1997) makes the point that Malinowski's decision to conduct fieldwork in the Trobriand Islands was not entirely a free one, faced as he was
   with the alternative of internment as an enemy subject (during the First
   World War) in Australia. In a literal sense then, the Trobriand Islands were
   for him a kind of prison.

2 Kahn (1996: 170) records that upon her arrival the Wamirans told her:
   'Someone like you should be in your own place with your family and friends,
   not so far away all alone.'

3 Kahn (1996: 187) says that when she returned to the United States she found
   a letter waiting for her from a friend in Wamira. It read: 'But when you are
   home again sitting in your room all alone, you will think about Wamira and
   cry. You will tell stories about our place to your friends and play our tapes
   for them. They will hear everything, but only you will really know. You will
   cry for Wamira. You will be homesick for Wamira. Only you have been to our
   place. Only you will really know.'

Glossary

The following glossary includes all Tok Pisin words that occur more than once in the text and may appear in untranslated form. For further information and etymology see Mihalic (1971).

bikboi: 'big boy'; a senior gang mate.

birua: 'enemy'.

bisnis man: 'business man'.

bus kanaka: 'bush man'; a person without knowledge of the way of the white men.

dak: 'dark'.

dak peles: 'dark place'.

dak rum: 'dark room'; cell cubes or screened corners.

disko meri: 'disco woman'; a woman who goes to nightclubs and has casual unpaid sex.

driman : 'dream'.

gavman : 'government'.

hap meri: 'half woman'; male prisoner who consents to anal penetration.

hausman: 'men's house'.

kalabus: prison.

kalabus man (kalabus meri): male prisoner (female prisoner).

klia ples: 'clear place'; a cell without screened corners or cubes.

lait: 'light'.

las ples: the 'last place'.

lus bodi: 'loose body'; a prisoner to whom no one claims a relation.

lus tingting: 'lose thoughts'; to forget.

munman (munmeri): 'month man' ('month woman'); convict with less than a year to serve of his or her sentence.

patna: 'partner'.

pes: 'face'.

ples : 'place'; ground of one's ancestors.

plesman (plesmeri): 'place man' ('place woman'); person who lives in the village or hamlet of his/her ancestors.

pren: 'friend'.

raskal: 'rascal'; spectral figure of criminal.

rot meri: 'road woman'; sex worker.

sel: prison 'cell'.

stilman: 'steal man'; a thief or a man who deliberately breaks the law.

tainim bel: 'turn emotions'; to convert to Christianity.

waitman: 'white men'.

wan: 'one'; persons animated by the same relation.

wangang : 'one gang'; gang mates.

wanlotu: 'one church'; denominational church mates.

wantaim: 'together'; persons who are implicated in each other's lives.

wantok: 'one language'; language group mates.

wan wan: 'one-one'; persons who are independent of each other.

wari: 'worry'.

wetkot: 'wait court'; a prisoner on remand.

yiaman (yiameri): 'year man' ('year woman'); convict with more than a year to serve of his or her sentence.

Bibliography

~~~

Annual Reports and other Archival Documents

British New Guinea Annual Report 1890–1891(held in the Royal Commonwealth Society Collection, University of Cambridge).

British New Guinea Annual Report, 1891–1892.

British New Guinea Annual Report 1892–1893/1893–1894.

British New Guinea Annual Report 1894–1895.

British New Guinea Annual Report 1897–1898.

British New Guinea Annual Report 1899–1900.

British New Guinea Annual Report 1900–1901.

British New Guinea Annual Report 1901–1902.

British New Guinea Annual Report 1902–1903.

New Guinea Annual Report 1914–1915 (held in the Royal Commonwealth Society Collection, University of Cambridge).

New Guinea Annual Report 1921–1922.

New Guinea Annual Report 1932–1933.

New Guinea Annual Report 1933–1934.

New Guinea Annual Report 1954–1955.

New Guinea Annual Report 1960–1961.

New Guinea Annual Report 1961–1962.

New Guinea Annual Report 1963–1964.

New Guinea Annual Report 1964–1965.

Papua Annual Report 1906–1907 (held in the Royal Commonwealth Society Collection, University of Cambridge).

Papua Annual Report 1907–1908.

Papua Annual Report 1908–1909.

Papua Annual Report 1911–1912.

Papua Annual Report 1912–1913.

Papua Annual Report 1913–1914.

Papua Annual Report 1914–1915.

Papua Annual Report 1916–1917.

Papua Annual Report 1917–1918.

Papua Annual Report 1919–1920.

Papua Annual Report 1924–1925.

Papua Annual Report 1925–1926.

Papua Annual Report 1926–1927.

Papua Annual Report1928–1929.

Papua Annual Report 1929–1930.

Papua Annual Report 1930–1931.

Papua Annual Report 1932–1933.

Papua Annual Report 1933–1934.

Papua Annual Report 1957–1958.

Papua Annual Report 1959–1960.

Papua Annual Report 1960–1961.

Papua New Guinea Annual Report 1970–1971 (held in the Royal Commonwealth
   Society Collection, University of Cambridge).
Papua New Guinea Annual Report 1971–1972.
Papua New Guinea Annual Report 1972–1973.
Papua Prisons Ordinance 1919 (Ordinances reproduced in annual reports, held in
   the Royal Commonwealth Society Collection, University of Cambridge).
Papua and New Guinea Corrective Institutions Ordinance 1957.
Annual Report of Papua New Guinea Correctional Services 1990 (reports, newsletter,
   draft bill and statistics held at the Department of Correctional Services, Port
   Moresby).
Annual Report of Papua New Guinea Correctional Services 1991.
Korek Nius: newsletter of the Correctional Services 1990.
Papua New Guinea Draft Correctional Service Bill 1995.
Prison Statistics of Papua New Guinea 1983–1988, Correctional Services.
Seligman, Charles. *Journal for New Guinea 1904* (held in the Archives of London
   School of Economics, London).

General Works

Banks, C. *Women in Transition: Social Control in Papua New Guinea.* Canberra:
   Australian Institute of Criminology, 1993.
Bateson, G. *Steps to an Ecology of Mind: Collected Essays in Anthropology, Psychia-
   try. Evolution and Epistemology.* London: Granada Publishing, 1973.
Battaglia, D. *On the Bone of the Serpent: Person, Memory, and Mortality in Sabarl
   Island Society.* Chicago: University of Chicago Press, 1990.
————, 'Displacing culture: a joke of significance in urban Papua New Guinea',
   New Literary History vol. 23 (1992): 1003–1017.
————, 'Retaining reality: some practical problems with objects as property',
   Man vol. 29 (1994): 1–15.
————, 'On practical nostalgia: self-prospecting among urban Trobrianders', in
   Battaglia, D., ed., *Rhetorics of Self-Making.* Berkeley: University of California
   Press, 1995, 77–96.
Baudrillard, J. *The System of Objects.* London: Verso, 1996.
Bellos, D. *Georges Perec. A Life in Words.* London: The Harvill Press, 1995.
Bénabou, M. 'Rule and constraint', in Motte, W.F., ed., *Oulipo. A Primer of Poten-
   tial Literature.* Lincoln: University of Nebraska Press, 1986.
Bergendorff, S. *Faingu City: a Modern Mekeo Clan in Papua New Guinea.* Lund:
   Lund University Press, 1996.
Bergson, H. *Time and Free Will: an Essay on the Immediate Data of Consciousness.*
   London: Swan Sonnenschein, 1910.
Biersack, A. 'Ginger gardens for the Ginger Woman: rites and passages in a
   Melanesian society', *Man* vol. 17 (1982): 239–58.
Blake, J. *The Joint.* Garden City, New York: Doubleday, 1971.
Borrey, A. *Ol Kalabus Meri. A Study of Female Prisoners in Papua New Guinea.* Port
   Moresby: Papua New Guinea Law Reform Commission, 1992.
Bosworth, M. *Engendering Resistance: Agency and Power in Women's Prisons.*
   Aldershot: Dartmouth Publishing, 1999.
Carroll, L. *Hacks, Blacks, and Cons: Race Relations in a Maximum Security Prison.*
   Lexington, DC: Heath and Company, 1974.

Clark, J. 'The incredible shrinking men: male ideology and development in a Southern Highlands society', *Canberra Anthropology* vol. 12 (1989): 120–43.
————, 'State of desire: transformations in Huli sexuality', in Manderson, L. and Jolly, M., eds., *Sites of Desire. Economies of Pleasure: Sexualities in Asia and the Pacific*. Chicago: The University of Chicago Press, 1997,191–211.
Clay, B. *Pinikindu: Maternal Nurture, Paternal Substance*. Chicago: University of Chicago Press, 1977.
Clemmer, D. *The Prison Community*. New York: Holt, Rinehart and Wilson, 1940.
Clifford, J. *The Predicaments of Culture. Twentieth Century Ethnography, Literature and Art*. Cambridge: Harvard University Press, 1988.
————, *Routes. Travel and Translation in the Late Twentieth Century*. Cambridge: Harvard University Press, 1997.
Clifford, J. and Marcus, G., eds. *Writing Culture. The Poetics and Politics of Ethnography*. Berkeley: University of California Press, 1986.
Cohen, S. and Taylor, L. *Psychological Survival: the Experience of Long-term Imprisonment*. London: Penguin, 1981.
Deleuze, G. *Bergsonism*. New York: Zone Books, 1988.
Díaz-Cotto, J. *Gender, Ethnicity and The State. Latina and Latino Prison Politics*. Albany: State University of New York Press, 1996.
Drumond, R. 'The sexual assault of male inmates in incarcerated settings', *International Journal of the Sociology of Law* vol. 20 (1992): 135–57.
Duncan, M. G. *Romantic Outlaws, Beloved Prisons: Unconscious Meanings of Crime and Punishment*. New York: New York University Press, 1996.
Errington, F. and Gewertz, D. *Articulating Change in the 'Last Unknown'*. Boulder: Westview Press, 1995.
Feld, S. Sound and Sentiment: birds, weeping, poetics and songs in Kaluli expression. Philadelphia: University of Pennsylvania Press, 1982.
————, 'Waterfalls of song: an acoustemology of place resounding in Bosavi, Papua New Guinea', in Feld, S. and Basso, K., eds, *Senses of Place*. Santa Fe: School of American Research Press, 1996, 91–135.
Fitzpatrick, P. *The Mythology of Law*. London: Routledge, 1992.
Flynn, T. 'Foucault and the eclipse of vision', in Levin, D., ed., *Modernity and the Hegemony of Vision*. Berkeley: University of California Press, 1993, 273–86.
Foster, R. *Social Reproduction and History in Melanesia: Mortuary Ritual, Gift Exchange and Custom in the Tanga Islands*. Cambridge: Cambridge University Press, 1995a.
————, 'Print advertisements and nation making in metropolitan Papua New Guinea', in Foster, R., ed., *Nation Making: Emergent Identities in Postcolonial Melanesia*. Ann Arbor: University of Michigan Press, 1995b.
Foucault, M. *The Order of Things: An Archaeology of the Human Sciences*. New York: Vintage Books, 1973.
————, *Discipline and Punish: the Birth of the Prison*. London: Penguin Books, 1977.
————, 'On the genealogy of ethics: an overview of work in progress', in Rabinow, P., ed., *The Foucault Reader: an Introduction to Foucault's Thoughts*. London: Penguin Books, 1984, 340–72.
————, *The Uses of Pleasure: the History of Sexuality Volume Two*. London: Penguin Books, 1985.
Friedman, L. M. *Crime and Punishment in American History*. New York: Basic Books, 1993.

Gewertz, D. and Errington, F. *Twisted Histories, Altered Contexts: Representing the Chambri in a World System.* Cambridge: Cambridge University Press, 1991.

Giallombardo, R. *Society of Women: A Study of a Women's Prison.* New York: John Wiley & Sons, 1966.

Gillison, G. 'Images of nature in Gimi thought', in MacCormack, C. and Strathern, M., eds, *Nature, Culture and Gender.* Cambridge: Cambridge University Press, 1980.

———, *Between Culture and Fantasy: a New Guinea Highlands Mythology.* Chicago: University of Chicago Press, 1993.

Goddard, M. 'Bedlam in paradise: a critical history of psychiatry in Papua New Guinea', *The Journal of Pacific History* vol. 27 (1992a), 55–72.

———, 'Big-man, thief: the social organisation of gangs in Port Moresby', *Canberra Anthropology* vol. 15 (1992b): 20–34.

Goffman, E. *Asylums. Essays on the Social Situation of Mental Patients and Other Inmates.* Chicago: Aldine Publishing, 1961.

Haney, C. Banks, C. and Zimbardo, P. 'Interpersonal dynamics in a simulated prison', *International Journal of Criminology and Penology* vol. 1 (1973): 69–97.

Harris, B. *The Rise of Rascalism: Action and Reaction in the Evolution of Rascal Gangs.* Port Moresby: Papua New Guinea: IASER Discussion Paper 54, 1988.

Harrison, S. *Stealing People's Names: History and Politics in a Sepik River Cosmology.* Cambridge: Cambridge University Press, 1990.

Heffernan, E. *Making it in Prison. The Square, the Cool, and the Life.* New York: John Wiley & Sons, 1972.

Herdt, G. *Guardians of the Flutes: Idioms of Masculinity.* New York: McGraw-Hill Book Co, 1981.

———, 'Selfhood and discourse in Sambia dream sharing', in Tedlock, B., ed., *Dreaming: Anthropological and Psychological Interpretations.* Cambridge: Cambridge University Press, 1987.

Hirsch, A. J. *The Rise of the Penitentiary: Prisons and Punishment in Early America.* New Haven, CT: Yale University Press, 1992.

Hirsch, E. 'Local persons, metropolitan names: contending forms of simultaneity among the Fuyuge, Papua New Guinea', in Foster, R., ed., *Nation Making: Emergent Identities in Postcolonial Melanesia.* Ann Arbor: University of Michigan Press, 1995a, 185–206.

———, 'The "holding together" of ritual: ancestrality and achievement in the Papuan Highlands', in de Coppet, D. and Iteneau, A., eds, *Cosmos and Society in Oceania.* Oxford: Berg, 1995b, 213–34.

———, 'The coercive strategies of aesthetics: reflections on wealth, ritual and landscape in Melanesia', *Social Analysis* vol. 38 (1995c): 61–70.

Hogbin, I. *The Island of Menstruating Men: Religion in Wogeo, New Guinea.* Scranton: Chandler Publishing, 1970.

Ignatieff, M. *A Just Measure of Pain. The Penitentiary in the Industrial Revolution 1750–1850.* London: MacMillan, 1978.

Inciardi, J. A. Lockwood, D. and Pottinger, A. *Women and Crack-Cocaine.* New York: Macmillan, 1993.

Inglis, A. *Not a White Woman Safe: Sexual Anxiety and Politics in Port Moresby 1929–1934.* Canberra: Australian National University Press, 1974.

———, *Karo: the Life and Fate of a Papuan.* Canberra: Australian National University Press, 1982.

Jacobs, J. B. *Stateville. The Penitentiary in Mass Society*. Chicago: University of Chicago Press, 1977.

Jameson, F. *Postmodernism or, the Cultural Logic of Late Capitalism*. London: Verso, 1991.

Jay, M. *Downcast Eyes. The Denigration of Vision in Twentieth Century French Thought*. Berkeley: University of California Press, 1993.

Kahn, M. 'Your place and mine: sharing emotional landscapes in Wamira, Papua New Guinea', in Feld, S. and Basso, K., eds, *Senses of Place*. Santa Fe: School of American Research Press, 1996, 167–96.

Kempf, W. 'Ritual, power and colonial domination: male initiation among the Ngaing of Papua New Guinea', in Stewart, C. and Shaw, R., eds, *Syncretism/Anti- Syncretism: the Politics of Religious Synthesis*. London: Routledge, 1994, 108– 26.

Kern, S. *The Culture of Time and Space 1880–1918*. London: Weidenfeld & Nicolson, 1983.

Küchler, S. 'Malangan: art and memory in a Melanesian society', Man n.s., 22 (1987): 238–55.

————, 'Malangan: objects, sacrifice and the production of memory', *American Ethnologist* 14 (1988): 625–37.

Kulick, D. 'Heroes from hell: representations of "rascals" in a Papua New Guinean village', *Anthropology Today* vol. 9 (1993): 9–14.

Lattas, A. 'Sorcery and colonialism: illness, dreams and death as political languages in West New Britian', *Man* vol. 28 (1993): 51–77.

Leach, James. 2003. Creative Land. Place and Procreation on the Rai Coast of Papua New Guinea. Oxford: Berghahn Books.

Levin, D. 'Keeping Foucault and Derrida in sight. Panopticism and the politics of subversion', in Levin, D., ed., *Sites of Vision: the Discursive Construction of Sight in the History of Philosophy*. Cambridge: The MIT Press, 1997, 397–466.

Lewis, Gilbert. *The Day of the Shining Red: An Essay on Understanding Ritual*. Cambridge: Cambridge University Press, 1980.

Levine, H. and Levine, M. *Urbanisation in Papua New Guinea: A Study of Ambivalent Townsmen*. Cambridge: Cambridge University Press, 1979.

Lindstrom, L. 'Personal names and social reproduction on Tanna, Vanuatu', *Journal of Polynesian Society* vol. 94 (1985): 27–43.

Malinowski, B. *Argonauts of the Western Pacific: An Account of Native Enterprise and Adventure in the Archipelagoes of Melanesian New Guinea*. New York: Dutton, 1922.

A Diary in the Strict Sense of the Term. London: Routledge & Kegan Paul, 1967.

Mathiesen, T. *The Defences of the Weak: A Sociological Study of a Norwegian Correctional Institution*. London: Tavistock Publications, 1965.

May, R., ed. *Changes and Movement: Readings on Internal Migration in Papua New Guinea*. Canberra: Australian National University Press, 1977.

Meggitt, M. 'Dream interpretation among the Mae Enga of New Guinea', *Southwestern Journal of Anthropology* vol. 18 (1962): 216–29.

————, 'Male-female relationships in the Highlands of Australian New Guinea', *American Anthropologist* vol. 66 (1964): 216–29.

Mihalic, F. *The Jacaranda Dictionary and Grammar of Melanesian Pidgin*. Milton, Queensland: Jacaranda Press, 1971.

Mimica, J. *Intimations of Infinity. The Cultural Meanings of the Iqwaye Counting and Number System*. Oxford: Berg, 1992.

Moczydlowski, P. *The Hidden Life of Polish Prisons*. Bloomington: Indiana University Press, 1992.

Monsell-Davis, M. 'Urban exchanges: safety-net or disincentive? Wantoks and relatives in the urban Pacific', *Canberra Anthropology* vol. 16 (1993): 45–66.

Morauta, L., ed. *Law and Order in a Changing Society*. Canberra: RSPacS, Australian National University, 1986.

Morris, T. and Morris, P. *Pentonville. A Sociological Study of an English Prison*. London: Routledge & Kegan Paul, 1963.

Mosko, M. *Quadripartite Structure: Categories, Relations and Homologies in Bush Mekeo Culture*. Cambridge: Cambridge University Press, 1985.

Motte, W. F., ed. *Oulipo. A Primer of Potential Literature*. Lincoln: University of Nebraska Press, 1986a.

————, 'Introduction. microhistory', in Motte, W.F., ed., *Oulipo. A Primer of Potential Literature*. Lincoln: University of Nebraska Press, 1986b, .

O'Hanlon, M. 'Modernity and the 'graphicalisation' of meaning: New Guinea Highland shield design in historical perspective', *Journal of Royal Anthropological Institute* vol. 1 (1995): 469–93.

Owen, B. *'In the Mix'. Struggle and Survival in a Women's Prison*. Albany: State University of New York Press, 1998.

Panoff, M. 'The notion of the double self among the Maenge', *Journal of the Polynesian Society* vol. 77 (1968): 275–95.

Perec, G. *A Void*. London: The Harvill Press, 1995.

————, *Species of Spaces and Other Pieces*. London: Penguin, 1997.

Poole, F.J. 'The ritual forging of identity: aspects of persons and self in Bimin-Kuskusmin male initiation', in Herdt, G., ed., *Rituals of Manhood: Male Initiation in Papua New Guinea*. Berkeley: University of California Press, 1982.

Rapport, N. *Transcendent Individual: Towards a Literary and Liberal Anthropology*. London: Routledge & Kegan Paul, 1997.

Reed, A. 'Contested images and common strategies: early colonial sexual politics in the Massim', in Manderson, L. and Jolly, M., eds, *Sites of Desire, Economies of Pleasure: Sexualities in Asia and the Pacific*. Chicago: The University of Chicago Press, 1997, 48–71.

————, 'Anticipating individuals: modes of vision and their social consequence in a Papua New Guinea prison', *Journal of the Royal Anthropological Institute* vol. 5 (1999): 43–56.

Rew, A. *Social Images and Process in Urban New Guinea: a Study of Port Moresby*. St Paul: West Publishing, 1974.

Robbins, J. 'Dispossessing the spirits: Christian transformations of desire and ecology among the Urapmin of Papua New Guinea', *Ethnology* vol. 34 (1995): 211–24.

————, '666, or why is the millennium on the skin? Morality, the state and the epistemology of Apocalypticism among the Urapim of Papua New Guinea', in Stewart, P. and Strathern, A., eds, *Millennial Markers*. Townsville: Centre for Pacific Studies, James Cook University of the North, 1997.

————, 'On reading 'World News': Apocalyptic narrative, negative nationalism and transnational Christianity in a Papua New Guinea society', *Social Analysis* vol. 42 (1998a): 103–30.

————, 'Becoming sinners: Christianity and desire among the Urapmin of Papua New Guinea', *Ethnology* vol. 37 (1998b): 299–316.

Rosaldo, R. *Culture and Truth: the Remaking of Social Analysis*. London: Routledge & Kegan Paul, 1989.

Rothman, D. J. *The Discovery of the Asylum: Social Order and Disorder in the New Republic*. Boston: Little, Brown, 1971.

————, *Conscience and Convenience: The Asylum and Its Alternatives in Progressive America*. Boston: Little, Brown, 1980.

Rubenstein, A. *Bad Language, Naked Ladies, and Other Threats to the Nation: a Political History of Comic Books in Mexico*. Durham: Duke University Press, 1998.

Schieffelin, E. *The Sorrow of the Lonely and the Burning of the Dancers*. New York: St Martin's Press, 1976.

Schieffelin, E. and Crittenden, R. *Like People You See in a Dream. First Contact in Six Papuan Societies*. Stanford: Stanford University Press, 1991.

Schifter, J. *Macho Love. Sex Behind Bars in Central America*. New York: The Haworth Hispanic/Latino Press, 1999.

Schiltz, M. 'Rascalism, tradition and the state in Papua New Guinea', in Toft, S., ed., *Domestic Violence in Papua New Guinea*. Monograph no.3. Port Moresby: Law Reform Commission, 1985, 141–60.

Schivelbusch, W. *The Railway Journey: Trains and Travel in the Nineteenth Century*. Oxford: Basil Blackwell, 1979.

Schlör, J. *Nights in the Big City. Paris, Berlin, London 1840–1930*. London: Reaktion Books, 1998.

Schwimmer, E. 'Friendship and kinship: an attempt to relate two anthropological concepts', in Leyton, E., ed., *The Compact: Selected Dimensions of Friendship*. Newfoundland: St Johns, 1974.

Sikani, R. *The Establishment of the Corrective Institution Branch, and Australian Colonial Detainee Rehabilitation Policies in TPNG Gaols 1950–1975*. NRI Discussion Paper Number 75. Port Moresby: The National Research Institute, 1994.

Sim, J. *Medical Power in Prisons: The Prison Medical Service in England 1774–1989*. Milton Keynes: Open University Press, 1990.

————, 'Tougher than the rest? Men in prison', in Newburn, T. and Stanko, E.A., eds, *Just Boys Doing Business? Men, Masculinities and Crime*. London: Routledge & Kegan Paul, 1994, .

Sloop, J. M. *The Cultural Prison. Discourse, Prisoners, and Punishment*. Tuscaloosa: The University of Alabama Press, 1996.

Spierenburg, P. *The Spectacle of Suffering: Executions and the Evolution of Repression*. Cambridge: Cambridge University Press, 1984.

Stephen, M. 'Dreams of change: the innovative role of altered states of consciousness in traditional Melanesian religion', *Oceania* vol. 50 (1979): 3–22.

————, 'Dreaming is another power! The social significance of dreams among the Mekeo of Papua New Guinea', *Oceania* vol. 53 (1982): 106–22.

————, 'Dreams and self-knowledge among the Mekeo of Papua New Guinea', *Ethos* vol. 24 (1996): 465–90.

Stewart, K. *A Space on the Side of the Road. Cultural Poetics in an 'Other' America*. Princeton: Princeton University Press, 1996.

Stewart, P. and Strathern, A. *Millennial Markers*. Townsville: Centre for Pacific Studies, James Cook University of the North, 1997.

Strathern, A. 'Crime and compensation: two disputed themes in Papua New Guinea's recent history', *POLAR: Political and Legal Anthropological Review* vol. 17 (1994): 55–65.

Strathern, M. *No Money on Our Skins: Hagen Migrants in Port Moresby.* New Guinea Research Bulletin no. 61. Canberra: Australian National University Press, 1975.

———, *The Gender of the Gift. Problems with Women and Problems with Society in Melanesia.* Berkeley: University of California Press, 1988.

———, *Partial Connections.* Savage, MD : Rowman & Littlefield, 1991.

———, *Reproducing the Future. Essays on Anthropology, Kinship and the New Reproductive Technologies.* Manchester: Manchester University Press, 1992a.

———, *After Nature. English Kinship in the Late Twentieth Century.* Cambridge: Cambridge University Press, 1992b.

———, *The Relation. Issues in Complexity and Scale.* Cambridge: Prickly Pear Press, 1995a.

———, 'Nostalgia and the new genetics', in Battaglia, D., ed., *Rhetorics of Self Making.* Berkeley: University of California Press, 1995b, 97–120.

———, *Property, Substance and Effect: Anthropological Essays on Persons and Things.* London: The Athlone Press, 1999.

Sykes, G. *The Society of Captives. A Study of a Maximum Security Prison.* Princeton: Princeton University Press, 1958.

Sykes, K. 'Raskalling: Papua New Guinea sociality as contested political order', in Banks, C., ed., *Developing Cultural Criminology for the Third World: Theory and Practice.* Canberra: Australian National University, 2000, 174–94.

Tatum, S. *Inventing Billy The Kid: Visions of the Outlaw in America 1881–1981.* Tucson: The University of Arizona Press, 1997.

Taussig, M. *The Nervous System.* New York: Routledge & Kegan Paul, 1992.

———, *Mimesis and Alterity. A Particular History of the Senses.* New York: Routledge & Kegan Paul, 1993.

Tsing, AL. *In the Realm of the Diamond Queen: Marginality in an Out-of-the-Way Place.* New Jersey: Princeton University Press, 1993.

Tuzin, D. *The Voice of the Tambaran: Truth and Illusion in Ilahita Arapesh Religion.* Berkeley: University of California Press, 1980.

———, *The Cassowary's Revenge: The Life and Death of Masculinity in a New Guinea Society.* Chicago: University of Chicago Press, 1997.

Wagner, R. *Habu: the Innovation of Meaning in Daribi Religion.* Chicago: University of Chicago Press, 1972.

———, 'Are there social groups in the New Guinea Highlands?', in Leaf, M.J., ed., *Frontiers of Anthropology.* New York: D. Van Nostrand Co, 1974.

———, 'Scientific and indigenous Papuan conceptualisations of the innate: a semiotic critique of the ecological perspective', in Bayliss-Smith, T. and Feachem, R., eds, *Subsistence and Survival: Rural Ecology in the Pacific.* London: Academic Press, 1977.

———, *The Invention of Culture.* Chicago: University of Chicago Press, 1981.

———, 'The fractal person', in Godelier, M. and Strathern, M., eds, *Big Men and Great Men: Personifications of Power in Melanesia.* Cambridge: Cambridge University Press, 1991, 159–73.

Wahidin, A. *'Life in The Shadows- a Qualitative Study of Older Women in Prison'.* Keele University, unpublished Ph.D. thesis, 2002.

Weiner, J. 'Substance, siblingship and exchange: aspects of social structure in New Guinea', *Social Analysis* vol. 11 (1982): 3–34.

————, 'Men, ghosts and dreams among the Foi: literal and figurative modes of interpretation', *Oceania* vol. 57 (1986): 114–27.

————, *The Empty Place: Poetry, Space and Being among the Foi of Papua New Guinea*. Bloomington: Indiana University Press, 1991.

————, 'Anthropology contra anthropology Part II: the limit of the relationship', *Critique of Anthropology* vol. 13 (1993): 285–301.

————, *The Lost Drum. The Myth of Sexuality in Papua New Guinea and Beyond*. Wisconsin: The University of Wisconsin Press, 1995.

Wetherell, D. *Reluctant Mission: the Anglican Church in Papua New Guinea 1891–1942*. Brisbane: University of Queensland Press, 1977.

Whitehouse, H. *Inside the Cult: Religious Innovation and Transmission in Papua New Guinea*. Oxford: Clarendon Press, 1995.

Index

CPSIA information can be obtained at www.ICGtesting.com
Printed in the USA
LVOW06s0014201115

463453LV00012B/86/P